CORPUS DELECTI

Corpus Delecti is an unprecedented event in the history of Latino performance art. Assembled and edited by one of the foremost practitioners and theorists in the field, it charts the extraordinary range of practices, narratives, and theories which make up this unique area of contemporary performance.

Using photos, scripts, essays, and poetry, *Corpus Delecti* explores the impact on performance of Latin American politics, popular culture, and syncretic religions. Nowhere else has such a vibrant and rich collection of writings and documents been fused into a comprehensive archive-volume.

Coco Fusco has brought together artists and scholars to bridge the theory/practice divide and to discuss a wide range of genres. They include:

- body art
- *carpa*
- vaudeville
- staged political protest
- tropicalist musical comedies
- the Chicano Art Movement
- queer Latino performance.

Corpus Delecti probes for the first time the specific contexts which have shaped Latin American performance. It is at once a significant intervention into the history and analysis of contemporary art and an ensemble piece of textual and visual work to treasure.

Coco Fusco is a New York-based interdisciplinary artist and writer and the author of *English is Broken Here: Notes on Cultural Fusion in the Americas* (1995).

CORPUS DELECTI

PERFORMANCE ART OF THE AMERICAS

EDITED BY COCO FUSCO

London and New York

First published 2000
by Routledge
11 New Fetter Lane, London EC4P 4EE

Simultaneously published in the USA and Canada
by Routledge
29 West 35th Street, New York, NY 10001

Routledge is an imprint of the Taylor & Francis Group

Typeset in Janson by Florence Production Limited, Stoodleigh, Devon
Printed and bound in Great Britain by St Edmundsbury Press, Bury St Edmunds,
Suffolk

British Library Cataloguing in Publication Data
A catalogue record for this book is available from the British Library

Library of Congress Cataloging in Publication Data
Fusco, Coco.
    Corpus delecti: performance art of the Americas/Coco Fusco.
      p. cm.
    Includes bibliographical references and index.
    1. Performance art–America.   2. Arts, Modern–20th century–
    America.   I. Title.
NX501.F87 2000
700'.98–dc21   99–26480
                                                         CIP

ISBN 0–415–19453–9 (hbk)
ISBN 0–415–19454–7 (pbk)

Contents

Part III
Stepping Toward An Oppositional Public Sphere

Illustrations

Contributors

Tania Bruguera is an interdisciplinary artist based in Havana, where she is also a professor at the Instituto Superior de Arte and directs the Espacio de Arte Tejadillo 214. She has presented her work in numerous international biennales and cultural institutions.

Maris Bustamante is a Mexican Non-Objectual visual artist and designer, a participant in the conceptualist grupos movement of the 1970s, the proud mother of Andrea and Neus, a feminist artist, university professor and researcher, writer, lecturer, and cultural promoter.

Nao Bustamante is a performance artist originally from the San Joaquin Valley of Central California. She has been living and working in San Francisco's Mission District since 1984. In addition to performance, Bustamante is a video and installation artist. She has presented her work in Mexico, Asia, Africa, Europe, Australia, New Zealand, Canada and the United States. View her websites at: www.slowburn.com/rosa.html and www.sfgate.com/nao1.html

Francisco Casas is a Chilean artist and writer currently living in Mexico.

C. Ondine Chavoya teaches in the program of visual and critical studies at Tufts University/School of the Museum of Fine Arts, Boston.

Roselyn Costantino is an associate professor of Spanish and Women's Studies at the Pennsylvania State University. She is completing a book-length manuscript entitled *The Body in Play:Contemporary Women's Theater and Performance in Mexico*.

Angel Delgado is an interdisciplinary artist based in Havana.

Ricardo Dominguez is the Senior Editor of *The Thing* (bbs.thing.net) and a co-founder of The Electronic Disturbance Theater. He is also a former member of Critical Art Ensemble, and a Fakeshop worker. He has collaborated with Francesca da Rimini on Dollspace and the Aphanisis Project with Diane Ludin. http://www.thing.net/~rdom

Felipe Ehrenberg's father gave him Da Vinci's biography to read when he was eleven years old, so he learned how to draw. After his own children arrived, he became a neologist. Henceforth, he intends to work on his garden and cultivate the ferns.

Maria Elena Escalona is a Cuban writer, curator and theater director based in Barcelona. Prior to moving to Europe, she spent three years working with Flora Lauten's Grupo Teatro Buendia in Havana.

Coco Fusco is a New York-based writer and interdisciplinary artist. She is the author of *English is Broken Here: Notes on Cultural Fusion in the Americas* (1995). She is an associate professor at the Tyler School of Art of Temple University.

Maria Elena Gaitan is a Los Angeles-based performance artist, musican and writer.

Guillermo Gómez-Peña is a Mexican performance artist and writer based in San Francisco. A recipient of numerous awards, he is the author of *The Warrior for Gringostoika*, *The New World (B)order* and *The Temple of Confessions*.

Felix Gonzalez-Torres (1957–1996) was born in Cuba, studied art in Puerto Rico and moved to New York to complete his studies in 1979, where he then settled and became a member of the artists' collective Group Material. Gonzalez-Torres's public artworks, installations, sculptures, prints and photographs have been exhibited throughout the US, Europe, Latin America and Japan.

María Teresa Hincapié is an artist based in Bogota, Colombia who has worked in the fields of theatre and performance for over twenty years. She is the only performance artist in Colombia to have received the country's top award for visual art. She has created solo performance works throughout Latin America and Europe. She teaches at the University of the Andes.

May Joseph is an assistant professor of performance studies at New York University. She is the author of *Nomadic Identities: The Performance of Citizenship* (Minnesota, 1999) and co-editor (with Jennifer Natalya Fink) of *Performing Hybridity* (Minnesota, 1999).

Cesar Martinez is an interdisciplinary artist based in Mexico City. He has participated in over sixty exhibitions world wide. He is a professor in the department of Graphic Design at the Universidad Autónoma Metropolitana-Azcapotzalco.

Raquel Mendieta Costa is a PhD candidate in the Department of Spanish and Portuguese of Stanford University.

Aldo Damian Menendez is a Cuban artist based in Miami.

Charles Merewether is an art historian and Collections Curator at the Getty Research Institute. His publications include *Art and Social Commitment : An End to the City of Dreams 1931–1948* (1984), *A Marginal Body* (1987) and the forthcoming *Anxieties of Revelation.*

Marta Minujín is an artist based in Buenos Aires.

Rafael Montañez-Ortiz is a an interdiscplinary artist and professor of art at Rutgers Unversity. He is also the founder and first director of the Museo del Barrio. His Destruction Art and Sratch Video works have been exhibited in seventeen museums and other cultural venues in the US and Europe.

José Esteban Muñoz is an assistant professor in the Performance Studies Deparment of the Tischo School of the Arts of New York University. He is the author of *Disidentifications* (1999) and the co-editor of *Pop Out: Queer Warhol* (1996) and *Everynight Life: Culture and Dance in Latin/o America* (1997).

Simone Osthoff is a Chicago-based Brazilian artist and writer. She is an instructor at the Art History, Theory and Criticism Department of The School of the Art Institute of Chicago.

Silvia Pellarolo is Assistant Professor of Spanish and Latin American Studies at the Department of Modern and Classical Languages and Literatures, California State University, Northridge, and a member of the Irvine Hispanic Theater Research Group. She is the author of *Sainete criollo/democracia/representación. El caso de Nemesio Trejo* (Buenos Aires: Corregidor, 1997).

Antonio Prieto is the co-author of *El teatro como vehículo de comunicación* (Mexico, 1992). He teaches in Stanford University's Department of Spanish and Portuguese, and is the project director for the DataCenter's Information Services Latin America (ISLA).

María Elena Ramos is a critic and the President of the Museum of Fine Arts in Caracas, Venezuela. She is the author of *Acciones frente a la plaza: Reseñas y documentos de siete eventos para una nueva lóica del arte venezolano* (1995).

Nelly Richard is a cultural critic and the editor of *La Revista de Crítica Cultural* in Chile. She directs the Cultural Criticism Seminar at the Universidad Arcis and the Program on Post-Dictatorship and Democratic Transition in Chile sponsored by the Rockefeller Foundation. She is the author of several publications, including *Metafora y Residuos* (*Metaphors and Residues*) (1998).

Lotty Rosenfeld is an interdisciplinary artist based in Santiago de Chile who has exhibited nationally and internationally for over twenty years. She is a founding member of the CADA art collective, one of the protagonists of the Chilean *avanzada*.

Leandro Soto participated in the renowned Volumen Uno art movement in Havana in 1981 as the first performance-installation artist in Cuba. He has participated in over 150 exhibitions throughout the world over the past twenty-five years. He currently teaches at Mount Holyoke College.

Merian Soto is Artistic Director of Bronx-based Latino arts organization Pepatian, and Associate Professor of Dance at Temple University's Esther Boyer College of Music and Department of Dance.

Carmelita Tropicana is a Cuban performance artist based in New York who received an Obie award for sustained excellence of performance in 1999. A book of her writings entitled *I, Carmelita Tropicana, Performing Between Cultures* is forthcoming from Beacon Press.

Evelyn Velez-Aguayo is a choreographer and performer and an assistant professor in the Dance department of the University of Michigan at Ann Arbor.

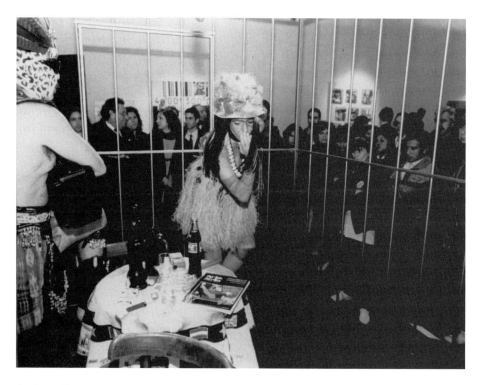

1. Coco Fusco and Guillermo Gómez-Peña
Two Undiscovered Amerindians Visit Buenos Aires, 1994
Fundación Banco Patricios, Buenos Aires, Argentina
Fusco's and Gómez-Peña's itinerant performance in which they exhibited themselves as exotic "savages" from an unknown island in the Gulf of Mexico explored the history of the ethnographic display of indigenous peoples and its influence in the shaping of images of cultural "Otherness" that informed European and American avant-gardes.

Introduction: Latin American performance and the *reconquista* of civil space

Coco Fusco

It is December 31, 1998, and I am sitting on the malecón, a stone wall that runs along the Caribbean sea in a tiny colonial village on the Venezuelan coast called Choroní. Nestled between sprawling cacao plantations at the edge of a magnificently dense rain forest, Choroní thrives on fishing and hosting eco-tourists and birdwatchers from Northern Europe. The clay-roofed houses built around interior courtyards here distinguish themselves by the inventiveness of the ironwork that covers their windows and entryways, the boldest of the designs resembling the hard-edged geometric patterns of the Kineticist art for which Venezuela became famous in the 1960s.

Each year during Holy Week the fishermen carry the Virgin Mary from their local church out to sea to ask for her protection. Their priest, an illustrious Jesuit called Padre Ignacio, in addition to offering Mass and baptizing babies, has transformed the nineteenth-century electrical plant in the rainforest where, according to the priest, he lives in a grandiose hall full of colonial furniture and religious artworks. Since it's Christmastime, at least five different nativity scenes complete with blinking lights are arranged around the hall. Next door is an artists' retreat where the American choreographer Bill T. Jones and company will soon arrive for a residency. The waterfalls that once provided energy for the electrical plant now serve as recreation for Padre Ignacio's guests and local children.

Between the humidity of the sea and the rainforest nothing dries completely. The pages of this manuscript have grown more and more damp each day since I've been here, and the worry that an unexpected power outage will erase the digital version that is lodged in my laptop has made me create several copies of everything I write. A small price to pay for the luxury of drifting off to sleep under the stars in a hammock, rocked by the breeze from the sea. Enveloped by the ebullient nature of this place I wait for the cannon on the malecón to be fired at midnight, after which the fishermen will spend the first day of New Year parading through the streets of the village, drumming in the doorways of each house just long enough to be awarded a bottle of rum. Locals and vacationers from Caracas and Maracay mingle with barefoot and sunburnt travelers from Germany and Italy, following behind the drummers. Some Irish visitors I've befriended are surprised to learn that the men are singing in Spanish. I wonder about the delicate balance that residents maintain between showcasing their world for others and enjoying the extraordinary beauty and abundance of their surroundings themselves. I also think about how these fishermen, descendants of slaves who once cultivated the finest cacao in the world, take obvious pleasure in recalling their history through the oral and physical gestures that catapult their chants into the air. The Caribbean, the cradle of New World syncretism, I decide, is the perfect place from which to reflect on the significance of performances that evoke multiple forms of *latinidad*. So from here, from the edge of south facing northward, I take a moment to remember how this project began.

Three years ago, I proposed to create a showcase of Latin American performance art for London's Institute of Contemporary Art. At the time the ICA's live art department was run by two visionary curators, Lois Keidan and Catherine Ugwu, who were interested in bringing the broadest spectrum of programming possible to the British public. I wanted to present an array of artists working in a variety of styles and strategies – first because I liked the work; and second because I wanted to break the tropicalist stereotypes about Latin American performativity and to unhinge the tokenist approach that characterized much "cultural diversity" programming, limiting it to the repeated presentation of one or two "name" artists. Luckily for me, Lois and Catherine instantly accepted my proposal, and I will always be grateful for their unfailing support.

In a way I was also looking at Britain as a sort of refuge from the virulent backlash against multiculturalism that had swept the US, on the one hand, and from the excessively instrumentalist versions of intercultural exchange that foundations and government initiatives had imposed on the other. Britain, after all, had welcomed several members of the Latin American avant-gardes of the 1960s and 1970s, many of whom were fleeing their countries, such as the Mexican artist Felipe Ehrenberg, who collaborated with members of Fluxus, the Brazilian Hélio Oiticica and Venezuelans Pedro Teran and Diego Barboza. Black Britain had also welcomed me in the 1980s, when I began a dialogue with black artists and intellectuals that has been absolutely fundamental to my sense of how to engage creatively with the politics of identity, and how to understand postcoloniality beyond the framework of American race relations.

When it came time to find a name for the program, I found myself browsing through the list of Latin expressions using the word "corpus" in my dictionary until I came upon "corpus delicti" which was defined as "the material substance, such as a body or a victim in a murder, upon which a crime has been committed." Given that so much performance I was interested in addressed, (albeit in an indirect manner), the illegitimately violent exercise of power over bodies, I thought the expression made a perfect title. Thanks, however, to my capricious memory, the message that I sent to London said "corpus delecti", which would mean something to the effect of "the body that derives or incarnates pleasure." Ironically enough, my slip evoked the tropicalist stereotype of the erotic Latin body propagated by touristic entertainment. Even the mistake – which I discovered much later – was recuperable.

During the festival, a short conference was held at which scholars and artists presented their views of Latin American performance, and it soon became clear that what all the participants shared was a lack of opportunities to discuss their work with each other and to see performances by artists from Latin countries other than their own. In response to that absence, then, I proposed to edit this book, which builds upon the original papers given at the conference. I sought to unite scholarly and creative interventions, to juxtapose performance by Latinos in Latin America, the US and Europe, and to bring together perspectives on performance that derived from visual artists' traditions as well as from theater so that body art, street actions and stage work could be compared and contrasted. I was not terribly concerned about coming up with a very strict definition of Latin America or of Latino performance – after decades of tedious semantic arguments on the subject I would rather concentrate on the work that artists make. Some artists might balk at the idea of being labeled by their nationality or regional affiliation, but I certainly did not mean to suggest that this territorial marker necessarily implies that a given artist *must* create a certain kind of work *because* of his or her having been born in a particular place. It is undeniable, however, that many artists have chosen to engage creatively with their contexts, for reasons that are explored by the writings in this volume. I also did not trouble myself much as to whether "performance" is a term that originated in Latin America – every Latino performance artist I have ever met knows what it means and how to use it, and many have offered alternative terms such as "plastic action," "non-objectual aesthetics," etc., vocabulary that is also explored here. And if Latin Americans who have spent the greater part of their lives creating work in the US and Europe still "represent" their nationalities of origin in international exhibitions, I see no reason why children and grandchildren of émigrés whose works evinced strong cultural ties to Latin America should not also be considered as fitting within the purview of this book.

I also purposely let self-consciously artistic performance take center stage in this volume. A good deal of scholarly debate in the US about "the performative" in Latin American culture and in US-Latino communities has been framed in anthropological terms, focusing on the study of rituals, on traditional and "everyday life" performances, and on the performative dimension of political action. This is due in part to the fact that since the field remains dominated by Anglophones, works that demand a knowledge of Spanish or Portuguese, and for which documentation exists largely in those languages, is largely ignored, or at least not systematically studied, by those who do not choose to do their field-work in Latin America. The anthropological bent of the focus on Latino performance artists has also meant that unless the work is perceived as serving a particular sociological agenda, whether it be feminism, queer theory, or cultural hybridity, it is less likely to be studied. While the appreciation of vernacular performativity derives in part from a desire that I sympathize with to dismantle highbrow definitions of culture, I do not believe that such anthropological incli-nations should lead to the symbolic erasure of artistic practices' role in the production of national and regional cultures, or that they should encourage us to misconstrue artists' work as essentially elitist. In addition, I have never under-stood why some scholars of performance seek to keep artists out of academic discussions of their work, preferring instead a formalist approach that privileges the written text or visual document. This seems peculiarly ironic, given how much effort has been made in the field of performance studies to analyze the power dynamics of conservative anthropological approaches that suppress, marginalize or objectify the subjects of study, or that replace the fluidity of time-based cultural forms with a fixed, static script.

Another somewhat overpowering paradigm is that of agitprop political theatre. As brilliant and necessary as the contributions of Paulo Freire and Augusto Boal have been to the understanding of radical pedagogy and social change, the desire to restrict the validity of Latin American cultural production to its capacity to politicize the underprivileged is a symptom of the frustration of leftist intel-lectuals and a way of ghettoizing Latin American cultural production. It has also been turned in the US into an insistence that all "authentically" Latino artists perform this function – even though the reality is that many Latin American artists' primary audience consists of their peers, other intellectuals, and audiences that do not respond receptively to what they perceive as outdated and dogmatic paradigms. Too many Latin Americans have suffered at the hands of authori-tarian systems that reduce all forms of expression – public, private, religious or aesthetic – to a certain political value or meaning for there not to be an enor-mous amount of skepticism about such approaches to culture. Other interpretative models and performance strategies are just as relevant to understanding Latin American performance art. On the other hand, much Latin American perfor-mance art that engages with the social does address traditions and themes that are not taken seriously by conventional theater scholarship in Latin America. As is explained in several of the essays in this volume, a good deal of Latin American performance recuperates and revindicates "low" theatrical forms such as *teatro frívolo*, cabaret and *carpa* to use them to address social and political issues from authoritarianism and censorship to sexuality.

Another issue that I wanted to explore in this volume is that of intercultural exchange, which I sought to demonstrate as a constant in the twentieth century rather than a product of the 1980s' multiculturalism or a program mandated by a foundation or a trade agreement. Interculturalism can imply many things: it can refer to dialogues among artists from different countries, the absorption of influences from other cultures, the syncretism of diverse sources within a given culture, or the history of theoretical debates about terms such as *mestizaje, creolité,* transculturalism, syncretism, etc. I am often shocked by how little awareness of the history of these debates enters into European and American discussions of the terms – I almost keeled over with laughter recently when I read a catalogue essay by a curator at a prestigious gallery about black British artist Chris Ofili in which it was suggested that "syncretism" was a term introduced by two young Latino scholars in an article published in 1991! I can only imagine the disdain I would incur if I were to publish a statement to the effect that Minimalism was a term invented by American critics in the 1990s.

Unfortunately in the US the term "interculturalism" has been limited largely to being conceived of as a corrective, a rubric that designates only the Latin American artists who address the colonial legacy of stereotyping as "useful" to bureaucrats and curators who want to solve the "problem" of racism and save a disenfranchised community from low self-esteem, or to scholars who seek to replace interculturalism introduced by European intellectuals such as Eugenio Barba with a postcolonially reconstructed one from the "margin" or from a "border." While it would be hypocritical for me to suggest that such an artistic project is utterly useless, it is crucial to understand when such strategies and orientations can become exhausted of their transformative potential through excessive use and institutionalization. It is all too easy to conflate cultural hybridity with political parity, and doing so can become a convenient perfunctory solution that substitutes tokenism for serious engagement with the power dynamics that shape specific intercultural relations at both the "centers" and the "margins" of global culture. Too often the strategy of Latin American governments has been to erase or suppress gross economic and political differences by insisting on the essential hybridity of their culture or a nation – thus generating a somewhat skeptical attitude on the part of the artists toward such gestures.

A similarly faulty logic has hampered cultural nationalism, which demands aesthetic product and interpretative models devoid of outside influence. These then would become the hallmark of an authentic national or ethnic culture and put an end to a supposedly colonial fascination with internationalism. Because so much performance art in Latin America and by Latinos in the US has implicitly and explicitly critiqued such cultural politics through their deployment of international avant-garde vocabularies, and because its ephemeral character has been an enabling factor for artists seeking to circumvent institutional control, performance art has rarely maintained a peaceful relationship with state-subsidized cultural institutions in Latin America or with conservative ethnic cultural organizations in the US. The exceptions occur when an institutional policy is established that posits certain modes of performativity as correctives (i.e., the multicultural mandate of the 1980s to educate Americans about racism, or in the case of 1990s' Mexico, to present a postmodern internationalist face for a country whose culture is associated with a pre-industrial pre-Columbian past) or as entertainment for openings and major art events.

In the present, the most common way of rejecting these imposed limitations has been for some Latin American artists to eschew all political concerns or social content in their work, and to reject invitations to present as members of a nationality, a minority, or a disenfranchised sector of humanity, and for curators and critics to downplay the sociopolitical subtext of the Latin American performances from the 1960s and 1970s that they chose to revindicate as part of a history of Latin American modernism. I would prefer to offer the panorama of perspectives in this volume as another way of addressing the intersection of ephemeral art and the social in Latin contexts. No self-respecting artist, Latin American or not, would want to restrict his or her sense of cultural identity to a bunch of vapid and trite stereotypes, nor would most artists be satisfied with recycling them ad infinitum – and the majority are offended by the facile reduction of cultural difference to stereotypes and rigid identity politics that often appear in uninformed appraisals of their work. But that reductiveness is a problem engendered by poor interpretation, and not of intercultural experimentation itself, even though the neo-formalists of the contemporary art world would deny this. Though some might chose to avoid these issues altogether, as long as global culture remains dominated by simplistic representations of cultural identity, the reception, comprehension, and interpretation of Latin American artists will be affected by that collective imaginary. It seems to me that the necessary antidote to facile interpretations of cultural difference, whether it arrives in the form of a Spanish-speaking Chihuahua who wants Taco Bell, or attempts to impose a single form of syncretism as a moral imperative, is to encourage awareness of just how much of the experimentation in Latin American visual art, literature, and theater in this century has adjudicated between national and regional influences and international vocabularies, and to demonstrate how these experiments cannot be reduced to any single formula. Concerns about cultural identity and interculturalism, then, do not constitute an evolutionary stage for Latin American art, but rather need to be conceived as ever-evolving constants.

It is always dangerous to generalize about Latin American cultural production, whatever the medium, but I would like to take that risk for a moment here and offer some observations about performance from the region and how it might differ slightly from work in other parts of the world that is recognized as constitutive of the performance "canon." The first generalization has to do with popular cultural influences. Most assessments of the Dadaist Cabaret Voltaire take into the account how important cabaret, vaudeville, the circus, and other popular theatre forms were for the Dadaists, who saw in them non-narrative structures, gestural vocabularies, anti-bourgeois sentiment, and interactive dynamics they sought to emulate in order to rupture the sanctity of salon culture and its contemplative reception model. As several of the essayists in this volume point out, analogous popular theatre forms, from the *sainete criollo*, to the Mexican *carpa*, to the tropicalist cabarets of the Caribbean and their televisual equivalents, have been key sources for many Latin American performance artists who also want to take advantage of them as storehouses of non-linear structures, anti-elitist attitudes, archetypal characters, and techniques for encouraging audience engagement. The tendency in gesture toward melodramatic exaggeration derives in large part from these traditions.

The second generalization I will make relates to rituals and religions as sources in the elaboration of corporeal vocabularies. The development of non-realistic dramatic styles in European and American avant-garde theatre in the twentieth century has relied heavily on the observation and adaptation of non-Western performance; Chinese acting for Bertolt Brecht, Balinese theatre for Antonin Artaud, and Indian theatre for Peter Brook, etc. Dadaist Hugo Ball declaimed poems from Africa and the South Pacific that he read phonetically. Surrealists studied the rituals, dances, and altered states of Native American shamans and Haitian voodoo priests. In the 1950s and 1960s, painters, poets, and theatre artists strove to emulate the improvisational style of black jazz musicians. In the 1960s the Living Theatre called upon its members to "become a tribe." In the 1970s, Performance duo Ulay and Abramovic stayed with Australian Aboriginals for a year to learn how to transform their existence into live art, and even today Abramovic continues to study the relationship between ritualized bodily movement and ecstatic states of consciousness in non-European cultures.

Latin Americans, on the other hand, have more often tended to look within their own cultures or to other Latin cultures for symbolic bodily gestures. They inhabit cultural landscapes with corporeal vocabularies derived from pre-Columbian, colonial, African, and Catholic traditions. Unlike the Prostestanism that underlies the aesthetics of the Euro-American avant-gardes, Catholicism proposes a greater continuity between the human and the divine, between the corporeal and the spiritual. The Catholic concept of the body as a receptacle of the Divine Spirit, and the many rituals of submission of that religion, which offer access to ecstatic states through the sacrifice of physical pain, functions as a conceptual backdrop and social subtext for many Latin American performers. In addition, the presence of African and indigenous traditions which codify collective history through the gestures of dance offer many Latin American artists sources of meaningful gesture. Finally, the extraordinarily rich adaptive processes of Afro-Latin syncretism have offered many Latin American performance artists models upon which to base their own attempts at assimilating Euro-American forms.

The last generalization has to do with what I will call the spatialization of power. Most histories of performance art point to key formal shifts wrought by the medium: from the object to the body as agent *and* object, from "atemporal" apprehension of a completed work to the intensified awareness of temporality through the participatory experience in the process of its making, from the primacy of the rational to the celebration of somatic expressivity. Some of those histories that focus on the social significance of the dematerialization of the object also stress that performance artists displaced the collector as ideal consumer, favoring instead an audience of peers, and sought to take their work outside the mechanisms of the commodification by situating it in non-institutional, and later in artist-run non-profit spaces. In light of the determinant role the art market has placed in the classification and evaluation of European and American art, it makes perfect sense that artists seeking to address the spatial articulations of this powerful institution would make such moves.

Latin Americans, however, have faced another series of problems that influence the relationships between art, society, aesthetic language, and the institutions that control the dissemination of creative expression. First, despite the initiatives of a few private patrons in Latin America who began to collect contemporary art in the 1980s, the art markets there do not play as central a role as they do in North America and Europe. In Cuba, Venezuela, Chile, Puerto Rico, and Mexico, the state continues to be the most important sponsor and patron of the arts, controlling networks of exhibition spaces, major collections, national and international competitions, fellowships, and awards. Whatever the attitudes of each government might be regarding the prevalence of the US in the international art market, official state rhetoric in each country defends the notion of a homogenous national culture, transmitted through its artistic production. Interestingly, Latino artists in the US with limited access to the international art market have also been subject, via the mandates of institutional initiatives targeted at ethnic minorities, to the totalizing discourse of cultural nationalism that dominates the realm of "community art."

The state in many Latin American countries not only plays a central role in determining the place and meaning of art in the public space of "cultural patrimony" but it also has a particularly physical way of exercising power on the bodies of its citizenry. During the period in which performance has flourished, the "presence" of the state in Latin American public space has been experienced as harsh, if not excessively physical. I am here referring to the disappearance of bodies, the brutality of the military and the police, the censuring of contestatory voices, and open warfare against political opposition. This state-sponsored violence reached startling proportions from the mid-1960s to the 1980s, when military regimes controlled much of Latin America; however, it has not entirely disappeared despite the shift to "democratic" governments in the 1990s. Furthermore, this approach to the exercise of power extends to the xenophobic treatment of the Latino subaltern in the US, relegated to *de facto* segregated neighborhoods, and mistreated by the border patrol, immigration authorities, the police, the owners of sweatshops, and neo-fascist groups. This North American situation is often overlooked by upper-class Latin American artists who emigrate or travel freely to the US, but it remains a reality for the majority of immigrants and their descendants, particularly those who are racially designated as "other" than the white American norm.

These factors have contributed to the tendency of many Latin American performance artists to infuse avant-garde strategies with social and political orientations, to address state institutions, and to envision the deployment of art in public space as a symbolic confrontation with the state. These factors also contribute to many artists maintaining the point of view that ephermeral, easily adaptable works constitute the ideal means of circumventing the power of the state. To an extent this not only explains, for example, why the Argentine artist Marta Minujín would build a Parthenon of banned books in the middle of Buenos Aires and invite the public to dismantle it and take home its parts; why, under the dictatorship of Augusto Pinochet, artists of the Chilean *avanzada* would consider the distribution of milk in poor neighborhoods a cultural gesture, or why the Cuban group ARTECALLE or the Chicano group Asco opted for ephemeral street actions, or why Juan Loyola in Venezuela chose to create actions that would generate a response from the police. It also explains why mail art – which provided many Latin American artists with a network of information exchange and exhibitions during a period of widespread censorship – played such an important role in the development of Latin American experimental art practice in the 1970s in addition to becoming a key precursor of telematic and Internet exchange in the 1980s and 1990s.

The material in this book is divided into three sections, corresponding to different spaces for the execution of performances and the imaginative terrains marked out therein. Interwoven with the critical essays are photographic documentation and excerpts of performance texts by artists whose works, though not specifically addressed by the critics in the book, nonetheless address similar issues. In conceptualizing the organization of the materials this way, I am indebted to Michel Foucault's concept of the heterotopia; that is, physical spaces that are symbolically charged, where social and political relations can be reconfigured.[1] While the majority of performances described in this volume address the need to expand or even to reinstate civic space and the failure of conventional aesthetic languages to engender this possibility, they do so from different sites, which I have designated here as the cabaret, the sacred space of ritual, and the street.

The cabaret as a venue has been critical to performance work in the past twenty years, particularly in the US. In downtown New York, San Francisco, and Los Angeles, for example, a scene developed out of clubs and tiny theatres that nurtured such solo Latino performers as Carmelita Tropicana, Marga Gómez, John Leguizamo, Nao Bustamante, Culture Clash, Luis Alfaro, the performance poets of the Nuyorican Poets Cafe and many others. In Mexico City, Jesusa Rodríguez and Liliana Felipe, Tito Vasconcelos, and Astrid Hadad present their ribald, politically charged performances in bars and cabarets. But the cabaret functions for many Latinos not only as a venue but as a tradition. Because of this, it was crucial to include the contributions by Silvia Pellarolo, which addresses the influence of the *sainete criollo* in the development of a melodramatic performative style that Evita Perón transposed to the political sphere, and the essay by Raquel Mendieta Costa, who explains how the mulatta archetype developed in nineteenth-century Cuban literature about slavery was carried over into popular theater, eventually became central to the tropicalist cabaret spectacles that enthralled tourists and moviegoers in the 1940s and 1950s. Mendieta reminds us also that the mulatta-rumbera as sign has re-emerged in recent years as tourist entertainment and prostitution have regained their central position in the Cuban economy. Pellarolo notes the importance of popular theater to the formation of a sense of identity for a new class of urban working women, and how Evita's body, in her public political performances, became "a synecdoche of [her] people's plight." Mendieta Costa notes how vaudeville and cabaret in Cuba have functioned as symbolic spaces where the drama of interracial encounters could be play out repeatedly and thus be made intelligible.

To an extent these spectacles created an intercultural, interracial, and inter-class framework within which Latin cultures became recognizable to most non-Latins – and, however distorted that framework was, its power has not abated. The cultural archetypes that evolved out of these traditions continue to be reworked by many Latino artists, such as Carmelita Tropicana, whose entire oeuvre could be interpreted as an homage to Cuban cabaret, Patricia Hoffbauer and George Emilio Sanchez, María Elena Escalona, and even my own collaboration with Nao Bustamante. In addition, essayists Roselyn Costantino, in her essay on Jesusa Rodríguez, and Antonio Prieto, in his work on Tito Vasconcelos, mention the importance of Mexican *teatro frívolo*, *teatro variété* and *carpa* to the work of those artists.

Though Jesusa Rodríguez sees herself more as a woman of the theater than a performance artist, her independence from Mexican government-supported theatre, her control of her material, the fact that she writes, directs, and performs, the fact that her sketches are often open-ended, and that she readily breaks with her scripts to interact with her audiences, makes her work resemble that of many performance artists in the US. As is described by Costantino, Rodríguez's El Hábito is an extraordinary example of an independent artists' space in Mexico City, a space for theatre and for dialogue about critical social and political issues in a country where the press is regularly censored. Costantino focuses on how Rodríguez uses her body to express the tensions in her social environment, drawing on the traditions of *teatro frívolo*.

Antonio Prieto looks at the cabaret spectacles by the legendary Mexican drag performer Tito Vasconcelos. He examines how the artist contributed to the nascent gay movement in Mexico City in the 1980s by convoking a community by the making-visible of gay issues, characters, humor, and sensibilities. Prieto demonstrates how Vasconcelos' version of camp corresponds to the dark camp of Charles Ludlam. It is a kind of camp that is grotesque, "displays an almost sadistic delight with cruelty," and verges on the aesthetic of French *théâtre guignol*. By pushing the irony and exaggerated theatricality of his camp drag to extremes, Prieto argues, Vasconcelos succeeded in unsettling conventional gender roles in a deeply *machista* society and a gay milieu that was resistant to effeminacy. He also engaged in a mode of symbolic terrorism parallel to the visual terrorism of street interventions by visual artists of the 1970s.

With José Muñoz's essay we move into the domain of the US. Muñoz examines how, in his stage piece "Cuerpo Politizado," Luis Alfaro renders social relations that shape Chicano life in Los Angeles through his performative acts. Muñoz's model for interpreting corporeal gesture is similar to that of Roselyn Costantino in her reading of Jesusa Rodríguez, but he concentrates specifically on how Alfaro dramatizes the interplay between categories of experience as a queer man and a Chicano. He posits a valuable notion of the theater space as an area in which memory is spatialized, and most importantly where it is presented as an anti-normative space where the self is continuously remade. In her stress on how performers Patricia Hoffbauer and George Emilio Sanchez use mobility and dynamism of their performative bodies to rupture static notions of identity and theatrical space, May Joseph's essay expands upon Muñoz's theoretical paradigm.

The second section of the book, entitled "Ritualizing the body politic," includes essays about Latin American body art. Most of the works discussed were presented in gallery spaces, even though some were designed as implicit critiques of the institutionalization of art and its reduction to a commodified object, or to an exponent of a given country's "true national culture." What emerges in these essays is just how the minimalist concerns of body art in the US and Europe were reconfigured in ways that allowed Latin American artists to address their specific social contexts. Also significant is how artists combined elements of a burgeoning international medium with performative rituals of Afro-Latin cultures, such as Ana Mendieta's incorporation of elements of *santería* in her actions, and Hélio Oiticica's transforming his sculptures into dynamic entities by creating his Parangolés for samba dancers.

Charles Merewether's essay on the late Ana Mendieta's early performances carefully reconstructs the creative steps that the young artist took which eventually led her to a poetics of exile. Examining her interest in everyday-life rituals, and particularly her study of anthropological writings that posited certain universal rituals that linked femininity and sacrifice, Merewether reveals how Mendieta was able to evoke her own experience of having been thrust unwillingly into exile from Cuba as a child and to elaborate an action-based practice that explored the aesthetic and sociological significance of disembodiment. Because Cuban artist Tania Bruguera began her career by reconstructing and continuing Mendieta's performances, I have juxtaposed an excerpt from one of her more recent performances against Merewether's essay. In addition, I have located Colombian artist María Teresa Hincapié in this section because her work focuses on everyday-life rituals and the sanctity of the most minimal human gesture. Her durational performances reinvest human relations and the natural environment with a sense of the sacred amidst the dehumanizing atmosphere of violence that surrounds her.

Simone Osthoff's analysis of the interactive dimension of Brazilian artists Lygia Clark and Hélio Oiticica traces the pre-technological origins of the avant-garde's interest in interactivity. She analyzes Clark's and Oiticica's investigations in the 1960s and early 1970s, which expanded in unique and original ways upon the rejection of the visual in favor of the experiential that was taking place on an international scale. Clark and Oiticica chose to render interactivity metaphorically as the constitutive moment of creation through their concentration on haptic experience. Clark's simple, even crude, gloves and masks were designed to catalyze and even liberate her engaged viewers' self-awareness. Oiticica's now famous Parangolés combined a new intermedia approach with an intercultural exploration of samba, which enabled him to propose an aesthetics of transformation via pleasurable engagement and simultaneously to reject a model of practice and reception based on rigid and imposed logic. Following this essay is the work of Puerto Rican artist Merian Soto, whose transformation of herself into an altar and her relinquishing of self-direction by blindfolding herself enables her to integrate her will with that of the crowd that directs her movement.

María Elena Ramos presents a panorama of Venezuelan body art from the period in which the medium flourished – the late 1970s and early 1980s. Ramos contextualizes the performances in her own country in light of the interest in "non-objectualist" practices that swept through many Latin American countries during this time. The term "non-objectualist," coined by Mexican critic Juan Acha, came to represent a set of ideas about aesthetic practice that paralleled those associated with the dematerialization of the art object in the US. This implied, in addition to a rejection of the focus on a finished object, a blurring of the art/life boundary and questioning of cultural institutions and policies. Venezuelans, Ramos also explains, were also responding to the visits in 1976 of Charlotte Moorman, Nam June Paik, Yoko Ono, Joseph Beuys, and Antonio Muntadas, as well as to the experiences many had studying and working in the US and Europe. In her essay, Ramos emphasizes how many Venezuelan artists addressed national issues such as the country's dependence on its oil industry and the political hypocrisy of the state, and combined an international vocabulary with knowledge of local anthropology.

The final section of this book is entitled "Stepping toward an oppositional public sphere." I am here alluding to social theorist Jürgen Habermas' notion of an ideal public sphere and its subsequent reformulations.[2] In the early 1960s, Habermas argued that the public sphere in a bourgeois democratic society was a domain between society and the state that consisted of a series of institutions through which citizens could engage in critical political discussions and thereby exert control over the state and hold it accountable for its acts. He believed, however, that this public sphere was eroded by the growth of mass media and the rise of the welfare state, as well as the incorporation into it of non-bourgeois groups. Radical cultural producers and theorists have since proposed that this public sphere, rather than being homogeneous, unified and rational, is better conceived of as fragmented and heterogeneous terrain that should remain open to oppositional cultural and political activity.

In this section of *Corpus Delecti*, artists and scholars examine performative interventions in public space that either call attention to the absence of such a domain or call it into being with their acts. These studies thus explore how performance artists use gestural forms, as Nelly Richard explains, and address the social imaginary through political representation. The works in question emanate from various situations in which political repression is spatially articulated: the military dictatorships in Argentina and Chile, the aftermath of the massacre at Tlatelolco in Mexico City, the forceful containment of Chicanos in East Los Angeles, the militarization of the US–Mexico border, the state censorship of news about the Zapatista Revolution, and the strict control of public space and cultural expression in Cuba. At the same time, in each case, the artists involved were equally concerned with the question of aesthetic strategies and how to effectively subvert the dominance of conventional approaches which were understood as simplistic and exhausted. The Chilean *avanzada* self-consciously distanced itself from traditional public artforms such as muralism, as did the Chicano group Asco. The Mexican *grupos* of the 1970s came on the heels of two decades of attempts to dislodge the retrograde notions of public art that had begun with the Rupture generation of the 1950s, but which were still propagated by governmental cultural institutions. As Leandro Soto describes in his testimonial account of the birth of performance in Cuba, it was the academicism imposed by teachers from the Soviet Union that prompted art students to begin rebelling by creating what he called "plastic actions." And the Electronic Disturbance Theater carries the guerrilla interventionist tactic of street graffiti into the domain of the virtual, through FloodNet actions in support of the Zapatista Liberation Army.

As I have already suggested in this introduction, these issues are ones that in a sense distinguish the thrust of much Latino performance art. But they also point to key differences in the relation of Latino performance to the aesthetic question of presence and materiality. Ephemeral actions can be read as a way of making one's work inaccessible to processes of objectification. However, artists who are trying to elude the repressive control of the state will also use them – hence the case of the Cuban group ARTECALLE, whose performances are described here by the group's founder Aldo Menendez. The Border Art Workshop, in its early actions in Borderfield State Park and at the San Ysidro checkpoint, also took advantage of the ephemeral quality of the performance medium to transgress laws that legislated exchange across the border without running a serious risk of arrest. And, as Ondine Chavoya aptly points out in his essay about the Chicano group Asco, the historiography of the Euro-American avant-garde generally links the aesthetic of dematerialization with a critique of the market, implying that the avant-garde ascribes "value" to the act of absenting oneself as an artist from art-institutional mechanisms. However, if one's exclusion from those mechanisms is not self-proclaimed but a byproduct of institutional racism, then perhaps the terms of what is properly understand as "radical" need to be altered to fit another context.

First published more than twelve years ago, Chilean-based critic Nelly Richard's study of the Chilean *avanzada*'s art produced during the Pinochet regime remains one of the finest studies of the relationship between experimental art practice and the social in Latin America. I have excerpted here two sections of her study that deal specifically with performance art – the first focuses on the street actions of the group CADA, which attempted to reclaim public space after the military regime destroyed civil life, and the second looks at the use of the body in the work of artists such as Carlos Leppe and Diamela Eltit, who engaged in acts of self-mutilation and self-sacrifice to represent the collective suffering of the Chilean people. Following her essay is documentation of more contemporary projects by Lotty Rosenfeld, one of the original members of CADA, and Las Yeguas del Apocalipsis (The Mares of the Apocalypse), two openly gay Chilean artists whose performances and political interventions address the marginalization of homosexuals in today's Chile.

Mexican artist Maris Bustamante, in addition to co-founding the conceptualist No-Grupo and the first feminist group in her country – Polvo de Gallina Negra (Black Hen Powder) – has for several years been conducting research on the development on non-objectual artforms in Mexico in the twentieth century. Her essay combines some of the materials she has unearthed and organized in the course of her research with a testimonial of her experiences during the *grupos* movement of the late 1970s and early 1980s. Her essay traces the impact of the arrival of the Surrealists to Mexico in 1940 and the creation of the first Live Art event that was part of their exhibition, the critique of stultified and localist public art by the Rupture generation in the 1950s and the "happenings" orchestrated by dramatist and filmmaker Alejandro Jodorowsky in the 1960s – all of which, she explains, lay the groundwork for the emergence of performance in Mexico.

I have no doubt that there will be readers who will wonder why I have chosen this particular group of artists and not others. As open as I may have tried to be in my selection process, there were points at which I did choose to draw the line. Work that was obviously closer to theater, in that the performers worked with directors and scripts they had not written themselves, I decided to exclude. I also left out stand-up comedy and performance poetry because it seemed to me that the centrality of verbal language as opposed to corporeal gesture placed these forms in a different realm from the kind of performance being studied here. For lack of space I could not include work by every single Latin American artist who has created a performance, but I did aim for a range that would be somewhat representative of the variety of work that has been and continues to be made. That women artists and gay artists are prominent in these pages says as much about the performance milieu (which has historically embraced social non-conformity and offered women a space for experimentation that is less encumbered by male-dominated art traditions) as it does about any conscious attempt to engage in affirmative action of any kind. I also limited my selection to artists who had developed a trajectory of work rather than ones who were just beginning. I do not intend this volume to be taken as definitive or exhaustive, but rather as a preliminary gesture. Those who want more writing about artists they are interested in but who are not between these covers should publish more books about Latino performance. They are certainly needed.

This book is the result of the efforts of many people, all of whom deserve acknowledgment. Without the talents of all the writers and artists whose works appear in this book, there would not be a publication, nor would it be such an extraordinary pleasure to be part of this corner of the performance universe. I give special thanks to Eduardo Aparicio, Juan Davila, Paul Foss, and Marcial Godoy for their fine translations. To Lois Keidan and Catherine Ugwu, for having helped me create the *Corpus Delecti* program, I am forever grateful. To Alan Read for his support for the original conference upon which this book is based, I am also greatly indebted. To Talia Rodgers at Routledge for her steadfast support and to Jason Arthur for shepherding me through the bureaucracy of book production, I offer my thanks. My former assistant Anoka Faruqee was tremendously helpful in transcribing texts and obtaining photos and permissions. A residency at the Yaddo Artists' Colony made it possible for me to concentrate on shaping this book in peace and comfort in the summer of 1998. I would also like to extend my gratitude to Diana Taylor and Jean Franco for lending a photograph of Jesusa Rodríguez; to Nelly Richard for also generously lending photos of Diamela Eltit and Carlos Leppe; and to Paul Foss of Art and Text, and Paul Dzus of MIT Press, for allowing me to reprint writings from their publications. I also thank all the artists and photographers who graciously provided me with photographs for this volume.

Finally I would like to close my introduction by offering thanks to some Latin Americans who helped to open my eyes to the power of performance art. The first person is my dear friend Leandro Katz, who, when I was his student nearly twenty years ago, first told me about his friend Hélio Oiticica, about his experiences working with Charles Ludlam, and who first took me to see *Chang in the Void Moon* at the Pyramid Club in the heyday of the East Village performance scene. The second is the Venezuelan artist known as the Black Prince, who I ran into at Documenta in 1987, and who tipped me off that he would create a surprise performance event at the opening press conference the following day. Sure enough, while European and American curators and critics were all congratulating themselves over the exhibition, Peña interrupted the conference to criticize them for ignoring the innovations of artists in Latin America, and began distributing tiny vials of crude oil with his signature on them. He was soon thereafter surrounded by throngs of journalists from all over the world, who would continue to raise the question of Latin American artists' contributions to cutting-edge artistic practices in their coverage of the event for years to come.

The third is not one single person but the residents of Tejadillo Street in Old Havana, where I performed in the spring of 1997 at a small gallery that Cuban artist Tania Bruguera runs out of her apartment. Tania and I decided to launch her gallery during the sixth Havana Bienal as part of a series of events taking place in a burgeoning circuit of galleries operating out of artists' homes. Tania was premiering her piece "The Burden of Guilt," which she describes in this book. I created a performance about the problem of repatriating the remains of Cuban exiles, "The Last Wish," which was based on the story of a woman who – after spending most of her life fighting her way out of poverty, a small town, a bad marriage, and finally her homeland – spent the last month of her life struggling unsuccessfully to return there to die. I was lying on the floor like a corpse set out for a country wake, but my eyes were open, and tears rolled out, one by one. The radio played *Radio Reloj*, a monotonous news show in Cuba that disseminates official history and is used for telling the time.

Tania and I knew that we would be visited by dozens of foreign guests of the Bienal but we had no idea that the barrio would spring into action. Her next-door neighbor helped her kill the goat she needed for her piece. Neighborhood kids ran around whispering to their friends and relatives that we were making art and that everyone had to see it. Neighbors came, watched, and commented. The bartender across the street from the house provided drinks and cigarettes for all the guests. By the time the police arrived to find out what the ruckus was, we had finished our performances, and even had an official permission slip for a party which Tania had shrewdly procured in advance to circumvent any measures that might be taken to stop us. The next day Tania's neighbors stopped by to congratulate us and the bartender thanked us for the extra business. I was deeply moved by these people's enthusiasm, curiosity, respect, and support, which made this into the most beautiful experience of performing in a community I have ever known.

The last person I will thank shall remain nameless. Suffice to say that in 1997 I was invited to attend the ARCO art fair in Madrid and deliver a paper at a conference that was part of it. In addition to preparing a talk on Latin American performance, I decided to organize one with two Cuban artists, Juan Pablo Ballester and María Elena Escalona, who had emigrated to Spain some years before. The three of us were concerned about the radical discrepancy between the new embrace of Latin American art by the Spanish art market and the steadily increasing hostility toward Latin American immigrants in Spain. So we invented a company named *Sudaca* (Spanish slang for "dirty southerner"), and designed a T-shirt on the front text of which we compared and contrasted the cost of Latin American artworks and of renting space to exhibit work at the art fair with the amounts of money that immigrants and refugees paid in bribes to enter the country, purchase false papers, rent apartments, etc. We ended our list with the amount of money that the Spanish government quietly paid the family of a Dominican woman named Leticia, who had emigrated to Spain to work as a maid and who was shot and killed for no reason by Spanish police in a bar frequented by Dominicans. The sum her relatives received monthly was the equivalent of what her annual salary had been as a domestic.

Then we donned ski masks and Peruvian knit caps, stormed the art fair in disguise, and proceeded to exhibit and sell our T-shirts on the floor – old-fashioned *tianguis*-style. We did brisk business on the first day and even sold a couple of T-shirts to museums. We even had a friend of ours dressed up as a policeman to deter the guards. This worked for a little while, but we were soon removed, and spent the next two days working our way back in, arguing with guards about whether we had the right to be present in the fair space if we were wearing masks. Once we sold all the T-shirts, we paraded around the fair wearing the last of them as if we were ambulatory sculptures, so that visitors could read our text.

There was a Mexican critic at the fair who had read a short piece I had written for the ARCO bulletin, in which I made a somewhat disparaging comment about a recent wave of what I saw as facile performance coming out of Mexico City, only to distinguish it from the work of Cesar Martinez, whose aesthetic proposals seemed much sounder to me. That critic sat in his room on the day of my arrival, so he could dial my number every half-hour. When I checked into the hotel, I was so jetlagged that I collapsed immediately. His phone call woke me, but his inexplicably accusatory tone and torrent of criticism made my body stiffen with shock. It seemed I had no right, first to be critical of anything Mexican at an art fair designed to promote Latin American art, and that, second, I should not be wasting space writing about performance. I soon gave up trying to discuss

2.   Juan Pablo Ballester, María Elena Escalona, and Coco Fusco
ARCO Art Fair, Madrid, 1997
Sudaca Enterprises, 1997
Ballester, Escalona, and Fusco set up an unauthorized stand at the first ARCO dedi-
cated to Latin American art and sold "art" T-Shirts with detailed information comparing
the costs involved in the sale of Latin American art to the costs of survival as an
undocumented Latin American political or economic refugee in Spain. The photo shows
Escalona in a ski mask and wool cap tending to customers.

anything rationally with the critic, realizing that, whether I liked his method or
not, he was doing the job he had been sent to do and I was too tired to fight.
He was there to deliver a paper on the Mexican art being sold at the fair, in
which he argued that there was no longer any need for Mexican artists to take
up political issues because the popular craftsmen did a better job with their bold
and bawdy curios.

When he saw the Sudaca performance, however, another side of him
emerged. Gone was the menacing phonecaller. Instead there was a rather daffy
gentleman who couldn't stop photographing us or yelling out my name so
all could hear, and finally he felt the need to deface a few of our T-shirts by
writing on them with his pen. We were in the middle of a performance that I
did not want to interrupt – plus, I was not about to give him the satisfaction of

acknowledging his presence. Later on, at the panel during which I was to give my paper on political street performance by Latin Americans, a group of his colleagues from Mexican art institutions systematically interrupted me with catcalls and hisses reminiscent of adolescents at a sports event. My hands shook while I read, but I didn't stop once to look up at them. It could not have been made clearer to me that there were kinds of performance that he and his colleagues really wanted to suppress. I thank them all for reminding me of the power of the medium. I hope they all read this book.

Choroní, Venezuela
December 1998

Notes

1   Foucault, Michel, "Of Other Spaces" in *Diacritics*, Spring 1986 issue, pp. 22–27.

2   Habermas, Jürgen, *The Structural Transformation of the Public Sphere: An Inquiry into a Category of Bourgeois Society*, trans. Thomas Berger with the assistance of Frederick Lawrence (Cambridge: MIT Press, 1989).

PART I

Heterotopic, homoerotic, hyper-exotic cabarets

The Melodramatic Seductions of Eva Perón

Silvia Pellarolo

This study explores the phenomenon of the libidinal attraction of the public figure of the actress Eva Perón – the extremely famous wife of Argentine president Juan Perón (1945–52) – and the following of her seduced audiences, under the light of current theories of gender construction and performance. I claim that in the fictional roles of her performing career Evita rehearsed the model of the political activist she would become during the Peronist administration, in which she starred as the protagonist of a flamboyant public theatricality. Her training as an actress resulted in a melodramatic style that could be traced from her first steps performing second-rate roles in the commercial theater and films, followed by the radio soaps she read passionately in the early 1940s, to conclude finally in her declamatory gestures at political gatherings.

This unexplored corporeal rereading of this public figure facilitates the recovery of her theatricality – and complexity – as a charismatic stage and political performer who embodied a modern feminine style which had already seduced mass audiences and thus received popular consent to promote much-needed reform in the society and legislation of her country.[1] For this revisionist approach to the understanding of Evita, Judith Butler's (1983) theories of the performative construction of gender become powerfully insightful tools.

In her introductory chapter to *Bodies That Matter*, Butler argues for the validation of a theoretical and epistemological reconsideration of the materiality of bodies. Her study traces the origins of Western metaphysics and the concept of representation in Plato via Irigaray, and discloses a number of exclusions in our received notions of materiality (i.e. women, animals, slaves, property, race, nationality, homosexuality), among which the materiality of the body of woman is underscored. Butler concludes by legitimating an inquiry critiqued many times for its "linguistic idealism" (p. 27), which would indeed serve as the groundwork for a political action validated by the reinscription of these exclusions in the Western truth regime.

Later in the book, she studies Slavoj Zizek's rethinking of the Lacanian symbolic in terms of the Althusserian notion of ideology in an innovative theory of political discourse, which "inquires into the uses and limits of a psychoanalytic perspective for a theory of political performatives and democratic contestation" (pp. 20–1). This theory which accounts for the performative character of political signifiers that, as sites of phantasmatic investment, effect the power to mobilize constituencies politically, could very well serve as a critical tool to understand the iconic appeal of Eva Perón, and the exchange engendered by her performing body and the enthusiastic reception of her adoring fans.

It could be said that, in a Butlerian sense, Evita's is a "body that matters," as I expect to prove in a book I am writing about gender construction in modern Argentina that focuses on the theatricality of "public women." I trace the trajectory that goes from the very popular women tango singers of the 1920s and 1930s and how their specific performative styles helped establish a modern feminine model that Evita would later incarnate, and thus take advantage of a vernacular type of female theatricality derived from melodrama, that facilitated an identificatory exchange with her audiences.[2]

It is impossible in such a study to disregard the issue of the "body" of Evita – considering her very public career and the overabundant dissemination of her iconography in the graphic propaganda of Peronism – and what this body represented for her constituencies (or the phantasmatic investments afforded to it). The strong symbolic value of this female body is ultimately proved by the anxious zeal of the Argentine military who overthrew her husband, president Juan Perón, in 1955, in "disappearing" her embalmed corpse from the public eye for almost twenty years.[3] Evita's is a body that matters because it becomes in the collective unconscious a synecdoche of the plight of a people, a screen onto which a community's desires, hopes, and needs for visibility and representation are projected.[4]

In fact, her performative body is all we have left from her to piece together the fragments of her private persona, which remained forever a façade: phantasms of a public figure, traces of a performing diva, specters of her volition in motion reproduced in different media (films, documentary footage, newsreels, photographs). A study of Eva's performing body will, then, following Butler, reveal its materiality and thus its political location as an exclusion of the pre-Peronist body politic. Eva Perón's mere physical presence served as a disruptor of the conservative political theatricality, used as it was to the austerity of male uniforms of institutionalized professions. In this context the body of an actress became a dangerous sign because it carnivalized received notions of propriety in political practices.

Argentine theater historians have noticed the discrimination actresses had to endure from a fanatically conservative society: "The independent life of the actress, as well as the dangers of work that involved public entertainment, had always made that profession somewhat disreputable for women" (Guy 1991: 157).[5]

3.   Peronist propaganda poster featuring Evita Duarte Perón, 1947. Text reads: "To Love is to Give Oneself, and to Give Oneself is to Give One's Own Life." *Photo courtesy of Silvia Pellarolo.*

This discrimination was evident since colonial times, as historian Teodoro Klein records in his well-documented history of Argentine performers (1994: 61), by a lack of actresses in theater troupes, due to the difficulty to attract women to a profession of ill-repute. An emblematic anecdote about the marginalization of actresses during the nineteenth century is told by the tragic story of a second-rate soprano surnamed Verneuil, who, while performing the role of the reverend mother of an abbey in the operetta *Mousquettaires au couvent*, transgressed the conventions of her role, and in what was perceived by the shocked audiences as an "attack of mental alienation" (Urquiza 1968: 25), raised the skirt of her habit and started to dance "a furious can can." Her punishment for such a sacrilegious subversion cost her her freedom: she was locked up in a lunatic asylum for the rest of her life.

Music-hall performers were said to be given to clandestine prostitution; as they received "absurdly low wages," they were obliged to "supplement their earnings . . . by practicing prostitution" (Guy 1991: 149). Actresses who sang in low-class music halls or theaters were frequently "obliged to associate with the audience . . . and to incite the men to drink" (p. 149). This practice became widespread with the success of the cabaret culture in Buenos Aires, during the second decade of the twentieth century. In venues such as the Royal Theater, which was situated in the ground floor of a very famous cabaret, in the context of which, and as part of the clauses of their contracts, "after the entertainment [wa]s over, . . . the young actresses [we]re expected . . . to 'entertain' the men who [we]re present" (p. 149).

These social values that condemned women performers, and perceived them as a threat to the hegemony of the patriarchal society, were the backdrop of the collective anxiety produced when the coupling of an actress as Evita and a disruptor of political conventions as her husband, Juan Perón, was shamelessly exhibited in the context of politically charged public performances. The evident disruption of the cozy boundaries between the private and the public that the Peróns promoted by means of their scandalous liaison is foregrounded by Donna Guy, who asserts that

> Much of the class anger directed at Evita and Juan Perón in the 1940s and 1950s derived from the same value systems that had generated the lively debates about prostitution and popular culture before 1936. That same fear of female independence, of lower-class and dubious women's taking control over their lives [and bodies], of their joining with society's most dangerous men in a social revolution, all came true within the context of the Peronist years, 1943–55, and in this way fiction became a reality.
>
> (1991: 173)

This blurring of the boundaries between reality and fiction, the overlapping of theater and life, that the carnivalization of Peronism represented in decorous Argentina, is even perceived in the historical accounts of that era. Such is the case of Navarro and Fraser's biography of Evita (1996), in which the use of the theatrical simile becomes redundant when describing the spectacular dimension of Peronism and the fascination produced on the audiences it summoned.[6] Probably modeling the spectacularity of fascism as an efficient way of staging a rustic vernacular theatricality repressed by the illustrated elite more prone to the mimicking of elegant French models, the propaganda machine of Peronism was a savvy interpreter of the benefits of the interconnection of mass culture and politics, with the intuition that in order to revert the hegemony of the oligarchy the ethic and aesthetic values and images of the rising class and emerging sector of consumers should be disseminated by means of the expanding culture industry. Thus, Peronism's revalorization of "popular national traditions, considered [by the Europeanized liberal class in power], to be synonymous with backwardness, obscurantism and stagnation" (Laclau 1977: 179), as efficient counterhegemonic practices and productions that would disrupt the coherency of a social imaginary constructed in opposition to its deepest cultural roots.[7]

In this epic play, Eva Perón assumed the role of the standardbearer of this rising class, her performing body an icon which – following a melodramatic tradition – fulfilled vicariously collective desires of representation and agency. The success of her acting career, her training field from 1935 to 1945, that consisted of twenty plays, five movies and twenty-six soap operas (Navarro and Fraser 1996: 48), could be read as a dress rehearsal the prominent role she would perform as the notorious wife of a popular president. Such was the case in the *radioteátro* scripts she performed for *Hacia un Futuro Mejor* (Towards a Better Future), an agitprop celebration of the 1943 revolution that had taken Perón and other reformist military men to power. Broadcasted by Radio Belgrano, and authored by the same men who would later write many of the Peróns' political speeches, the program aired on the night of August 14, 1944, titled "The Soldier's Revolution will be the Revolution of the Argentine People," presented Eva's debut as a Peronist militant. "Over the sound of a military march" a speaker announced

> Here, in the confusion of the streets, where a new sense of purpose is coming to be born ... here, among the anonymous mass of working, suffering, thinking, silent people ... here, in the midst of exhaustion and hope, justice and mockery, here in this shapeless mass, the driving force of a capital city, nerve centre and engine of a great American country ... here she is, THE WOMAN ...
>
> (Navarro and Fraser 1996: 43)

With a melodramatic tone, Evita talked next about the wonders of the Revolution, which she claimed had come to cure "the sense of injustice that makes the blood rush to one's hands and head"; a Revolution that "was made for exploited workers," due to the "fraud of dishonest politicians," because the country was "bankrupt of feeling, at the verge of suicide" (p. 43). Her training in this excessive verbal style, with its virtuosity of gradiose hyperboles and contrasts, the strong enunciation of a Manichean worldview, and the delivery of clear didactic and moralizing messages, would prove to be extremely effective during her forthcoming public appearances, in which she spoke to the hearts of the masses, thus satisfying, as it happens in populist regimes, the "rising expectations" of the people, with an ideology and a style that appealed directly to their emotions (Laclau 1977: 152).

Another interesting illustration of this "rehearsal" of her political role is the movie *La Pródiga* (The Prodigal; completed in October 1945, but sequestered from public viewing until 1984), in which she portrayed a repentant sinner who, as part of her penitence performs acts of charity; a rich widow who, in a very feudal way, is prodigal with the good peasants of her domains, who address her in anticipation to her political career as "*hermana de los tristes, madre de los pobres*" (sister of the sad, mother of the poor). "Evita liked the film and also the stereotype of suffering, sacrifice and destruction she had portrayed," declare Navarro and Fraser (1996: 48); this was said to be her favorite role in her performing career, a "memory of the future" in Alicia Dujovne Ortiz's words (1995: 96). No wonder that in the fiction of Eloy Martínez's *Santa Evita* the first lady is presented delighting in the solitary pleasures of its private screening.

Evita's female agency, charisma, and stage presence undoubtedly derive from her desire to please the public, to perform legitimacy and thus become visible before a captive audience. As an illegitimate child, she carried inscribed on her body the unsurmountable desire to be acknowledged, to be seen; a desire that, according to Dujovne Ortiz, became the mobilizing force which propelled her forward (1995: 95). In her autobiography, *La Razón de mi Vída*, Eva confesses that since her early childhood, she always wanted to recite (*declamar*): "It was as if I always desired to say something to others, something big, that arose from the bottom of my heart" (1996: 24). In fact, there is a very interesting childhood photograph that captures "the creative Duarte children" dressed up in costumes for the Carnival celebrations in the town of Los Toldos (de Elía and Queiroz 1997: 23). To the left of the group appears a shy 2-year-old Evita, attired with a ballerina costume, ready to entertain the fantasy of being someone else, an attempt to escape from her daily misery and illegitimacy.

Her road towards stardom, before her political career, was documented in the insinuating photos reproduced in movie magazines *Sintonía*, *Antena*, and

Radiolandia, which portray the new model of Argentine beauty: a blend of Hollywood screen allure with the earthy nature of vernacular melodrama heroines. And why was this melodramatic style so appealing to her constituencies? Although lacking in sexual appeal, Eva's withdrawn and calculated performance of modern feminity, which is captured at its best in the studio portraits taken by society photographer Annemarie Heinrich, satisfy the expectations of her popular audiences pampered by spectacles carefully tailored to their tastes since the times of the colonial *circo criollo*.[8]

The movie *La Cabalgata del Circo*, released in May 1945, which marked Evita's debut as a blonde movie star, illustrates the transformation of this melodramatic style by the cinematic representation of a theater troupe of rural origins in the *circo criollo*. With an extremely innovative narrative style, this film, directed by Mario Soffici, unearths the undergound trajectory of a vernacular popular culture that the advent of Peronism was rendering visible at that time. Usually remembered for the famous dispute that arose between Eva and co-star and tango singer Libertad Lamarque, which remained in the popular imagination as the cause of the prolonged exile of the latter in Mexico, its storyline traces the process of modernization of the *criollo* popular theater from its silent pantomimes that celebrated an agonizing *gaucho* culture to the urban *sainetes de cabaret* of the commercial theater of the 1920s.[9] In its scenes we see Evita at her melodramatic best, performing the role of the betrayer in a semi-incestuous sentimental triangle with screen partner and tango singer Hugo del Carril.

In her studies of Latin American *telenovelas*, Nora Maziotti considers melodrama as a "hypergenre that contaminates different practices, even everyday life" (1993: 154). Its emphatic representational and performative syles, geared towards the triggering of sudden emotions in its audiences, can be traced in tango singers, and, its choreography, and even in public speeches of political performers. Melodrama as a nineteenth-century theater genre was characterized by its poliphony of signs, produced by spectacular *mises en scène* which boasted of technical resources: contrasting lights, emphatic make-up, music used to foreground the different episodes of the action, and a sophisticated stage machine (Maziotti 1993: 154–55). This "rhetoric of excess" – as Peter Brook has denominated the flamboyant gestuality and theatrical language of melodrama – continues, according to Jesús Martín-Barbero, the performing tradition of country fairs and travelling troupes which combine "the presentation of farces and comic interludes with acrobatics, puppetry . . . juggling" and pantomime (1993: 114). The "metonymical stylization" of this performing style, with its "often exaggerated symbolism of facial and other personal characteristics" continues the "strong codification that corporeal appearance and gestures have in popular culture," as is the case in Commedia dell'Arte.

Martín-Barbero traces the origins of melodrama to the French Revolution, and claims it is the "portrayal of the transformation of the rabble into an organized public . . . which could not read and who looked to the stage not for words but for action and great passions" (1993: 112–13). Furthermore, he adds that the melodramatic excess was a victory over the repression of bourgeois patrons and consequently the genre's complicity

> with the new popular culture and with the cultural space which this public marked out for itself provide the keys which help us situate this form of popular spectacle at the turning point of the process which moved from the popular to the mass. Melodrama provided a point of arrival for the narrative memory and gestural forms of popular culture and the point of emergence of the dramatization of mass culture.
>
> (1993: 113)

La Cabalgata del Circo, successfully transferring this popular tradition to the culture industry supported by Peronism, validated a "regional expressive system," as Angel Rama has denominated the gestuality of *circo criollo gaucho* dramas (1982: 135), a corporeal performativity influenced by melodrama, which, mirroring the popular sectors of the Argentine community since colonial times, prepared the ground for the creation of a popular national theatricality that later spilled over the film industry and the spectacular language of modern political actors.

María de la Luz Hurtado studies the structural characteristics of the melodrama genre, which she claims is a type of fiction which "gains popularity in times when the modes of production and social relations are transformed, the historical institutionalization of which had meant an integrated and culturally legitimized world" (1986: 124). This narrative structure is as follows. Given an initially harmonious situation centered around a humble family of traditional values, a conflict is introduced whereby the traditional family order is broken. Based on Manichean values, the party responsible for this disintegration is the bad boy/girl:

> an external element to the biological family . . . which exerts a negative influence on one of its members. The attractions with which the "bad guy" lures his prey are based on the modern values of a capitalist consumer society in its moment of speculation, not of production. The accepted goal of this life is the conquest of status, profit, ostentatious luxury, and the cult of physical attraction (i.e. women who use jewelry and makeup, who rely on their eroticism, and who, naturally, always need money , are the "bad girls" of this melodrama . . . The main symbol of the fall provoked by the disintegration of the family is the loss of "virtue" in the case of the young woman and the "neglect" of the mother in the case of the son.
>
> (1986: 123)

The progression of the narrative widens the abyss between the values still held in the heart of the family and the new "licentious" life led by the "bad boy/girl." The dramatic tension leads to a climax that usually represents a turning-point in which the pre-existing order is reestablished. The resolution follows the mythical theme of the prodigal child, as we have seen, a favorite fictional role of Evita's.

The commercial theater of the 1920s and 1930s, in the context of which Eva had been trained, had found a very popular topic in the representation of poor women who, in search of a better social position, would leave their suburban tenements to work in downtown cabarets, where rich men from the upper classes learned to dance tango. Following a melodramatic narrative structure, numerous *sainetes* (brief farce-type plays) dramatized, amplifying them, the narrations of the tangos included in these works, which constituted the "hook" to attract audiences. Many famous tangos were introduced in these *intermezzos cantabiles*, and the young women who performed them – and would eventually become international figures favored by the radio and recording industries – made their debuts singing in these venues. The magnitude of this phenomenon created by the roaring popularity of these plays and the symbolic impact they produced in the collective psyche makes of this rich corpus an attractive document which recorded the transformations undergone by traditional feminine roles during modernization.

The tangos sung by these women show a clear intertextuality with French melodramas. Repeating the fictional plight of the serial novels' heroines, who end up abandoned by their lovers after being displaced from their class origins, these young women accuse the tango for their destruction. This topic, repeated in so many other plays, is presented in *Canciones Populares* (Popular Songs) of 1920. Its first vignette, titled "Damned Tango," is a didactic piece which represents the disillusionment of Ivonne, an alleged French prostitute, who blames the tango for her licentious life, and laments in her final confession and recognition of her hybris:

> It is always the eternal story, always the same and always different. The cabaret, with its luxury and pleasures ... The folly, the gay hours, and the vertigo to forget the bitter moments ... And le "tangó!" ... oh le "tangó!" ... I have thus fallen ... Le "tangó" is a bad friend ... I have forgotten all ... all ... mother ... family ... home ... All ... And meanwhile, I am the favorite of many men without belonging to none ... The business of love has killed love ... In fact ... I could never live without the cabaret ... without the music ... without the champagne ... without the long night of madness ... (pauses) Le "tangó" ... ! Le "tangó"! ... It gives me life killing me slowly ... I curse it! And ... nevertheless ... I can't, I can't abandon it.

The multifaceted film mentioned above, *La Cabalgata del Circo*, provides a screen version of this topic. In one of the scenes that portray the urbanization of the rural theater troupe, Libertad Lamarque, in the role of a cabaret singer, performs the famous "Maldito tango," displaying a gestuality of excess influenced by the old pantomimes. The incredible success received as an international tango singer by "La Reina del melodrama" – a privilege with which her Mexican fans have recently awarded her – helps to deconstruct the threat of doom that tango signified for the character she played in the famous film.

These women tango singers were able to achieve the impossible: while singing mostly male-authored lyrics, which delivered a message of control over modern women's independence, the public availability of their performing bodies, which interacted mainly with female audiences, contradicted the representation of abjection, prostitution, and destruction suffered by the women of the tangos they sang. With the classical tactic of the weak, which Evita also knew so well how to manipulate, these singers gladly staged a collective warning to young women that it was better to stay in their suburban tenements laboring as dressmakers, and to resist the illusions of grandeur that the tantalizing center of the city with its tango culture and its opportunities of social mobility lured them with. In any case, the female audiences who witnessed, for example, Azucena Maizani performing tangos with these type of messages, such as "No salgas de tu barrio" (Don't leave your barrio) in the "Porteño" theater, clearly understood that the physical presence of this woman on the stages of downtown Buenos Aires was an implicit message of disobedience to the song's advice.[10]

In addition, the artistic personas of these female performers – the *arrabalera:*, the tough yet glamorous woman of the suburbs who had learnt to deal with modern life and men, and who many times had to cross-dress in order to be allowed to perform as tango singers – became an acceptable alternative to a more radical type of woman for the conservative sectors of society. Most of the time these singers had to legitimize their access to the masculinized public space of the tango culture through the impersonation of male roles, dressed up as *gauchos* or *compadritos*, as is evident in the case of Azucena, known popularly as the "*la ñata gaucha*" (pug-nosed gaucha). The public support that these women tango singers constantly received, particularly from their female audiences, proves that this feminine model, skillfully transferred from the living theater of the city to actual theater stages by this constellation of talented performers, had become a viable alternative for modern urban women. The visibility and popularity of successful, independent, professional women performers provided by the mass culture was effectively internalized by a society which rejected a more radical feminine style.

It is not surprising, then, that this theatricality that had trained audiences in the acceptance and adoption of this gendered model was later adopted by Eva Perón, who was able to impersonate and institutionalize this feminine style as the charismatic first lady who pushed for the female vote and an end to discrimination against women in the workforce in the late 1940s. As Julie Taylor affirms when exploring the myths of Eva Perón, her figure "confronts us with the enigma of power attributed to a woman in a traditionally and formally patriarchal society" (1981: 10). To trace the prehistory of this powerful female model, it is delusive to look at the feminists and left-wing women who were politically active in Argentina since the turn of the century. These elite women, who refused to support the empowering of women by Peronism – i.e., the passing of the law that granted them the right to vote – due to their suspicion of the reformist and demagogic characteristics of this movement were never able to attract a massive following of women because of their class alliances and their allegiance to international interests. The genderless austerity that many of them displayed, modeled by international feminists, was collectively perceived by the fanatically heterosexual Argentine society as a dangerous model of femininity due to their lack of "feminine charm." Moreover, as Kathleen Newman's article on the modernization of Argentine women demonstrates, this austere female model was construed as a "foreign threat" (1990: 85).[11] These masculinized foreigners did not satisfy the expectations of Argentine audiences instructed to value beauty in the mysteriously feminine availability of Hollywood silent-screen divas or native melodrama heroines.[12]

Women tango singers, on the other hand, provided a strong vernacular model that was not devoid of gender contradictions, the most notorious of which was their interest in crossdressing, as so many women did in the 1920s. Their defiance to standard canons of female beauty when they crossdressed was accepted naturally by their audiences, who were probably pleased to see mimicked on stage forlorn vernacular types: the slick *compadrito*, and the more exotic *gaucho* style. This embracing of a national popular aesthetic diverted the attention from the mischievous gender play that Argentine audiences would forever deny as being the reflection of a hidden gender ambiguity that some recent studies are bringing to the fore.[13] What was evident to these audiences was the strong model conveyed by these women, many of whom would become sympathizers with Peronism, such as the cases of Azucena Maizani and Nelly Omar, who authored the tango "La descamisada" which celebrated the loyalty of "*la mujer argentina*" (the Argentine woman) to the Peróns. Others, like Juanita Larrauri, a fervent militant of the feminine branch of the Peronist party created by Eva, served as senator from 1952 to 1955, and was later elected president of this political organization (Santos 1983: 230–4).

Re-enacting the same trajectory of tango and melodrama heroines, Evita follows the path of so many poor women, who, lured by the lights and opportunities of the modern city, abandon their marginal postition in society confident that they will succeed in a performing career. After triumphing as an actress and becoming quite visible as the wife of the president, Eva discards the glamorous Hollywood style she had adopted at the beginning of her acting career and which reached a peak during her spectacular trip to Europe in 1947, as Perón's goodwill ambassador. Empowered after her return by the interest of the international media in disseminating her public image, her old needs of visibility therefore satisfied, she then adopts – as many women tango singers before her – what is perceived by most of her opponents as a masculinized public image when she finally becomes a political actress with a strong social agenda.

Her training in the performing styles of the late 1930s and early 1940s is clearly perceived in her public appearances in mass rallies. As Davis and Dulicai have shown in a movement signature study of Hitler's public performances, which they describe as "melodramatic actions" (1992: 160), Eva Perón demonstrated remarkable skills when performing her political persona in a public setting. If we analyze the footage of newsreels of her last years (e.g., the August 22, 1951 Cabildo Abierto del Justicialismo, when the unions offered her the vice-presidency, and her last public appearance for the act of the International Workers' Day on May 1, 1952), we can detect the same excess in language and gestuality that she had used when performing a melodramatic style. Angrier than before, due to the urgency of her political message and the awareness that her body was being devastated by uterine cancer, her rare apparitions in this footage are wonderful illustrations of the seamless transition from her fictional roles to the political. Second in importance to "the people" – the collective body of the masses that were construed by the Peronist lens as the protagonist of these multitudinous rallies – it is her strong and hoarse voice (as in her radio days), which emphatically addresses her faithful followers, that is foregrounded.

As in tangos and cheap serial novels, or the radio plays she used to perform before she became a political figure, Evita died young, endowing her fellow countrywomen with a strong public model of femininity and activism. Just as her vandalized embalmed corpse was returned after twenty years of concealment, it is high time Evita recover her (performing) body.

Notes

1.   I had a confirmation of the importance of this revisionist approach by the recent opposition of wide sectors of the Argentine society to the representation of this political and

social icon by US actress and singer Madonna. Their rejection of the US sex icon to impersonate Evita indicated to me – beyond legitimate concerns to uphold decolonization – that for Argentinian audiences this was an explosive (gender/performative/popularity-based) combination that intersected in the performing body of Madonna. In a metonymic twist the media-disseminated spectrality of this "loose" corporeality threatened to demystify the flat "saint–whore" dichotomy that pro- and anti-Evita sectors had grudgingly accepted as a safe way of immortalizing (and disembodying) her memory.

2.   In his "Closing Remarks" to *Negotiating Performance: Gender, Sexuality and Theatricality in Latin/o America* (1994) Juan Villegas favors the concept of "theatricality" to the more accepted one of "performance" in US academia. He claims that, as "performance" cannot be translated into Spanish, a less colonial term to explain the visuality of certain Latin/o/a American performance practices could be used by the translatable concept of "theatricality" or "theatrical discourses," terms that allow for the inclusion of theatrical activities beyond the "dominant culture's traditional view of 'theater'" (p. 316). "Theatricality" would then be understood "as a means of communicating a message by integrating verbal, visual, auditive, body, gestural signs to be performed in front of an audience . . ., codes which are integrated in the cultural system and the social and political context" (pp. 316–17) of the producer and the receiver. The obvious focus on the reception of that encoded visuality afforded by the term "theatricality" is shifted to the agency of the performer in the concept of "performance." My work will meander between both points of view, as I am interested in studying the theatrical apparatus of Peronism, its "theatricality" as a political strategy for claiming public space and political visibility for the empowerment of traditionally erased sectors of society, and Eva's predominant role in this *mise en scène*; and affirming and foregrounding Eva's performing skills, her agency as an efficient (political) actress, and the use she made of well-established acting styles in modern Argentina.

3.   Diana Taylor, co-editor with Villegas of the volume mentioned above, in her article "Performing Gender: Las Madres de la Plaza de Mayo," included in the collection, studies the politicized staging of motherhood in Argentina during the last repressive military dictatorship (1976–81) as a legitimate site of contestation to the military regime and an efficient political strategy for the searching of these mothers' "disappeared" loved ones. The concealment of Evita's body, seen in this context, would anticipate the infamous practice of the military junta of "disappearing" suspicious individuals construed as threatening diseases of the body politic. See also Taylor's *Disappearing Acts: Spectacles of Gender and Nationalism in Argentina's "Dirty War."* In her works, Taylor privileges the concept of "performance," due to the fact that it "allow[s] for agency, which opens a way for [the inclusion of] resistance and oppositional spectacles" (1997: 14).

4.   Even after her death her body became the contested site and trophy of pro- and anti-Evita sectors, as is fictionalized in the famous novel by Tomás Eloy Martínez, *Santa Evita* (1996). Moreover, her beatification by her adoring fans responded to the need to construct her death as a sacrifice that, in some magical sense, would redeem the whole membership of the society from class and race conflicts.

5.   At the beginning of this century, as Guy notes, "all independent women were [considered] potential prostitutes because they symbolized social decay and the loss of social and

personal virtues" (1991: 154). These "problematic," "dangerous" women, like actresses and other breadwinners, became a threat to the very conservative and patriarchal society due to their financial and sexual independence.

6.   Navarro and Fraser claim that Perón "was to become a great exponent of the theatrical in politics, its ceremonies and spectacles" (1996: 38). Referring to his and Evita's protagonic role in the politics of their time, the historians recurringly use theatrical analogies: they were "actors in the drama" (p. 49), Perón's speeches represented a "theatrical statement of hatred, group against group, class against class" (p. 51); the semiotics of his public appearances are foregrounded, and references to theatrical styles or genres constantly mentioned. For example, the grandiose outcome of his release from prison due to the spontaneous mobilization of the masses on the historical October 17, 1945, is portrayed as a operatic script: Navarro presents him "dressed in civilian clothes," standing "in the glare of the lights which were trained on him," "aware . . . of the almost invisible presence of the enormous crowd, its size exaggerated by the night" (p. 66). Unlike Navarro's, anti-Peronist accounts of this event foreground its farcesque character; such as the case of Félix Luna, who described this empowerment and visibility of the people flooding the public space of elegant Buenos Aires as "a curious pantomime, something quite unique in the history of any country" (Navarro and Fraser 1996: 66).

7.   I thus agree with Ernesto Laclau's understanding of populism, which he considers is "not an expression of the ideological backwardness of a dominated class but, on the contrary, an expresion of the moment when the articulating power of this class imposes itself hegemonically on the rest of society" (1977: 196).

8.   The *circo criollo* (creole circus) had been since colonial times a privileged entertainment of the popular classes. Consisting of two parts – the acrobatics of the first and the pantomime of the second – this performative genre is considered one of the earliest expressions of a vernacular theatrical tradition. It originated in the rural areas surrounding the port-city of Buenos Aires and suffered a transformation with the modernization and urbanization of the country in the last decade of the nineteenth century. On the arenas of the *circo criollo* was staged the rebelliousness of the outcasts displaced by the modernizing economy: the *gauchos malos* (bad cowboys), and the transculturation of the different characters provided by the massive European immigration, thus adding an ethnic dimension to its lower-class appeal. For further information on this genre and its transculturation, see Beatriz Seibel's (1993) and Raúl Castagnino's (1953) studies on *circo criollo*, and my *Sainete criollo/democracia/representación. El caso de Nemesio Trejo* (1997).

9.   Libertad Lamarque complains in her memoirs of the abuse of power that she claims Evita exhibited during the shooting of the film, a power that came from her liaison with the most important man in the country. In spite of this clash of personalities of two competing divas (Libertad had been named the "Queen of Tango" some years before), this conflict should be seen under an ideological light. Libertad belonged to an anarchist family, and had been trained in the rich tradition of libertarian theater groups that performed social dramas, a tradition that she translated into the cinematic medium when she became a film star (Maziotti 1993). Her notorious dislike towards the reformism and demagogy of Peronism was manifested against Eva, who bragged about her proximity and political solidarity to Perón and his ideas.

10.   "No abandones tu costura,/ muchachita arrabalera,/ a la luz de la modesta/ lamparita de kerosene . . . / No la dejes a tu vieja,/ ni a tu calle, ni al convento,/ ni al muchacho sencillote/ que suplica tu querer./ Desechá los berretines/ y los novios milongueros,/ que entre rezongos del fuelle,/ te trabajan de chiqué./ No salgas de tu barrio, sé buena mucha- chita,/ casate con un hombre que sea como vos/ y aún en la miseria sabrás vencer tu pena/ y ya llegará un día en que te ayude Dios./ Como vos, yo, muchachita./ era linda y era buena; era humilde y trabajaba,/ como vos, en un taller./ Dejé al novio que me amaba/ con respeto y con ternura/ por un niño engominado. que me trajo al cabaret;/ me enseñó todos sus vicios,/ pisoteó mis ilusiones,/ hizo de mí este despojo,/ muchachita, que aquí ves" (Gobello 1995: 130).
   Eva did the same when in her autobiography she summoned women to stay at home and procreate, two things she never did (pp. 205–07).

11.   In "The Modernization of Femininity: Argentina, 1916–1926," Kathleen Newman analyzes some photographs of North American feminists published by the periodical *Plus Ultra,* targeted to an elite readership. Attired "in dull dress – long, masculine jackets and matching long skirts of a heavy material, plain, full-brimmed hats," the caption concludes that this was "the uniform of the National Army of Women" (1990: 83).

12.   Even Eva in her autobiography, has something to say about these masculinized "femi- nists." In the chapter titled "Women and My Mission," there is a brief section that explains her personal view of these women, whom she describes as "ridiculous." She starts out by confessing that the alternative of "a 'feminist' path" scared her, for, as she continues, exclaiming with a false modesty that recalls the tricks of the weak used by Sor Juana four centuries earlier, "What could I do, humble woman of the people, where other women, more prepared than me, had failed?" (1996: 200). She then reflects, "I was not an old single woman, nor so ugly as to occupy a position like that one . . . which, generally, in the world, since the English feminists until now, belongs almost with exclusive rights, to this type of women . . . women whose first vocation should undoubtedly have been to be men" (p. 200). It is evident that what Eva dismissed of the English feminists was their Puritanism, what she perceived as their lack of sexuality, and the threat they posed as international agents to the nationalist vision espoused by Peronism.

13.   Canonic tango studies have seldom included reflections on gender issues. Only very recently, and mostly abroad (with some exceptions in Argentina) have such approaches been undertaken, due to the fact that the discipline has been historically monopolized by a sexist male scholarship reluctant to accept dissident views (i.e., feminist). The Bay Area Tango Association newsletter, *Gotán,* dedicated its summer 1996 issue to "women and tango." Among recent academic approaches, see dos Santos (1978), Pellarolo (1997), Salessi (1995), Savigliano (1995).

References

Butler, Judith. *Bodies That Matter: On the Discursive Limits of "Sex."* New York and London: Routledge, 1993.

Castagnino, Raúl. *El Circo Criollo.* Buenos Aires: Lajouane, 1953.

Davis, Martha and Dianne Dulicai. "Hitler's Movement Signature." *The Drama Review* 32.2 (Summer 1992):132–52.

de Elía, Tomás and Juan Pablo Queiroz (eds). *Evita: An Intimate Portrait of Eva Perón*. New York: Rizzoli, 1997.

Demitrópulos, Libertad. *Eva Perón*. Buenos Aires: CEAL, 1984.

Dujovne Ortiz, Alicia. *Eva Perón, la biografía*. Buenos Aires: Aguilar, 1995.

Eloy Martínez, Tomás. *Santa Evita*. New York: Alfred A. Knopf, 1996.

Gobello, José. *Letras de Tangos; Selección (1897–1981)*. Buenos Aires: Nuevo Siglo, 1995.

Guy, Donna. *Sex and Danger in Buenos Aires: Prostitution, Family and Nation in Argentina*. Lincoln and London: University of Nebraska Press, 1991.

Hurtado, María de la Luz. "El melodrama, género matriz en la dramaturgia chilena contemporánea: constantes y variaciones de su aproximación a la realidad." *Gestos* 1 (April 1986): 121–30.

Klein, Teodoro. *El actor en el Río de la Plata; de la colonia a la Independencia Nacional*. Buenos Aires: Asociación Argentina de Actores, 1984.

——. *el actor en el Río de la Plata II; de Casacuberta a los Podestá*. Buenos Aires: Asociación Argentina de Actores, 1994.

Laclau, Ernesto. *Politics and Ideology in Marxist Theory: Capitalism, Fascism, Populism*. London: Verso, 1977.

Martín-Barbero, Jesús. *Communication, Culture and Hegemony: From Media to Mediations*. London: Sage, 1993.

Maziotti, Nora. "Intertextualidades en la telenovela argentina: melodrama y costumbrismo." *El espectáculo de la pasión: Las Telenovelas Latinoamericanas*. Nora Maziotti (ed). Buenos Aires: Colihue, 1993: 153–64.

Navarro, Marysa and Nicholas Fraser. *Evita: The Real Life of Eva Perón*. New York, London: W. W. Norton, 1996.

Newman, Kathleen. "The Modernization of Femininity: Argentina, 1916–1926." In *Women, Culture and Politics in Latin America*. Seminar on Feminism and Culture in Latin America (ed.) Berkeley, Los Angeles: University of California Press, 1990: 74–89.

Pellarolo, Silvia. "Performing Melodrama/Performing Gender in Modern Argentina: Tango, Crossdressing, Eva Perón." *Feministas Unidas* 17.2 (Fall 1997): 16–21.

——. *Sainete Criollo/Democracia/Representación. El Caso de Nemesio Trejo*. Buenos Aires: Corregidor, 1997.

Perón, Eva. *La razón de mi vida y otros escritos (Evita por ella misma)*. Buenos Aires: Planeta, 1996.

Rama, Angel. *Los Gauchipolíticos Rioplatenses*. Buenos Aires: CEAL, 1982.

Sábato, Néstor (ed.). *Libertad Lamarque. Los grandes del tango* 14, 1991.

Salessi, Jorge. *Médicos, maleantes y maricas: higiene, criminología y homosexualidad en la construcción de la nación Argentina (Buenos Aires: 1871–1914)*. Rosario: Beatriz Viterbo, 1995.

Salessi, Jorge and Patrick O'Connor. "For Carnival, Clinic, and Camera: Argentina's Turn-of-the-Century Drag Culture Performs 'Woman.'" In *Negotiating Performance. Gender, Sexuality and Theatricality in Latin/o America*. Diana Taylor and Juan Villegas (eds). Durham: Duke University Press, 1994: 257–75.

Santos, Estela dos. *La historia del tango. Las cantantes*. Buenos Aires: Corregidor, 1978, vol.13.

—— *Las mujeres peronistas*. Buenos Aires: CEAL, 1983.

Savigliano, Marta. *Tango and the Political Economy of Passion*. Boulder: Westview Press, 1995.

—— "Whiny Ruffians and Rebellious Broads: Tango as a Spectacle of Eroticized Social Tension." *Theatre Journal* 47 (1995): 83–104.

Schaeffer Gallo, Carlos. *Canciones populares. La Escena* 13 year III (October 1920).

Seibel, Beatriz. *Historia del Circo*. Buenos Aires: Ediciones del Sol, 1993.

Taylor, Diana. *Disappearing Acts: Spectacles of Gender and Nationalism in Argentina's "Dirty War."* Durham: Duke University Press, 1997.

—— "Performing Gender: Las Madres de la Plaza de Mayo." In *Negotiating Performance: Gender, Sexuality and Theatricality in Latin/o America*. Diana Taylor and Juan Villegas (eds). Durham: Duke University Press, 1994: 306–20.

Taylor, Julie. *Eva Perón: The Myths of a Woman*. Chicago: University of Chicago Press, 1981.

Urquiza, Juan José de. *El Cervantes en la Historia del Teátro Argentino*. Buenos Aires, Ediciones Culturales Argentinas, 1968.

Villegas, Juan. "Closing Remarks." In *Negotiating Performance: Gender, Sexuality and Theatricality in Latin/o America*. Diana Taylor and Juan Villegas (eds). Durham: Duke University Press, 1994: 306–20.

4.   Carmelita Tropicana in "Chicas 2000" as Pingalito Betancourt, 1998, New York
Photo: Dona Ann McAdams
Cuban-born Tropicana (Alina Troyano) began her career in the 1980s as a performer at the WOW Cafe in the East Village and soon became a fixture of the performance-art milieu that blossomed around such sites as the Pyramid Club and PS 122. She has written and performed dozens of shows that draw on the *variété* sketch structure and satiric style of Latin American popular theater, and she often uses cross-dressing and cross-gender casting while poking fun at tropicalist stereotypes.

Chicas 2000

An excerpt
Carmelita Tropicana

Pingalito Betancourt, a Cuban man with cigar, is played by Carmelita Tropicana.

Good evening ladies and gentlemen. My name is Pingalito Betancourt. I am a retired public transportation official. As a matter of fact in Cuba in 1955 I was the conductor of the Ml5 bus. I was called the Socrates, the philosopher king of the M15. It is an honor to be here at opinions of the Hoi Polloi. First when I see the sign I get excited, I think it is Spanish, *Hoy Pollo* (today chicken), but no. Hoi Polloi is an expression that means, mi gente, the people, the masses.

I want to discuss with you my philosophy about Puritanism. I started investigating Puritanism last Thanksgiving when I was eating turkey and watching *Pocahontas*. I know you look at me and see a very Puritan kind of guy, a regular John Smith. That is correct. I have many of the components of Puritanism: self-reliance, frugality, and industry.

Let's take self-reliance. You see these glasses of mine are broken; I relied on myself to put on duck tape and fix them. Industry, yes, America should have many factories. And frugality, *el dos por uno*, two for the price of one, when I can go to the A & P and get two containers of Tropicana orange juice for the price of one, that floats my boat and rocks my boots. But where I part company with Puritanism is with the sexuality stuff. I think there is a little hypocrisy here. How many of you remember Joceleyn Elders? Come on, raise your hands. For those of you who don't know, Joceleyn Elders was the Surgeon General who dared to mention masturbation. And what happened to her? She got fired. I want to take a poll today. Raise your hands ladies and gentlemen if you have never ever touched yourselves. Come on. OK.

So, people, Puritanism has some good things some bad. How do we save it? We cannot throw the baby out with the bathwater. How do we create a gentler, kinder Puritanism? I was thinking about this when the answer came to be watching a PBS special on the Bonobo monkeys of the Congo. These monkeys are incredible. Distant cousins you say? Not so distant. We share 98 percent of the same genes. Like us they got tools. You should see these monkeys with the Black & Decker power saw. And culture! These monkeys have culture. One monkey, Jane, was taught to paint; she already has two shows at a SoHo art gallery. The critics call her painting Japanese Simian.

But the Bonobos excel in two areas. First Government. The ERA, they got it. A boy or girl Bonobo can become king or queen. And sexuality. These monkeys have sex for procreation, recreation, to relieve stress anxiety and boredom. Can you imagine ladies and gentlemen, what a world this could be if you get up in the morning, you are tired sleepy, the doorbell rings. It's the UPS girl and to wake you up she starts to rub up against you and then you go to the post office, you lick your stamps and the postal employee licks you. And then you go to the bank, you are overdrawn on your checking account, you are so upset that the bank teller to make you feel better starts to fondle your genitals. What a world this could be ladies and gentlemen. Let us invigorate America by creating a real Banana Bonobo Republic!

Exotic Exports: The Myth of the Mulatta

Raquel Mendieta Costa

Translated by Eduardo Aparicio

Ochún's blessing and curse[1]

> *Caminando por las calles del pueblecito natal*
> *Con su tipo espiritual ella va luciendo el talle.*
> *Con la bata arremangá, sonando sus chancleticas,*
> *Los hombres le van detrás a la linda mulatica.*
>
> (Strolling down the streets of her home town,
> With soulful demeanor she hands out flowers.
> With her robe tucked up, and her thongs clapping,
> Men go chasing after her, the pretty little mulatta.)
> | *Los Zafiros* quartet

In Cuba, as in the rest of the countries where plantations were established with African slaves, the myth of the mulatta as the embodiment of female sensuality is widespread. Gilberto Freyre's quoting in *Casa-grande y Senzala* (1942: 2: 109) of the traditional Brazilian adage that states that "white women are for marrying, mulattas are for fornicating, and black women are for working" could easily be applied to Cuba, and Cubans do not tire of making the naughty remark that the best invention produced by our country is the mulatta.

Why the mulatta and not the black woman? Why not the blonde woman, so highly prized as a standard of beauty in countries where racial prejudice has been such a determinant influence? Why has the mulatta attained such a special role in the collective imaginary of Cuba, the Caribbean, and Brazil?

Without discounting the beauty of many mulattas (and also that of many mulattos), it is undeniable that a mesh of mythical exoticism and sensuality has been built around the mulatta, and that it transcends reality. Racial mixing in and of itself is no guarantee of beauty or sensuality. The origin of the myth lies in the slave society itself. Prostitutes in port cities such as Havana were mostly enslaved black women and mulattas. As early as in the eighteenth century, the presence of bordellos in the city of Havana caused such a scandal that the captain general of the Isle of Cuba, in a moralistic outburst, attempted to close them.

But the interesting point in this is that enslaved black women and mulattas were forced to practice the oldest profession.

Enslaved black women and mulattas were also the sexual object of attraction for the white males in slave-owning families. Obviously, these men were mostly responsible for the production of mulatto babies. Many free blacks in Cuba's slave society were mulatto. This was no mere coincidence: city slaves were usually chosen from among the Creoles, those born into slavery in Cuba, because they were considered more docile and malleable. Slaveholding families therefore preferred to have mulattos for domestic service inside the home. But being a Creole slave was not enough: they were also considered for their good health, youth, skills, and beauty. That beauty was based on a white model. Mulattas were, no doubt, strong candidates. As seamstresses, laundry women, nannies, personal servants for the ladies, and docile lovers for the gentlemen, many of these mulattas were able to buy their freedom, or earn it by some other means.

By the nineteenth century, the mulatta no longer represents the image of the slave as much as that of the *free colored woman*. She was part of a growing middle sector, urban and free. She was already the sensual, exotic, volatile woman, and a huntress of white men. Cigar labels and popular prints by Landaluce have left us a visual testimonial of coquettish mulattas of colonial times. A woman good for dancing rumba, the life of the party, the woman coveted by both black and mulatto men, the mistress of the white man, who aspired to be his wife – a wish seldom attained. She is the antithesis of the white woman; the latter being the very image of prudishness and virtue, to whom the male-dominated and racist Cuban society reserved the role of faithful wife and mother of the family.

Cecilia Valdés, the title character of the most widely known nineteenth-century Cuban novel of the same name, is among those most responsible for consecrating the image of the beautiful sensual mulatta. And this is not coincidental: the myth of the mulatta has been the invention of Cuban men's imagination. Its author, Villaverde, though he attempts to hand us a morality tale to teach us how dangerous interracial relationships can be, transcends, perhaps without intending to, the initial contemptible objective of his novel, forever consecrating in the collective imaginary the myth of the beautiful, sensuous, charismatic, ambitious mulatta, who also poses a danger to the health of stratified Cuban colonial society.

But the most criticized aspect in the mulatta in racist, colonial Cuban society is her ambition to *possess* a white man. The role reserved for the mulatta was that of *mistress* in a reality where social mobility was limited by skin color and, further, by *the purity of the blood*. To *improve the breed* was good – within a society that aspired to become more white – since the threat of Cuba's being dominated by a black majority was one of the biggest ghosts in Cuban colonial history. But for them to aspire to equality, that was an entirely different matter.

Interestingly, Villaverde's vision does not in fact correspond to Cuban reality in the second half of the nineteenth century. *Cecilia Valdés* was written and published when slavery as an institution in Cuba was already in total decline and its abolition was eminent. Further, and particularly among popular sectors of Cuban society, an emerging process of racial interaction without precedent was taking place in the western part of the country, where racism was much stronger due to the establishment of a sugar-producing slave plantation system. The cause of this increase in interracial relations was the massive arrival, beginning in the second half of the nineteenth century, of Galicians, Asturians, and Canarians, originating from the most dispossessed regions of Spain. They arrived in waves of single men, without the ability to return (due to lack of means) and without the racial prejudices of the receptive society.

It is no coincidence that vaudeville theater took up as its main characters the black "boy," the mulatta, and the Galician man. As aptly stated by Rine Leal (1975: 17), ". . . what's valuable is that racial differences are erased in that marginal broth and the longing for interracial living arrives to the stage before it does so in real life." The mulatto condition was, at this point, not only the result of racial mixing, but more than that, a cultural product. In 1880 we are treated to the birth of *danzón*, the first completely hybrid or mulatto music in our cultural history.

With the rise of vaudeville theater during the period between the two wars of independence (1878 through 1895), we already see the mulatta within a context that is *vaudevillian and ambiguous* (Leal 1975: 34), and which consecrated her in the theatrical space.[2] Without a doubt, vaudeville theater helped to accentuate and perpetuate the myth of the mulatta.

As if the wish of Ochún had been to bless her black half and curse her white half, the mulatta was split in two. As no other Cuban woman, she became the bearer of goddess-like attributes: passion, sensuality, eroticism, the desire for the forbidden or the exotic. As no other Cuban woman, she has been abused and vilified; she also became the symbol of opportunism, the huntress of white men, the source of discord, the prostitute.

Harvesting exoticism

> *Mulatta, I know you like to party.*
> | *Las D'Aida* quartet

Vaudeville theater fixed the image of the mulatta as a popular figure, living in tenements, wearing thongs, a troublemaker, and a rumba dancer. Around her,

5. **"Esmeralda"**. A classic example of the exoticization of the mulatta, from the Cuban magazine *Bohemia*, 1956

was a web of double-entendres that in some cases verged on the pornographic.[3] This image is transferred at the very onset of the twentieth century from traditional vaudeville to the new popular theater set up in traditional theater halls, such as the Alhambra and Martí, to name two of the better-known.

Thus, theaters continued to keep on stage the image of the witty mulatta well into the 1930s, when cabarets begin to replace traditional theater such as *zarzuelas* (musicals) and *sainetes* (one-act farces) as the preferred form of nightly entertainment among the public.

Cabarets brought the appearance of vedettes, who came to replace *sainete* actresses, such as Blanquita Amaro. Vedettes, like *sainete* actresses before them, would sing, dance, rumba, and act, and were surrounded by an aura of sensuality and eroticism. But the image of the vedettes was constructed based on a stereotype influenced by big Broadway and Hollywood productions. This American influence arrived with film, and the traffic of Cuban tourists in New York and American tourists in Havana. Cubans appropriated all the fantasy elements from American musical productions, while recreating the tropical and Caribbean exoticism that could satisfy the expectations of the growing numbers of American tourists.

Mexico became one of the primary markets for Cuban artists, particularly for musicians and female rumba dancers. Major figures in Cuban music, such as Bola de Nieve, Rita Montaner, Benny Moré, Dámaso Pérez Prado, José Antonio Méndez, Elena Burke, or reciter Eusebia Cosme, just to name a few, were able to penetrate the Mexican market in the 1940s and 1950s. They were joined by female rumba dancers and vedettes, some of whom succeeded in securing a major role in Mexican artistic circles, particularly in cinema, such as Lina Salomé, known as the Dancing Sphinx, Amalia Aguilar, Ninón Sevilla, and Rosita Fornés. Mexican cinema definitely internationalized for the Latin American market the image of the Cuban woman as vedette and rumba dancer. Whether white, mulatta, or black, what was being exported was Caribbean exoticism and the *sensuality* of the Cuban woman.

A typical case of how this image of the exotic mulatta is constructed for export is that of *Wuananí*. Who was *Wuananí*? Her real name was Alina Ferrán, who, having little or no success in Cuba, left for Mexico, where she began her exotic trajectory. In Mexico, this Cuban mulatta appeared totally transformed physically, wearing platinum hair that contrasted with her dark skin. After her success in Mexico City, she got a contract to sing in a famous Hollywood nightclub. There, according to the legend woven around her, a movie was made with the title *Sangre Negra* (Black Blood), which no one was able to see because it had supposedly been censored. From Hollywood she went to Paris – one of the biggest centers for consumption of exoticism at the time. She arrived by way of Rome and it was in Paris where *Wuananí's* self-parody reaches the point of delirium: for some she is Afro-Chinese, with a touch of Hindu; for others she carried the name of an old Central American tribe to which she belonged, which was entirely dedicated to singing and dancing before the Spanish conquest. She was the daughter of a Chinese mother and a *patoa* father, who has arranged for her songs taken from Cuban folklore which make up her repertoire. *Wuananí*, without a doubt, was the sum total of everything exotic that the feverish imagination of a first-world country could consume in its prejudiced gaze of the Other: African, Chinese, *patuá*, member of a mysterious Central American tribe. But the truth behind the delirious myth of *Wuananí* was a raunchy mulatta with platinum hair. It is not difficult to imagine how much fun this savvy Cuban mulatta by the name of Alina Ferrán must have had constructing the character of *Wuananí* to sell it, without the least reserve, to the uninformed Parisian public.

Wuananí was not an isolated case. By the 1940s and 1950s, Cuba had become a big exporter of exoticism for the international market. It did not matter whether this market was outside or inside its own borders, as in the case of tourists who began to visit the island in increasing numbers each year. The tourist sector of the economy grew to such levels in the 1940s that much data was published in the Cuban press pointing to the fact that earnings stemming from tourism were beginning to compete seriously with those from the traditional sugar industry.

But for Cuban artists there was a clear delineation between the *exotic* for tourist consumption and what was authentically Cuban. One of the most revered representatives of authentic Cuban music during the years of the Republic was Rita Montaner. She was the daughter of a middle-class mulatto family from Guanabacoa, and received a solid education as a pianist and singer from Peyrellade Conservatory. Rita was a beautiful mulatta with extraordinary green eyes. She possessed not only one of the finest singing voices ever in Cuban history, but also had extraordinary acting talents, leading her to become the queen of stage shows and concerts, of variety theater and musical *zarzuelas*, of radio and film, of cabarets and television, of opera and stage comedy. For over three decades she was the idol of Cuban music: Rita the Unique One, Rita of Cuba.

Josephine Baker arrived in Cuba in 1951. When this famous black American vedette arrived – she who had first enraptured Paris and later the rest of Europe – Rita Montaner played a trick on her. La Baker, as well as Cuban vedettes and rumba dancers, had conquered Europe by selling their *exoticism* to an avid European public. As Cuban artists had done (and here I am thinking of *Wuananí*), Baker had constructed for Parisians a stereotype of the exotic that fulfilled their prejudiced expectations of what they considered *the Other*, the non-European.

But on this occasion, Baker should not have tried to show off in front of the experts. Exporting exoticism was one of the most prosperous businesses led by Cuban women. And, more importantly, it was not produced for domestic consumption, but for the same public that had been fascinated by Baker in Europe. When the *Black Venus*, better known as *La Platanito* inside the Cuban entertainment circuit, appeared on stage, Rita immediately captured the satiric side of Baker's show in the Cuban context. So, Rita immediately staged the musical review *Se Cambia, Se Cambia*, (Change, Changes) at the Teatro Martí, where she imitated the famous vedette. It was not hard to achieve hilarity, Rita's histrionic abilities notwithstanding. Josephine Baker was a construction of black exoticism for an elitist, uninformed public, but could not hold ground in front of a public versed in mulatta culture, in a context where her exoticism became pure fiction while Rita's mocking of her was pure caricature.

However, to the extent that the tourist industry kept growing, so did the pressures to produce a *Cuban ambience* to fulfill the expectations of the increasing number of tourists. By the 1950s, Havana had become one of the biggest tourist spots in Latin America, and by the end of the decade income generated from tourism exceeded that for sugar exports.

We should not be surprised if the press regrets that "many of those nice places lack the magical touch that would make them a bit more Cuban." But what is that concept of "a bit more Cuban"? More Cuban means not playing jazz, since it has no exotic enchantment for American tourists. But more Cuban also means not playing *guaguancoes* and *guarachas de locura*, which tourists would not know how to dance to. More Cuban is, in fact, making a Cuban music that tourists can recognize and dance to: rumba. And, of course, "Rumba means danzón. It means son. It means conga. It means mambo. And it means chacha" (*Bohemia* 1951).

Expressed in those terms, the request was for the production of a well-packaged and appropriately labeled Cuban culture that would serve as a product that could be easily digested by the tourist.

The 1950s represented, within the Cuban context, the epitome of this trend. The choreographer known as Rodney had made the Tropicana cabaret internationally famous, with its extravagant productions, such as: *Diosas de Carne, Canciones para Besar, Rumbo al Waldorf* (Flesh Goddesses, Songs to Kiss By, On to the Waldorf). The last one premiered in Havana after its staging at the Waldorf Astoria in New York. This production aimed to dazzle Americans with a show of Cuban women who were so exceedingly beautiful, so delicately coifed, so delightfully dressed, and so sculpturally undressed (*Bohemia* 1957).

Large cabarets, such as Tropicana, Sans Souci, and El Salón Rojo at Hotel Capri, and Alibar, El Sierra, and El Parisién at Hotel Nacional, among others, were in the business of selling an elitist, pretentious, exuberant exoticism.

As a counterpart to these, there were small, run-down late-night cabarets filled with the stench of brandy in the Playa district of Marianao. They often presented sordid and pornographic shows, where one could find anything from a black man exhibiting his extraordinarily large penis, to groups of men and woman fornicating, whether mulattas, white women, or black women, or, for that matter, mulatto, white, and black men – all placed in the tourist market.

Interestingly, in this last category of sordid dives, in spite of their marginal nature, one could find, next to the black man with the biggest penis, musicians of extraordinary caliber, such as Chano Pozo and Tata Güines, who used their drums to make a type of Cuban music that went beyond the rumba made for tourists.

But this does not mean that there was no good Cuban music in luxury cabarets. Benny Moré, Las D'Aida, Elena Burke, Omara Portuondo, José Antonio Méndez, Portillo de la Luz, Celeste Mendoza, La Lupe, Olga Guillot, Celia Cruz, Felipe Dulzaide, and dozens of other musicians made Havana a sleepless city where cabaret girls were the queens of the night.

On the journey back to the source

> *The fun is over.*
> *The Commander arrived and ordered it stopped.*
> | Carlos Puebla

In reality, fun could never end altogether with the Revolution. The intensity of Havana's nightlife was so great, and was such an integral part of the city's spirit, that even upon closure of the casinos in 1959, to which many of the luxury cabarets in Havana were attached, cabaret shows and jam music sessions in the nightclubs continued with relative energy. However, the dives in the Playa district of Marianao quickly disappeared as part of the social *cleansing*.

I remember that, in the 1960s, when I was a teenager, one could still hop through Havana's nightclubs and cabarets and even stay until morning at El Gato Tuerto, listening to jam sessions by all-night musicians who came to this last refuge for Havana's sleepless crowd.

The most luxurious cabarets and nightclubs, almost all of them located in El Vedado area, kept their shows with good productions and included vedettes and major musical figures. Rosita Fornés would do her season at Hotel Internacional in Varadero, accompanied by the Meme Solís quartet. Juana Bacallao was queen at Parisién. El Pico Blanco, at Hotel St. John, was the place for late sessions by the singers of the *feeling* movement, although José Antonio Méndez retained his special place at Club Scherezada. Tropicana continued to offer its large productions in the style of Rodney, but now without him. And Mulatas de Fuego at Parisién continued to play havoc with the imagination of the Cubans.

Not even the Revolutionary Offensive of 1968 or the The Gray Quinquennium (1971–76)[4] were able to do away with all nightlife in Havana, despite the prevailing moralist chauvinism which considered cabarets a remnant of the past, a cultural expression of American influence, and a place where Cuban women had been exploited. Cabarets were thus seen as being in contradiction with the new *socialist morality*, whereby women ceased being objects of sexual luxury to become *active comrades*, representing new values: exemplary mothers, militia women in defense of the motherland, outstanding workers.

The best expression of this new perspective was to be found in Wilson's *Las Criollitas* from the 1960s. This cartoonist created the characters known as *Las Criollitas* to embody the new values of the socialist society. Interestingly, even when *Las Criollitas* contained an obvious political, moralizing *message*, they were portrayed as stunning mulattas who did not lack any of the sensual and sexual attributes that Cuban tradition had ascribed to them: shapely legs and thighs, wide hips, small waist, pointed breasts (not too big, not too small), fashionably dressed, wearing bell bottoms or miniskirts, always marking their sex, tight T-shirts highlighting a tight waist, wide hips, and perfect breasts, and platform shoes. Whenever they were presented in a sitting position, their feet were pointed in a feminine way. Of course, there were other physical, decorative attributes: sensual lips, long eyelashes and big eyes; always wearing bracelets, watch, necklace, and big earrings. *Las Criollitas* were the socialist morality in the body of a sensual mulatta – a kind of rehabilitated mulatta, as whores had been rehabilitated in the early years of the Revolution.

Although The Gray Quinquennium did not totally do away with cabarets, they undoubtedly went through a real stage of decline. The country was going through one of its biggest economic crises and, above all, the tourist industry, to which cabarets had been linked from the onset, had fallen to the lowest levels. The decline was otherwise obvious: costumes were of the worst quality, chorus girls who would never had been able to aspire to a dancing career in large cabaret productions – fat, thin, tall, short – paraded unenthusiastically down runways, and the furniture started to deteriorate in an alarming way.

But, little by little, almost imperceptibly, surreptitiously, foreign tourists made a new comeback. The first to arrive in Varadero were the Canadians, in the second half of the 1970s. During that time they were still kept apart, isolated in a luxury ghetto, for fear of moral contamination. Those were years of xenophobia and self-isolation, when the Cuban government was beginning to feel strong after its entry into the former Eastern-bloc common market Comecon, but not enough to do away with its need to stimulate the tourist industry.

Almost at the same time began the arrival of tourists of all nationalities from socialist countries in Europe, particularly Soviets but also Germans, Bulgarians, Czechs, etc. These tourists were considered less important, since they did not pay *with freely convertible currency*, a euphemism used to refer to the dollar.

The year 1978 marked the arrival of the *butterflies*, a name wittily given to Cuban exiles and their children, who until then had been referred to as the *worms*. They were returning to see their families, but the Cuban government required, as a condition, that they had to buy a tourist package in order to visit the country.

Following these early groups came those who would become the *mainstay* of Cuban tourism: Western Europeans, mostly Spaniards and Italians, plus Mexicans, Venezuelans, and Argentineans, although in smaller numbers.

By the end of the 1980s, the Cuban economy began to feel the first ravages of the political crisis in the Eastern-bloc socialist countries. Cuba went, sooner rather than later, from economic fear to panic. The standard of living of the population, which had been relatively prosperous in the 1980s, took a steep decline. In July 1991, the Special Period was officially announced. And Cuba was thus put up for sale to foreign investors.

With tourism, Cuban nightlife began to prosper. As is always the case, in the face of compelling economic needs Morality yielded the way. Havana's nightlife has had a rebirth, as well as that of Varadero (the other tourist stronghold), in addition to other cities, such as Santiago de Cuba. Traditional nightclubs and cabarets were refurbished. Some new ones were created and others, such as Palacio de la Salsa, have already become the hubs of fashionable nightlife in Havana. As cabarets prospered, prostitution bloomed. The thunderous fall in the standard of living and the growth of the tourist industry also brought prostitution. Cuban *jineteo*, or hustling, became the basic source of income for many Cuban families. The legalization of possession of dollars for Cubans in 1993 consecrated the prosperity of this old private industry.

History began to repeat itself. What was the best product of our exoticism that we could sell to tourists? The exoticism of our sun and our Caribbean beaches; the exoticism of our old and beautiful capital city, even as it lay in ruins; the exoticism of our *habano* cigars and our rum with a name in English, Havana Club; the exoticism of our beautiful and sensuous mulattas. Cuba, like many other tourist destinations, sells the exoticism of its women, and not even socialist morality could interfere with this: Cuban mulattas, now promoted by the state, appear in *Playboy* magazine or stroll their fabulous, partly naked bodies in theater halls around the world, during tours of *Tropicana*. Others can be found under contract at cabarets in Cancun or other major tourist destinations in Latin America.

Finally, the industry of the exotic has been reborn. And here it is likely to stay, as well as the exporting of the mythical Cuban paradise, where mulattas, as personifications of Ochún, reign in the nights of Havana and in the feverish imagination of its visitors.

Notes

1.   Ochún is a primary orisha, or deity of the Yoruba pantheon. She is the guardian of love, femininity and the rivers. She is represented as a beautiful mulatta, who likes to dance and be festive. She is joyful, but she also likes to incite conflicts between men. Her color is yellow, and because of this her children or followers wear necklaces made of Amber or yellow beads. In the process of syncretization with the Catholic religion, Ochún became identified with the Virgen de la Caridad del Cobre, who is the patron saint of Cuba. For more information, consult Natalia Bolivar's *Los Orishas de Cuba* (Cuba's Orishas) (Ediciones Unión. Unión de Escritores y Artistas de Cuba. Ciudad de La Habana, 1990).

2.   *His counterpart [that of the black "boy"] was the mulatta, that copper-skin Venus who emerges out of beer head. She was not only presented as the apple of discord, but she was also given the role of a woman of easy morals, scatterbrained, a prostitute, a real danger to the sacrosanct peace of "decent families." The myth of the mulatta, which started much before Demajagua, reaches now an extreme, because the intent is to show that social evils stem from people of color, who should not be living on an equal level with white people . . .*
            (Leal 1975: 37)

3.   The Alhambra theater entered fully into what was frankly a pornographic repertoire. For lack of texts as definite proof, some titles still remain. The following titles are taken at random: *A Physical Defect, No Pants, Plastic Scenes, Balls to End the Century, Pussycats, The Clarinet, A Husband to End the Century, . . ., The Dead Snake, The Effect of the Spanish Fly, Married But Virgin, Three Under the Covers, Mr. Rod, Should I Undress?, My Wife and the Jewel, The Large Pickle, The Baron of Dry Stick, Cuckold on the Moon, Man and Chicken, . . . , Nervous Excitation, A 6 and a 9, A Question of Balls, My Bunny, Hide Repairs, Carlotta's Pastime, She Thought the Tool Funny . . .* and other similar titles fill the billings for the Alhambra theater between 1892 and 1893.
            (Leal 1982: 315–17)

4.   "The Gray Quinquennium" is the term used to refer to the period from 1971 through 1976. It started with the First National Congress on Education and Culture, held in Havana in April 1971. The establishment of the Ministry of Culture in 1976 is considered the event that ended this period. The Gray Quinquennium is an allusion to the censorship and repressive policies implemented by the Cuban government against intellectuals. Likewise, repression against homosexuals was legalized. The term "The Gray Quinquennium" was coined by Ambrosio Fornet (1987) in "A propósito de las iniciales de la tierra," in *Casa de las Américas*, La Habana, 164, pp. 148–53.

References

Freyre, Gilberto (1942) *Casa-grande y Senzala: Formación de la Familia Brasileña Bajo el Régimen de Economía Patriarcal.* Biblioteca de Autores Brasileños, vols 1 and 2, Buenos Aires.

Leal, Rine (1975) *Antología del Teátro Bufo del Siglo XIX*, vol. 1, Editorial Biblioteca Básica de la Literatura Cubana. La Habana.

—— (1982) *La Selva Oscura*, vol. 2, Editorial Arte y Literatura. Ciudad de La Habana.

Villaverde, Cirilio (1984) *Cecilia Valdés*, Editorial Letras Cubanas, La Habana.

Journals

Bohemia (years: 1947, 1948, 1949, 1950, 1951, 1957, 1958, 1959).

Carteles (years: 1941, 1942, 1943, 1944).

She is a Virgin and She Awaits You

An excerpt

By María Elena Escalona

A fascinating way of proving yourself
to be able to transport yourself back a hundred years
Situated in the semi-savage landscape
to be able to transport yourself back a hundred years
A fascinating way of proving yourself
Fantasy beaches
bathed in warm waters
Villages with a tropical flavor
Impregnated with melodious rhythm
a real melting pot of races
of races and customs
A refuge of varied flora and fauna
A diverse and singular microcosm
near and distant culture simultaneously
aesthetic nourished by extravagance and color
neo-colonial fantasy
desert of sand, devoid of emotion
bikinis of encouragement,
swimsuit of impact
another world
beautiful, austere, savage, natural, and mystical
The nightlife is exciting
You will play a sophisticated version of hide-and-seek
Come to the pearl of the Caribbean
which is an irresistible magnet
Live the other nature
be a seeker of rarities
renew your existential argument
sharpen your culture profile
have a new experience
ratify your difference

with the litheness of a palm
She is a virgin and she awaits you

Tropical flavor

Look at me and contemplate your power
that I am your mythical animal
I am the memory of what precedes you
and the great myth of your origin

I am your guarantee to ancestry
so utilized as possessed
and with this grace which is so mine
I calm your thirst for authenticity

I don't mind being enslaved by my limited freedom
If it is I that am the mirror of your masculinity
I feel as is appropriate, captured and conquered
and my freedom is enclosed by your gaze

With my tropical flavor
and my cultural level
I go on and on
in my transcendental anonymity

Heroically strong and miraculously sweet
When you arrive in Cuba your luck changes
and it could be that even your subconscious gets alarmed

With my tropical flavor . . .

I am the nature of your culture
On the outside you escape, on the inside you like it
Ay! Papi tell me what tortures you . . .

6.   Lucrecia Perez in "She is a Virgin and She Awaits You" by Mariá Elena Escalona,
1996 Barcelona, Spain
Photo: Juan Pablo Ballester
Escalona studied theater in Cuba before emigrating to Spain in 1991. In the past
eight years she has written and directed several solo works for cabarets and small
theaters in Spain and other parts of Europe that comment humoristically on the lingering
effects of stereotypes of exotic female sexuality on Cuban women currently living in
Europe. Lucrecia Perez, the first actress to star in "She is a Virgin and She Awaits
You," is a popular Cuban singer who resides in Spain.

Darling, wish that you were here!

The Beach is Nice

Felix Gonzalez-Torres

This apparently undialectical performance was conceived in the middle of a great deception, with the return to decorative art or the return of the artists to the studio in the most traditional way. It is evident that the majority of the artists are not aware that this return to "artists making art" is just another strategy of the dominant ideology in a moment of economic crisis. It eradicates any contradiction about the production of art within this society, therefore it isolates the artist from any social context (and content). Art is nice, let's buy art! It looks good in my decorated living room!

For thirteen consecutive days I played my favorite role: the tourist (an example of metaphorical escape). The piece was performed right into the "real" world, and in complete anonymity. No press release, no specific props, actions, or text. Only trivia. A newspaper, *Artforum*, a bottle of Hawaiian Tropic suntan oil #3, a black bathing suit, and a few Piña Coladas. I simply laid under the sun for the duration of the performance.

Once more the performance never happened, it was forgotten. In the island, memory is prohibited. Greetings!

7. **Felix Gonzalez-Torres**
"The Beach is Nice," 1983
Santurce, Puerto Rico
Photo: Dionysis Figueroa
Cuban artist Gonzalez-Torres is best known for his sculptural and photographic works and for his collaboration with the New York-based artists collective Group Material in the 1980s. However, as an art student in Puerto Rico prior to his arrival in the US, he created several performances. He submitted documentation of this piece to *High Performance* magazine in 1983.

STUFF!

An excerpt

Coco Fusco and Nao Bustamante

Judy
(a Cuban transvestite)
Begins to style her hair and primp "herself"
Voiceover

Me puedes llamar Judy. ¿Me preguntas si me deprimo? Por supuesto que me deprimo.
Pero esto es un trabajo, vieja. ¿Qué puedo hacer? Nadie escogió vivir en medio de esta
mierda. Trato de no pensar mucho en estas cosas. Cuando me siento mal, pienso en un
peinado nuevo. A los italianos les fascina el pelo rizado, asi que me hize este permanente
para estar más morena. ¿Qué te parece? Es que chica, ¿hay que comer, no?

¿Mi familia? Ya estan acostumbrados. Cuando traigo un gallego a la casa, mi familia
no lo ve a él – ven un pollo, arroz, frijoles, y plátanos, ven un refri lleno. Les digo a los
pepes que estoy haciendo esto para comprarme una libra de picadillo, y así se sienten más
culpables de mi situación y entonces me dan más plata. No digo que me gusta estar en un
lugar con aire acondicionado. Yo pudiera estar en una oficino todo el día, como hacia cuando
trabajaba en el banco. ¿Pero qué saqué de eso? Ay mi cielo, absolutamente nada.

(You can call me Judy. Depressed? Sure I get depressed. But it's a job, honey.
What can I do? Nobody chooses to be born in the middle of a mess like this
one. I try not to think about things too much. When I feel down, I start thinking
about a new way to fix my hair. The Italians like wild hair, so I permed mine
to look more *morena*, what do you think? We have to eat, right?

8. Coco Fusco and Nao Bustamante
STUFF!, 1996–98
Photo: Hugo Glendinning
Coco Fusco as "Judy," a transvestite prostitute in Havana. Portions of the script of
STUFF!, Fusco and Bustamante's exploration of tourism and its impact on Latin women,
were based on interviews with actual *jineteros* and *jinteras* in Cuba and child street
vendors in Chiapas, Mexico. Other sections were derived from foreign-language manuals
specially designed for sex tourists.

My family? Oh, they're used to it. When I bring a Gallego home, my family doesn't see him, they just see a chicken, rice, beans and *plátanos* – a full fridge. When I tell the guys that I'm doing it to buy a pound of ground beef, they feel better about giving me money, and they leave me more. I don't say I like to be in a nice room with air conditioning for a change. I could sit in an office all day – I did that when I was working in a bank. What did I get then? Oh darling, absolutely nothing.)

Visibility as Strategy: Jesusa Rodríguez's Body in Play

Roselyn Costantino

"Cameleón" is a term frequently applied to Mexican director, playwright, actress, scenographer, entrepreneur, and social activist Jesusa Rodríguez (b. 1955, Mexico). This "legend of Mexican theater" (Avilés) moves effortlessly across the spectrum of cultural forms and theatrical traditions. Her *espectáculos* incorporate "elite" forms such as Greek tragedy and opera as well as popular genres of cabaret, *teatro de carpa* (itinerant theater, literally "under a tent"), indigenous ritual, and political resistance. Constant are humor, satire, parody, linguistic play, and historical recreation and recuperation, along with gender-bending, and interaction with and participation of the audience. One might argue that her work is postmodern or Brechtian, but Rodríguez emphasizes that her choices have more to do with Mexican history, culture, and people than with broader aesthetic or theoretical discussions.

Jesusa and her Argentine companion, Liliana Felipe, first established the theater-bar El Cuervo (1980) and then, in 1990, the theater-bar El Hábito with an adjacent theater, La Capilla, in Coyoacán, Mexico City, which together they own and manage. In 1983 they formed the theater cooperative Divas (the name a play on the female sex symbols of revue, cabaret, and *carpa)*, a mixed group of mainly females, some males, and a variety of sexual preferences. Directed by Jesusa, they have produced some 200 shows from 1990 to 1997, including sixty-eight *farsas* (farces) and seventy-five *espectáculos músicales* (musicals). From 1993 to 1995 Rodríguez directed thirty cabaret shows, for which Felipe wrote and performed the music. Printed scripts of some works, such as the Christmas *pastorelas* (a shepherd's play) and episodes of *telénovelas* (soap operas), appear along with other satirical and parodic writing by Rodríguez and songs composed by Felipe in *Debate feminista*, an important feminist journal in Mexico, the editorial board of which she is a member.

Belonging to a generation of Mexican women artists, writers, activists, and feminists born in the 1950s who have transgressed traditional women's roles in a patriarchal society, Rodríguez chooses theatrical forms which permit her to render corporal and, thus, visible, the tensions among the ideological, religious, social, political, and economic discourses operating on and through the individual and collective human body. In her performances, that body engages in transgression and experiencing pleasure as natural acts.

With the motive of "making seen" that which has been kept in the closet, the kitchen, the mountains, the confessional, and the barrios, Rodríguez uses the body – often female and nude – as a point of departure for her explorations and creations. She interrogates the nature and reception of performance, and foregrounds the politics of representation. At the same time she does not negate or erase totally the "real" body or the reality of its lived experiences. In her work, the body is never taken as value-free; on the contrary, it is a primary signifier, a site for meaning, a location and sign of itself.

Rodríguez's ideological and aesthetic choices express her sense of the connection between performance and politics. Her strategies take on a particular significance in relationship to the history of theater, spectacle, and theatricality in Latin America. As has been argued by Jean Franco (1989, 1992), Diana Taylor (1991), and Carlos Monsiváis (1981, 1988), since the pre-Columbian civilizations, performance, theater, and spectacle have extended beyond symbolic representation on the proscenium to play an active – albeit contradictory – part in the politics of self-affirmation and in the empowerment of those contesting that domination. As defined by Taylor in *Theatre of Crisis*, spectacle – being an especially prepared or arranged display of more or less public nature, that which is seen or capable of being seen – and theatricality – which includes the mechanics of spectacle or theater, the manipulation of images and events behind the scenes which are also capable of not being seen – are ingrained in the dynamics of all social relations: political and religious, on the collective level, and familial in the private sphere (1991: 4).

Taylor studies the connection between theatrical performances, and the "wider uses and abuses of social spectacle" dating from before the sixteenth-century Spanish conquest (1991: 1). Marí Sten asserts that "theater was for the spiritual conquest of Mexico what horses and gunpowder were for the military conquest" (quoted in Taylor 1991: 14). Franco and Monsiváis trace the long roots of performance through the temporal and spatial configurations of the societies and cultures inhabiting la República Mexicana, and describe how social interaction is scripted, pre-assigned roles dramatically performed, and rituals re-enacted incorporating established images and icons as sets and props. In Mexico, for instance, that process entails the use of the national flag and its colors incorporated into the image of the Virgin of Guadalupe in order to generate responses of patriotism and religious reverence. Nonetheless, as Franco, Taylor, and Monsiváis reveal in their studies, a simultaneous resistance to these systems of control existed in the margins of society – a space to which women were relegated by Hispanic, Roman Catholic, indigenous patriarchal traditions. Because this resistance was articulated through marginal forms and spaces, the resulting cultural production has been overlooked in historical accounts. Studies like those mentioned above fill that gap as they investigate and analyze that part of the Mexican landscape.

Rodríguez revives the forms on the stage in order to arrive at similar ends – recording, performing, and advocating a strategy of resistance that she hopes will lead to the empowerment of individuals and, ultimately, changes in the system. It is no coincidence that she has selected theatrical styles that have always been outside "mainstream" theater; that is, styles of so-called *teátro frívolo* (frivolous theater, as opposed to "serious" art), or what is referred to today as performance art. In reference to her choices, Jesusa offers:

> In Mexico right now, there's a lot of interest in performance art and cabaret, but that's to be expected. We're in such a profound crisis, and cabaret always flourishes in crisis – remember the Nazis, how cabaret boomed then? In Mexico, we're in an impossible spectacle, beyond Ibsen or the absurd. We're in a kind of perverse fiction. . . . This is how we inform each other about what's going on. The media in Mexico are controlled by the government, which everyone knows is corrupt, so you can't believe what you read in the newspapers, what you hear on the radio or see on TV.
>
> (quoted in Obejas, 1996: 8)

Teátro frívolo became popular during the nineteenth century as a way of appealing to the needs and tastes of Mexicans from all social classes. A growing urban population mingled at and participated in the ritual of *teatro frívolo*; these were truly "public" spaces. Popular theaters, Socorro Merlín affirms in *Vida y milagros de las Carpas*, were "the space of the religion of satire, criticism, jokes, and laughter. The public (. . .) saw in it the manner in which to exercise its freedom" (1995: 19). Spectators would engage in linguistic duels with actors. Not passive, audience members shouted opinions and reactions that became part of the show. The resulting improvisation and audience interaction made each show an unique experience.

Merlín explains that during this crucial time in Mexican history, due to the intimate, interactive nature of *carpa*, sketch, revue, and cabaret, a sense of nationalism and civic participation was generated by the entrepreneurs and artists who entertained the masses while, simultaneously, creating in individuals a feeling of belonging and of empowerment as they saw themselves and their worldview represented on stage (pp. 20–24). A variety of social types, including students, the vedette, the drunk, the young virgin, *rancheros*, soldiers and generals, politicians, and prostitutes, was constructed through audio and visual signs, and spoke through popular language. This oral tradition also found music (boleros and ranchera) at the center of popular culture and thus at the center of popular performance. As writers drew their material from daily events in Mexico City and throughout the provinces, theater and song transmitted news and information (to a mostly illiterate populace), voiced sociopolitical criticism, and created a sense of nationhood and national identity:

> These theaters, characterized by their informative content in a satirical-humoristic tone ... kept the population up-to-date of the sociopolitical events in Mexico, even in the far corners of the country. They served as forms of entertainment with didactic ends as well as of a certain type of political activism during this period of Mexican history.
>
> (F. E. Rodríguez 1988: 1–4, 28)

This activism was facilitated by the accessibility of performances, especially to the growing class of poor and illiterate urban dwellers, and by the difficulty in censoring popular song or stage productions – as these could be altered in the presence of censors and in the absence of written scripts – a characteristic not missed by Jesusa. As the economic, social, and political landscape changed, these artists stood opposite growing cultural and intellectual elitism. They challenged the increasing *no-participar* (non-participatory) character of the emerging ruling party, a policy known then as "listen, see, and be quiet" (Merlín 1995: 39). Then, as now, the ruling party (Partido Revolucionario Institucional or PRI) was an institution whose structures – hierarchical, patriarchal, and ethnocentric – permeated all social and political spaces.

It is no coincidence that Jesusa opts for the style of *teátro frívolo* and that the theater cooperative she directs selected the name Divas. The group plays on the contradictory versions and roles of the divas, the sex symbols of early cabaret. For instance, in Pablo Dueñas' *Las divas en el teatro de revista mexicano* (1994), one of the few studies on divas, Enrique Alonso describes the women as passive objects of sexual desire and commercial interest, victims of their lifestyles and of the men who controlled them. In *Escenas de pudor y liviandad* (1981), Monsiváis, however, provides a different view of the role of these women, not only in the theater but also on the social stage. He insists that the women on the popular stage were instrumental in providing alternatives to mainstream images of women as far back as the emergence of modern Mexico in the late nineteenth and early twentieth century. They offered models for women and men of all economic classes by establishing economic autonomy and defying authority. In the manner described by Monsiváis, early divas performed in theaters as well as on the social stage.

Like her contemporaries, Mexicans Astrid Hadad and Maris Bustamante, and Brazilian Denise Stoklos, Rodríguez is among a growing number of Latin American and Latina female artists who find in performance a space for artistic freedom and a strategy to interrupt social systems. Humor is the tone of choice, as Rodríguez sees it, particularly in its political form, as a tonic for the sense of "betrayal" by their government and a survival strategy for dealing with the difficult reality which is life in Mexico (Iliff 1995). She offers these reflections on the subject:

> We all need to go and laugh right there, *en vivo*, with other people who are laughing. The line I propose is a line full of humor, not as gratuitous or frivolous jokes, but humor as a manner in which to see the world from distinct angles, to stop and see the infiniteness of this world, to permit us to see it in all its ambiguity and its ridiculousness, from a distance. I propose: let's be ambiguous, let's break with the tabu of ambiguity as something we permit ourselves only in dreams, like incest; let's be ambiguous, not as something involuntary, but full of intention, as objective; let's assume the ridiculous and failure as an option in order to grow, to get to know ourselves. Against order, against precision, against the rigidity of putting on a play, against the solemnity of Mexican theater, I propose ambiguity in order to achieve, not 'theater of the masses' but in order to satisfy the vital necessity – like that of eating – of public expression.
>
> (in Seligson 1989: 158–59).

Víctimas del pecado neoliberal (Victims of Neoliberal Sin; 1994) consists of a series of fast-paced sketches, in which a strong dose of humor is coupled with audience participation in dialogue touching on some of the raw, painful social issues that Mexicans face in a decade of perpetual crisis. The presidency of Carlos Salinas de Gortari (1988–94) was one of the most corrupt in modern Mexican history. This, together with the North American Free Trade Agreement – seen by many as an economic policy benefiting a small elite while devastating most sectors of society and widening the gap between the rich and poor – provided ample material for criticism, and for poking fun at the idiosyncrasies of urban society.

Rodríguez played adeptly the roles of then-president Salinas and Adolf Hitler. Without disturbing her portrayal of the historical figures of both men, she makes obvious the process of performance – both her performance and the performances rendered by them. She does this while explicitly demonstrating her interpretation of the similarities – not only physically, but in word and deed – between the two.

During the show, Rodríguez leans over the stage and speaks directly to the spectators. Frequently, she moves freely among the spectators, asking questions, in dialogue with them about what has just happened on El Hábito's or Mexico's stage that day, taking surveys, calling for votes for or against politicians or their platforms; she teases out, from even the shyest members of the audience, their thoughts on key issues. She takes advantage of the physical layout of El Hábito, which is a relatively small space with rows of couches, chairs, and low coffee tables that surround the stage on three sides, the rows usually ten deep.

Rodríguez and her cohorts spend time each day combing news sources for material that is incorporated into that night's performance, with urgency, commitment, and humor, regardless of the severity or tragic nature of the event. Either woven into the personal exchange with the audience or flashed onto a screen at the back of the stage, the script is adjusted daily, and the objective realized: in a city where urban sprawl is rapidly diminishing the interpersonal, El Hábito provides community members with the opportunity to discuss, express rage, recognize shared interests, and formulate strategies for change. Audience reaction is unpredictable, and there have been tense moments, especially since the 1994 presidential elections, when some bureaucrats, politicians, and government officials whom Jesusa openly criticizes began to attend her shows. President Ernesto Zedillo – then Secretary of Education – came to see what was being said about him, as have other major political figures from various parties. Verbal parlays have erupted during performances, at times breaking into emotional give and take with audience members. Jesusa recounts the attendance of the daughter of Fernando Rodríguez González, a legislative aide jailed on charges he allegedly helped arrange the assassination of José Francisco Ruiz Massieu, brother-in-law of Salinas de Gortari. The young woman yelled insults at the character portraying her father (played by Jesusa) with such insistence and volume that Jesusa stopped the performance, called the woman up on stage, and gave her the opportunity to explain her family drama (Rodríguez PI).[1]

In her production, *La Diana casadera* (1993), the mayor of Mexico City, Apolo, falls in love with La Diana Cazadora, goddess of the hunt, a statue-fountain in Mexico City of a beautiful, strong, full-bodied naked woman. Motivated not only by love, but by politics, Apolo proposes marriage. He aspires to be selected by the president as the PRI's official candidate or, as critics say, successor. The outgoing president handpicks a candidate through *el dedazo* (the huge finger signaling), an undemocratic process in which no one so designated has ever lost a presidential election in modern Mexican history. Apolo, however, is single and needs a wife to complete the correct official image. (In patriarchal Mexico, the male-dominated family is the holy union upon which all other institutions are fashioned.) Diana, with her own agenda, accepts Apolo's proposal, in spite of their brother–sister relationship. She receives from him, as a gift and wedding dress, Mexico City's

Palacio de Bellas Artes – a majestic, white marble, European-style palace of fine arts begun by dictator Porfirio Díaz at the end of the nineteenth century as a symbol to the world of Mexico's achievement of progress and civilization. On stage, the palace-dress was an elaborate to-scale replica constructed in foam rubber, with a gilded dome hat. Together Diana and Apolo plot to utilize each other and their power for personal gain. In return for agreeing to marry her brother, Diana demands that he declare her, ironically, the "Goddess of Democracy."

Other characters, however, offer their own interpretations of Diana: El Angel de la Independencia (the Angel of Independence) calls her a nymph and icon of whores; the mayor's male secretary, a "symbol of subversion." El Angel, a bronze statue propped atop a tall marble column pedestal in downtown Mexico City, is another of the city's principal landmarks and the site of post-game soccer celebrations. In a costume similar to Diana's bronze-colored body stocking of foam rubber that gives the illusion of nudity, Liliana Felipe as El Angel wears only gold wings and gold body paint that obscures, yet reveals, the nude body. In one scene, frozen on stage in statuesque poses, these two symbols of Mexico's spirit discuss their views of current events from the special vantage point afforded them by their strategic locations. Humor, wit, and biting criticism fill their conversation; visual and verbal *albures* (witty plays on words often with sexual overtones, particularly characteristic of Mexican Spanish) abound, keeping the audience members in laughter, as they are reminded of their roles in the ongoing drama which is life in the megalopolis. Not missed are the opportunities to criticize men who see Diana only as a sexual object, missing her symbolic value, and thus, when they pass her on their way to work, end up arriving to their jobs "excited." The fanaticism of tens of thousands of soccer fans who converge at El Angel after matches, frenzied to the point of violence, is noted, as are police corruption (often involving abuse of women), *mordidas* (bribes), and the air, noise, and traffic pollution characteristic of urban life.

The production of *La Diana casadera* demonstrates Rodríguez's strength as a creator of theater of images in which sets and props are as revealing as dialogue. The first scene takes place in Apolo's office, which contains only a map of Mexico City and a bed from which Apolo's head emerges. Each of the headboard posts (made of foam rubber) is adorned with one-foot miniatures of the statues of our main characters: La Diana Cazadora and El Angel de la Independencia. These reproductions, however, are puppets with interior mechanisms so that, when a small handle at the base is turned, the female figures seductively rotate their hips in imitation of the miniature dolls of skimpily clad cabaret dancers popular since the early 1900s. The bed, with one easy movement, flips up and converts into a office desk, upon which the miniature statues serve as desk ornaments. The multiple interpretations of the easily converted bed-desk (sites of male power and prowess) and of the statue-dolls (posed in traditional female roles) contribute equally to the levels of criticism and humor of the show.

Mexico City appears as a character in the play, portrayed as a seven-foot green and pink dragon (made of foam rubber) with highly visible genitals of both sexes. Mexico has five heads, each depicting a different social type: politician, blue-collar worker, intellectual, yuppie, and *chavo banda* or gang member. Each head speaks in colloquial jargon that reflects its specific socio-economic status. The head of the monster designated as a yuppie has a cellular phone attached to it and speaks in pretentious and pseudo-intellectual jargon with an occasional dash of English. The working-class head speaks and moves in more of a jiving, street slang, filled with *albures* and so-called "bad" Spanish. The five-headed dragon represents the heterogeneous multitude that converts individuals into the mass – the monster – which is Mexico City.

The spectators in El Hábito easily recognize the visual and linguistic references in these scenes; although, due to the mix of ideological perspectives, their interpretations may vary so that, to some, Rodríguez is reflecting positive aspects of Mexican society and, to others, the biting satire coincides with their views. To certain sectors of the population, for instance, commentary on the soccer fans could bring chuckles of self-recognition or embarrassment over a fanaticism that has been shown to form part of a strategy of control of the elite to keep the masses content and entertained, and to give them a false sense of empowerment (Levine 1980: 463). To some, the Palace of Fine Arts is a fitting salute to Mexico's rich cultural heritage, particularly those elements that bear European traces. To others, the building that took several decades and enormous resources to construct, reflects Mexico's identity crisis and its inability to value its indigenous or mestizo culture – realities resulting in internal conflict.

In Mexico City in 1997, protests ensued over plans to build over the Indian ruins of Cuicuilco to make way for a golf course and country club. Rodríguez was very active in this campaign – appearing personally, organizing, and using El Hábito's Internet connection to rally citizens. Though she has been brought to police stations on several occasions, Rodríguez is unwavering in her commitment to orchestrating such civic participation and to fighting what Mexicans themselves call their "sheepish acceptance of authority and capacity for meekness and manageableness"(Cazés 1994: 9).

In her own manner of ignoring tradition, Diana, an idealized version of Woman, manifests physical human needs and desires, sometimes in an "unlady-like" manner: she insists that she loves her freedom to live "*desnuda*" (naked), and with very discreet movements, suggests she needs to "*hacer pipi*." The binary opposition of the real/ideal woman is literally watered down as the reality of

physical body is foregrounded by the suggestion of Diana urinating in her fountain. The mythical lover is further humanized when she dons her Palace of Fine
Arts wedding dress. Due to its size, weight, and style, Diana Cazadora, the Hunter,
is transformed into Diana Casadera of the play's title, meaning "Diana the housewife." The dress and, by extension, matrimony, confines her, domesticates her,
and makes her look ridiculous.

   This final scene can be read as a parody of popular narratives of soap operas
and romantic novels with moralistic story-lines in which the "bad" girl is either
punished or saved from herself. Through the negation of a binary division of categories of identity, Rodríguez promotes "myriad possibilities of ways of being" in
which good complements bad; male, female; aggressive, passive; body, spirit; myth,
history. For instance, in *La Diana casadera*, El Angel de la Independencia refers to
himself/herself as the symbol of progressive thought, while Diana notes that the
statue looks like an exaggerated phallic symbol with breasts. Is El Angel male or
female? In Spanish, *el* is a grammatical marker for masculine gender, but the statue
in Mexico City and in Jesusa's production has breasts. Liliana Felipe with only
bronze body paint, wings, breasts exposed, and a bronzed cloth draped over her
hips, leaves no doubt about her "sex" from a traditional reading of the category.
The blurring and confusion are amplified when, in a passing remark in conversation, El Angel implies interest in a relationship with Diana (explicitly female) soon
after calling her a whore. Such ambiguity in categories of identity and sexuality is
a central element in much of Jesusa's artistic production. She further reveals her
concepts of identity in "El Génesis," a script published in *Debate feminista*, in which
a progressive God converses with a confused Mother Nature:

> God: Since, if in body, material, and being, there didn't exist, besides men
> and women, varieties and variations, nothing would be good, nothing
> convenient, nothing delectable.
> Mother Nature: Very well, Eternal Father, but, why, if you are my creator,
> did you make the "strange ones," the ones called *"queers"*? Why did you,
> the origin of origin, create unnatural beings? I can accept that there are
> bastards, eunuchs, crazies, brain-damaged ones, but why *queers*, My Father?
> God: Given that it's bothersome and sad that there only exist people who
> have two testicles, unpleasant and boring that there are only beings with
> two ovaries, well then, that which gives us pleasure is the move across
> from one state to the other and ambiguous "intersex."
>
> (1997: 401, 403)

The inscription of discourses of power on the female body is brilliantly represented by Rodríguez by her casting women protagonists as objects, as scenery

and props. Women's bodies thus function simultaneously as the vehicle and the message. They are monuments, buildings, plants, animals, stone statues. In *La gira mamal de la coatlicue* (The Mammary Tour of Coatlique – a satiric reference to the Pope's visit to Mexico) and *Cielo de abajo: cabaret prehispánico* (The Sky Below – a pun on the female body), Jesusa performs enveloped in a foam-rubber replica of the giant stone statue of the goddess Coatlicue.[2] Coatlicue is activated; she speaks and dances with her skirt of live serpents and necklace of skulls. She is a symbol of fertility as well as destruction: *la última madre* – mother of all deities and of creation, frightful and loving, unforgiving and nurturing, life-giving and life-taking, from whom we all came and to whom we all return. It is Jesusa's real (naked) female body upon which the monument is set; the myth of the origin is literally mapped and weighted onto her body.

Jeanie Forte suggests that "women's performance art operates to unmask this function of 'Woman,' responding to the weight of representation by creating an acute awareness of all that signifies Woman or femininity" (1990: 252). Rodríguez moves us beyond a simple awareness of Woman as architectural base to an escape from that position: she emerges from the depths of the beautiful and horrific stone; she is born. It is a rebirth, for Jesusa had, in earlier scenes, completed travels through the underworld, successfully making the journey to Coatlicue to re-enter the cycle of life with her female lover. Naked and painted green, Liliana and Jesusa travel as deceased lovers through the Mayan under-world; in the few scenes in which they are semi-clothed, Jesusa drapes herself in a Greek-style toga and Liliana wears a half-body cactus costume, fusing her body with the cactus from which Jesusa sucks nourishment. This scene is a light moment in this recreation of Mayan myth, as Rodríguez incorporates traditional Mexican song and dance and a dancing skeleton into the cycle of creation and destruction, of life and death.

Rodríguez's investigation of the body is perhaps most explicit in her adaptation of Marguerite Yourcenar's texts in *Yourcenar o cada quien su marguerite* (1989). Entailing one year of rehearsal, Rodríguez and the Divas "explored the visceral – accessed through the body's surface – by interrogating the relationship in movement of the naked body to the four elements: earth, wind, fire, and water" (PI). Employing enormous rocks, wind, fire, and water, the actors performed ritualized motions which required agility, strength, and understanding of the properties of the elements and how the body could perform with and react to them. Learning to move freely, safely, and adeptly among, and communicate through, the gigantic stones, water pools, and fire was a challenge. Rodríguez speaks of "exercising" the human being as "body of love" and of "a journey through time, of recuperating pure instinct through rock, not the machine, of the surface of the body, reconnecting it to the natural elements of fire, water, earth and wind" (PI).

Based on Greek myth, *Yourcenar o cada quien su marguerite* re-enacts the encounter at the gate of death of the Minotaur (representing pure instinct) and Theseus (the interpretation of the modern man who chooses reason over instinct). Desire and passion intertwine with power and death as Theseus's wife, Phaedra, and her sister, Ariadne, become instruments of vengeance. Of interest here is the role of the set design, which acts as a protagonist. For the production, more than twenty tons of rock were transported to the stage of the Foro Sor Juana Inés De La Cruz of the National Autonomous University of Mexico in Mexico City. Choosing this performance space was Rodríguez and the Divas' attempt to recuperate the human body from the "frenetic, paved, and polluted city which is Mexico," as well as from the censoring social codes which impinge on all that is "natural" (PI). Dialogue was minimal and the visual primary, a reversal that left audience members confused but intrigued. From Rodríguez's perspective, the process of creation, including the year of rehearsal, was more rewarding than the final product – the performance (PI).

While *Yourcenar* exemplifies Rodríguez's version of the eternal exploration of the human body and spirit, in *El concilio de amor* she blasts with gusto the dogmatism and hypocrisy, fraud and corruption that permeate the institutions and individuals responsible for imposing rules and regulations. Considered her most controversial piece, *El concilio de amor* is an adaptation of Oskar Panizza's *Council of Love*, which was immediately banned and Panizza jailed upon its publication in Bavaria in 1894. No less polemic in Mexico in 1988, *El concilio* triggered threats and physical violence by right-wing conservatives, Pro-Vida and neo-Nazi groups, against Jesusa, the actors, and El Hábito. In response, an organized reaction by the intellectual and artistic community, orchestrated by Rodríguez, resulted in public demonstrations for artistic rights, and protection for El Hábito and the cast of *El concilio* guaranteed by then-president Salinas de Gortari.

In *El concilio*, Jesusa, wearing only wings and a glittering G-string (thus her female body foregrounded), plays the Devil, who is summoned for consultation to Heaven by an angry God (forgetful, unmotivated, yet lustful) and the Virgin Mary (moody, a bitch) to devise a manner in which to punish Man's lascivious behavior. The Devil devises the perfect scourge: AIDS, which he/she will pass onto humans by copulating with a human who is traditionally represented as a symbol of the very behavior to be punished – Salomé.

In this production, Rodríguez exposes two operations: the masculization of the origin of power and authority in patriarchal Hispanic society, and the disembodiment of authority through modern technology. Jesus Christ had a sex: male.

Except in regard to his relationship to the archetypical fallen woman, Mary Magdalene, he is rarely discussed in this way despite his manhood's being the key to his position of power within Western Christian symbolism. In *El concilio*, a naive Jesus asks the Devil about his wet dreams. He/she comments, "that's right, they never tell you about your body," foregrounding how sexuality and knowledge are bound within language. At another moment, in Heaven (depicted through simultaneously functioning levels of the stage) God the Father chases Marilyn Monroe (Tito Vasconcelos), while Jesus makes a trip "down" to Hell to consult the Devil. The G-stringed Devil greets Jesus, dresses him(her)self, and then explains to Christ the functions of his male body and sexual desires. Ignorance perpetrates violence, so the Devil offers Jesus a lesson on condom use. In the play, Jesus will be saved from AIDS by using condoms, while his Church on Earth, in real time, fights against educating the masses with the same information, thus setting the stage for another battle to be waged by Rodríguez through her art.

Rodríguez exposes the disembodied nature of knowledge, power, and truth as she turns the systems on themselves. On stage, the use of "voice-off" and film and slide projections ironically punctuate the "live" drama. Images interacting with the performance appear on a large screen above the rear of the stage: clips ranging from old Hollywood, Mexican Golden Age, or sci-fi movies, speeches by Mexican presidents (or filmed parodies of those appearances), cut-and-pasted pieces that include traces of Internet surfing. In *Víctimas del pecado neoliberal* there is redundant live coverage of what is being presented on stage: Rodríguez as the mustached ex-president Salinas de Gortari (presently in exile, supposedly to escape prosecution) dressed in a nun's habit, pleading innocence to any and all offences against the nation – a hilarious play that mirrors the bizarre nature of actual – not virtual – events.

The powers, visible and invisible, involved in the ascribing of meaning are as central to Jesusa as they are to a study of her work. Whether artistic creation circulates in Mexico and becomes part of its cultural history has everything to do with the meaning it is given. Over the last two decades, Rodríguez's work has been at the center of Mexico's artistic milieu. With enthusiasm, members of Mexico's literary, theater, and artistic elite have frequented El Hábito. Nonetheless, in major

9.   Jesusa Rodríguez
"The Council of Love," 1988
Mexico City
Photo courtesy of Jesusa Rodríguez
Jesusa Rodríguez (below) and Liliana Felipe in Rodríguez's adaptation of Oskar Panizza's *Council of Love*. The play, published in Bavaria in 1894 and immediately banned, also caused an uproar in Mexico City in the 1980s.

studies, she has been relegated to footnotes and passing comments instead of in-depth analysis. At times her work, like the styles she draws from, has been classified as "frivolous" (Avilés 1992: 30), paratheatrical, commercial, popular entertainment, but not art – all of which is fine with Rodríguez, who prefers to remain in the margins to avoid distractions and the antagonism that often ensues within the Mexican intellectual and artistic elites (PI).

Rodríguez has been censored – on occasion, violently – but survives through equally bold tactics that include bringing to the public sphere the facts, forcing the government and citizens to take responsibility. Her actions are part of a feminist project Rodríguez might refer to as Corruption Interruptus. El Hábito, whose name is a clever play on a nun's habit as well as "the habit of attending or the habit that does or does not make the man" (PI), is frequently a site of gatherings of non-governmental organizations and other groups including the Zapatistas rebels, feminists and other political activists, or common citizens who unite in opposition to the political structures. Rodríguez has led demonstrations in the plazas and streets of Mexico City, helped organize and addressed meetings in the jungles of Chiapas, writes regularly in *Debate feminista*, and encourages not only the participation in civic resistance, but also the use of technology to increase visibility and record events to avoid the erasure not uncommon in Mexican politics. An August 7, 1997, e-mailed plea from El Hábito announces a series of public actions against the "rape" of the archaeological site of Cuicuilco, and urges, "Call your friends, send faxes, e-mails to the world! Don't allow them to destroy what is ours! Bring your camera and video cam!"

Rodríguez's actions are neither didactic nor prescriptive, neither aggressive nor self-righteous (although these adjectives have been used on occasion by some reviewers). Her work, at least momentarily, suspends not the codes or institutions that inscribe themselves violently onto the individual and collective body, but the fear and the guilt – self-induced and therefore "curable" – that cripples. For her, performance is not about power but empowerment. She would agree with director Lina Wertmuller: "It is a wonderful revelation for a child that authority exists only at the moment when you believe in it" (quoted in Waller 1993: 14).

Notes

1.   *PI* refers to personal interviews conducted from 1991 to 1997 in Mexico City. Throughout this essay, all translations are mine.

2.   For further discussion of *El Concilio de Amor* and *Cielo do Abajo*, see Franco (1992), Taylor and Nigro (1993).

References

Avilés, Jaime. "Jesusa y Liliana reinauguran esta noche el teatro de la capilla." *La Jornada*, June 2 (1992): 30.

Cazés, Daniel. "Subestimar para saquearnos y volvernos a saquear." *La Jornada*, December 31 (1994): 9.

Dueñas, Pablo. *Las divas en el teatro de revista mexicano*. Mexico City: Asociación Mexican de Estudios Fonográficos, A.C., 1994.

Forte, Jeanie. "Women´s Performance Art: Feminism and Postmodernism." *Performing Feminisms: Feminist Critical Theory and Theatre*, ed. Sue-Ellen Case. Baltimore and London: Johns Hopkins University Press, 1990. pp. 251–69.

Franco, Jean. *Plotting Women. Gender and Representation in Mexico*. New York: Columbia University Press, 1989.

—— "A Touch of Evil" *TDR* 36.2 (1992): 48–62.

Iliff, Laurence. "Poking Fun at Mexico's Political Woes." *Dallas Morning News*, September 3 (1995): 1C.

Levine, Robert M. "The Burden of Success. Futebol and Brazilian Society Through The 1970s." *Journal of Popular Culture* 14.3 (1980): 453–64.

Merlín, Socorro. *Vida y milagros de las carpas: La carpa en México 1930–1950*. México: INBA/CITRU, 1995.

Monsiváis, Carlos. *Amor perdido*. 10th ed. México, DF: Biblioteca Era, 1988.

—— *Escenas de pudor y liviandad*. México, Buenos Aires, Barcelona: Grijalbo, 1981.

Nigro, Kirsten. "Un revuelto de la historia, la memoria y elgénero: expresiones de la posmodernidad sobre las tablas mexicanas." *Gestos* 17 (1994): 29–41.

Obejas, Achy. "It Hurts to Laugh; Even Performance Artists Are Numbed by Mexico's Crisis". *Chicago Tribune*, April 11 (1996): 8.

Rodríguez, Francisco Escarcega. *El teatro de revista y la política nacional: 1910–1940*. Tesis de Licenciado en Literatura Dramática y Teatro. Mexico City: UNAM, 1988.

Rodríguez, Jesusa. Personal interviews. 1991–1997. Mexico City.

—— "El Génesis." *Debate feminista* 8.16 (1997): 401–03.

Seligson, Esther. *El teatro, festín efímero. reflexiones y testimonios*. Mexico City: Dirección de Difusión Cultural, 1989.

Taylor, Diana. "'High Aztec' or Performing Anthro Pop: Jesusa Rodríguez and Liliana Feliipe in Cielo de abajo." *TDR* 37.3 (1993): 142–52.

—— *Theatre of Crisis: Drama and Politics in Latin America*. Lexington: University of Kentucky Press, 1991.

Waller, Marguerite R. "'You Cannot Make the Revolution on Film': Wertmuller's Performative Feminism in Mimi Metallurgico, Ferito nell'Onore." *Women and Performance* 6.2 (1993): pp. 11–25.

"Border Brujo," 1988

Guillermo Gómez-Peña

Photo: Max Aguilera-Hellweg

Mexican artist Guillermo Gómez-Peña's award-winning performance "Border Brujo" is most often characterized as a prime example of 1980s' American multiculturalism and autobiographical monologue. However, as a university student in Mexico City in the 1970s, Gómez-Peña was mentored by Mexican conceptual artists and performers such as Felipe Ehrenberg and Maris Bustamante. While his work with the Border Art Workshop/ El Taller de Arte Fronterizo invoked the strategies of the artists of Mexico City's *grupos* of the 1970s, who revindicated the aesthetic value of urban popular culture from wrestler masks to *carpa* comedians to comics and presented their work in public spaces, "Border Brujo" is closer in its stage setting and blistering social critique to Jesusa Rodríguez's politically charged cabaret.

"Oh Goya! Goya!" 1996

An excerpt
Evelyn Velez-Aguayo

And now a little Christmas Carol ... In the 1950s a legendary mayor of San Juan, perhaps what they called a typical colonial leader, like one of those that you might know, decided that the essential problem to the educative process of the Puerto Rican children was that as inhabitants of the tropic and not of temperate zones, they have never seen Christmas in Vermont, Fifth Avenue Tree Lights, *Bing Crosby White Christmas Special*, they did not know SNOW.

Her master plan to save our poor children who had never played in the snow – no angel wings, no igloos, no little round men with carrot noses – consisted in renting, a day before the Three King's Day, *víspera de los Tres Reyes Magos*, or Epiphany's day, that is, January the 5th, an airplane – calling Eastern Airlines, calling Eastern Airlines, flight ... an airplane ...

In upstate New York, pretty, blonde, blue-eyed children were called upon to stuff giant sacks with charitable snow that would arrive to the Puerto Rican capital, San Juan!

That day school buses on the island transported children from public schools to the airport. They were instructed to bring with them any empty can they could find in order to play with the snow, to sing "Jingle Bells" and to play with sweaty Santa Clauses who were welcoming the plane. That day the children arrived to the airport in a tropical eighty degrees to see for the first time the snow.

They swear to anyone that does not believe this, *en eso no me meto*, that it was snow, not ice, that the children were going to see for the first time; it was

11. Evelyn Velez-Aguayo
"Oh Goya! Goya!," 1996
Photo: Adam Oranchak
After studying modern dance in Puerto Rico Velez-Aguayo dabbled briefly in body-building and dancing for Las Vegas-style spectacles before settling in the US to pursue a career in modern dance and performance. Her performance "Oh Goya! Goya!" explores the experience of isolation she experienced as a Puerto Rican living in Arizona, where not even the commercial goods targeting the Puerto Rican market on the East Coast of the US were available.

going to happen in San Juan and not in Macondo, they swear so you know, *y que venga el resto, que esto no era cuento*, this was not fiction but history, I mean her-story.

The airplane came full of snow. The municipal band played military marches and more "Jingle Bells". The mayor, honored and proud of her strategy of saving our underdeveloped children who have not seen snow, *ay bendito!*, opened the door of the plane to start the unpacking and revealing of the imported educational bread, imported educational bread, imported educational bread, educational bread, educational bread, educational bread ... Wonder Bread!

Guess what? The snow immediately adapted to the tropics and in few minutes it became melted and dirty water. One observer said that the act was saved by a boy who uncovered the reality by yelling that the melted and dirty water looked like shit. Immediately a chorus of children started hitting the cans together and singing along: *mierda, mierda, mierda*!

[This text was inspired by the writings of Efraín Barriado.]

Camp, *carpa* and cross-dressing in the theater of Tito Vasconcelos

Antonio Prieto

In a way, this essay is an act of retrospection.[1] Remembering a theater production staged fourteen years ago in Mexico City takes me back to a particular time within Mexican political life, but also to a time when attending that play was an act of identity-quest. In 1985, I was barely becoming aware of a thriving gay world in Mexico City. Tito Vasconcelos' *Mariposas y Maricosas* (a play on words that roughly translates as "Butterflies and Fag-Things") was to me an enthralling experience of seeing that homosexuality could be publicly and openly celebrated. Though the audience began as a primarily gay one, this long-running show soon became a "crossover" success and was attended by many heterosexuals, some of whom were brought by gay relatives as a way of coming out of the closet.

One of the best-known and respected gay public figures in Mexico, Tito Vasconcelos, has deftly combined art and activism since the beginning of his career. With playwright José Antonio Alcaraz, he is credited with having initiated Mexican gay theater in 1980, with the production of *Y Sin Embargo, Se Mueven* (And Yet, They Move).[2] In this essay I will focus on *Mariposas y Maricosas*, which ran from September 1984 to June 1985. It represents a high point of this extraordinary artist's career, and was the best-received gay performance in Mexico during the 1980s.[3] Vasconcelos wrote, produced, directed, and starred in the show and its two sequels in 1988, *A Otra Cosa Mariposa* and *Mariposas de Bar*. All were variety shows that mixed dance, singing, poetry, monologues, and sketches on gay and drag themes, performed by Vasconcelos and two supporting actors – Sergio Cassani and Sergio Torres Cuesta.

The most memorable segments were a parody of *Mommy Dearest* – featuring Vasconcelos in a now-legendary impersonation of Joan Crawford – and a cooking lesson by *la doctora* Tatiana Ilhuicamina. This character was based on Chepina Peralta, an icon of Mexican housewives (and gays), whose noontime cooking lessons were watched by millions during the 1960s, 1970s, and 1980s. Vasconcelos added a significant twist to Chepina's image of the quintessential middle-class *comadre*:[4] his Tatiana was also a militant feminist, and a champion of gay rights.

While the Crawford impersonation was played to the limits of grotesque camp, the Tatiana segment displayed a sharply contrasting tone in its use of *carpa*, a popular comedy genre that thrived in central Mexico from the early 1920s to the late 1950s. *Carpa* became popular through its particular mixture of musical numbers (featuring voluptuous vedettes), and sketches performed by clown-like characters involving sexual puns and political parodies.[5] While *carpa* did not include professional transvestites among its repertoire, at times its male actors would cross-dress for the sake of parody. In his Tatiana Ilhuicamina sketch, Vasconcelos created a sort of *carpa* drag, doing what no other drag performer had done before on a Mexican stage: explicitly advocate gay issues. I am interested in the way Vasconcelos used the icon of a stereotypically *normal* kitchen-bound woman to disrupt categories of gender role-playing, to empower the Mexican gay community, expose homophobia *within* that community, and suggest the possibility of resistance from the heart of domestic space. Homophobia was directly addressed, not only in the Tatiana segment, but also in a poignant monologue by Torres Cuesta towards the show's middle section about solitude, oppression, and fear that ended with the straightforward call: "let's do away with silence, let's fight for the right to live our love in the daylight!"

In an interview,[6] Vasconcelos spoke about his longtime interest in cross-dressing which began in an award-giving ceremony in 1978, where he performed his first drag character, Sarah Bernhardt, about which he recalls:

> It was fantastic! I had all the audience at my feet, including people who previously would not speak to me. That way, I discovered my potential as a trans-gender actor, that incredible alchemy that I can achieve in feminine characters.

In *Maricosas*, Vasconcelos sought to move beyond the conventional "lip-synch" transvestite, widespread in Mexican clubs since the 1940s. At the same time, he sought to address "the phobia directed towards the feminine part of the homosexual group." Vasconcelos' work broadened public awareness of the aesthetic possibilities of drag as a medium, as well as the situation of gays in Mexico.

The political climate

When *Maricosas* opened in 1984, Mexico was in the middle of yet another economic crisis, with the drop of oil prices leading to the peso's devaluation. The conservative policies of President Miguel de la Madrid's administration (1982–88) were in full sway, and the Catholic Church was gaining ground in the political sphere. The homosexual movement had become visible in a historic 1978 march in Mexico City, during a larger demonstration to commemorate the 1968 student movement's tenth anniversary.[7] Unlike US gays, Mexican homosexuals did not need to fight for reforms in the state's laws, since same-sex acts between consenting adults are not illegal. However, oppression and homophobia in society at large did need to be addressed, as did the constant (often violent) harassment at the hands of the police. Bars were regularly raided, and extortion and blackmail were daily affairs. Groups such as the militant Frente Homosexual de Acción Revolucionaria (FHAR) and the Grupo Lambda de Liberación Homosexual (which included a large lesbian contingent) sought allegiances with leftist parties, and for some years obtained their support. However, internal disagreements led to the dismemberment of these groups and the virtual disintegration of the movement by 1984 (Lumdsen 1991: 68). This was very unfortunate, since AIDS was starting to spread, and the gay community was not organized at the time to contend with this crisis. Some groups did respond, such as the Colectivo Sol and Cálamo, offering legal and psychological assistance, but their outreach was very limited. Key spokespeople for the gay and lesbian groups during the late 1970s and the 1980s were Nancy Cárdenas, Carlos Monsiváis, Juan Jacobo Hernández, Luis González de Alba, José María Covarrubias, and Tito Vasconcelos.

In spite of the bleak sociopolitical landscape, gay and lesbian writers and artists were quite productive during this period. Authors Luis Zapata and José Joaquín Blanco were publishing groundbreaking novels that addressed the urban middle class. Jaime Humberto Hermosillo's film *Doña Herlinda and Her Son*, an endearing comedy about the relationship of two men in Guadalajara, one gay and the other bisexual, opened in 1984. Young playwrights Jesús González Dávila and Carlos Olmos were producing gay-themed dramas that were staged to much acclaim. All this indicated an increasing acceptance of gay art and literature within the generally conservative society of Mexico City.

On camp, cross-dressing and "terrorism"

Maricosas was one of the first shows to be staged in the recently opened (1983) Foro Shakespeare, a 170-seat theater located in the middle-class Condesa neighborhood, close to the Chapultepec park. The small stage was built on what used to be a home's backyard, and the house itself accommodated a cafeteria and the only theater bookstore in the city at the time. Vasconcelos' show set the tone for the Foro's following productions, usually gay-themed and subject to protest by right-wing watchdog groups such as Pro-Vida. The Foro's limited seating provided for an intimate environment and a feeling of proximity with the actors on stage. This is a feature that Vasconcelos exploited, especially in the Tatiana Ilhuicamina sketch, in which he directly addressed the audience. Another opportunity for participation occurred during Vasconcelos' memorable rendering of

"Take a walk on the wild side" (translated as "*Vamos a callejear*," an invitation to cruising), in which he would direct his microphone to specific audience members and coax them to join the imaginary chorus of "beautiful black men" (which in the original song are "colored girls").

Vasconcelos' Joan Crawford is remembered by many as being his *tour de force*, since he so perfectly impersonated the diva's fulminating gaze and overbearing personality. He based the segment on the 1978 biography by Christina Crawford – *Mommy Dearest* – and its popular screen version of 1981. Sergio Cassani impersonated Joan Crawford's daughter, who takes every opportunity to put her famous mother in ridiculous situations. Their camp performance exhibits most of the characteristics that Susan Sontag assigned to that sensibility in her much-quoted 1964 essay "Notes on Camp" (1966/1990): it revels in style, exaggeration, sentimentality, theatricality, and irony. But Vasconcelos' is not a light camp; it is imbued with a sense of the grotesque, and displays an almost sadistic delight with cruelty. That darker aspect of camp is inspired on the sensibility developed by Charles Ludlam's Ridiculous Theater Company during the mid-1960s in New York City. The Ridiculous aesthetic is a combination of "pastiche, parody, intertextuality, crossdressing, camp and theatrical self-reflexivity" (Dasgupta 1998: viii), whose images and themes are drawn from the mass media, popular culture, and classic drama texts. Vasconcelos read about the Ridiculous Theater in the late 1970s, and was immediately taken by its theatrical use of drag. He never saw a play, but he did meet Ludlam shortly before his death in 1987.

Mariposas y Maricosas shares Ludlam's fascination with American popular culture and his satirization of the media, while adding important aspects of Mexican *cultura popular*. In Mexico, the term refers not to mass-mediated culture, but to folk traditions, of which *carpa* is an example. In the Tatiana Ilhuicamina segment, Vasconcelos framed *cultura popular* (in this case, an indigenous-cuisine recipe delivered in *carpa* idioms) within a live television show. This allowed him to satirize the way Mexican mass media exploits folklore, while at the same time to use "folklore" to subvert the claims to modernity of televised cooking lessons. The use of American popular culture and Mexican *cultura popular*, of references to national and international mass media, makes for a hybrid performance that is perfectly in tune with a society that daily negotiates its local traditions with American imports of all kinds.

The Crawford segment opens[8] with the familiar Twentieth Century Fox fanfare, as Christina and Joan rehearse a remake of *Snow White*. Christina plays Snow White, while Joan plays the Evil Queen, who asks her mirror who is the fairest of them all. Realizing that she is to be transformed into a witch, Joan quips that Bette Davis would be better suited for the role. Christina insists the

12. Tito Vasconcelos
"Mariposas y Maricosas," 1984
Mexico City
Photo: Jesús Carlos
Tito Vasconcelos (right) as Joan Crawford and Sergio Cassani as her daughter Cristina
in Vasconcelos' high-camp version of *Mommy Dearest.*

role is perfect for her mother, who then slaps her with an exaggerated gesture
that is repeated throughout the segment.

Christina produces a script "just sent by Brian De Palma," and convinces
her mother to go over it. As it turns out, the scenes acted are the ones that open
De Palma's *Dressed to Kill*, and the audience laughs at the sight of Joan Crawford's
hyper-melodramatic rendering of the "rape" scenes in the shower and the taxi
("Christina, these are too many rapes for one morning!"). Her daughter gleefully
directs, with an *in crescendo* tempo, until Joan's character is brutally murdered in
an elevator. The rest of the film, Christina announces as she skips across the
stage, will feature a murderous transvestite acted by herself. Joan glares at her

daughter and asks with a menacing growl: "And exactly how much screen-time do I have?," to which she happily answers, "Eight minutes!!" Joan removes her gloves and again slaps Christina. The girl nonetheless brings out another script, this time a Broadway musical based on the Greek tragedy of Electra. Of course, Christina plays Electra, accomplice to her brother Orestes' matricide.

To Joan, this is definitively the last straw, and she drags Christina off stage, where we hear a violent fight take place. Joan finally emerges with the decapitated plastic head of Christina dangling from her outstretched hand. Horrified by her handiwork, she throws the head to the floor, turns to the audience, and reiterates her desire to make a grand return to the screen. The spotlight closes in on her face to better appreciate her eyes bulging with madness, as she dramatically intones: "Mr. DeMille, I'm ready for my close up."

It is no accident that these actions recall a "Punch and Judy" performance, since Vasconcelos was precisely seeking to create an *estética guiñolesca*; that is, an aesthetic derived from French carnivalesque marionette traditions known as *théâtre guignol*. In the Crawford sketch, he mixed glamor and horror in what he calls a "Hollywood guignol" that would adapt Euro-American camp to the Mexican sense of humor.

Vasconcelos has long been inspired by divas such as Joan Crawford, and his personal favorite, Sarah Bernhardt, whom he impersonated in the groundbreaking 1980 production of *Y Sin Embargo, Se Mueven*. For that show, he evoked Bernhardt's Hamlet, as an act of, in his own words, "double transvestism" (a man playing a woman playing a man), but adding the extra twist of Hamlet as a rock star. Vasconcelos is fascinated by the power of drag to woo and seduce his audience, but also feels it's important to remember the crucial role transvestites (called *travestis* or *vestidas* in Mexico) have played within the gay community. In his words:

> There tends to be an unwillingness to understand differences, even within the gay community. But it's drag queens who have always been the most radical within the ghetto, since they are the ones who start the cultural and political demonstrations. Transvestites were the first to confront the police and get their jaws broken at the Stonewall riots. *Travestis* have always been the cause of scandal, the ones who get murdered, the ones to appear in tabloid newspapers. They are, so to speak, the tip of the iceberg, and that's why they are the most maligned.

Vasconcelos remarked that transvestites' subversiveness lies in the way they "take their femininity to the last consequences of sophistication, of mannerist contortions," in what amounts to a form of symbolic terrorism. In that respect, he alludes to the terminology of some Mexican avant-garde artists, who in the 1970s used the term "visual terrorism" to describe their aggressive street interventions.[9] It might be more appropriate to characterize the transvestite's performative strategy as one of seduction, but here Vasconcelos evokes his explicit political aims to unsettle conventional gender roles. As a middle-class artist and intellectual, Vasconcelos deliberately engages in cross-dressing as a guerrilla strategy. However, his shows don't address the "real" terrorism and repression that working-class *travestis* are subjected to by police and gay-bashers. During the 1980s, bars where *travestis* performed were frequently raided or closed, while Vasconcelos' show never suffered any kind of censorship. The venues that would be closed were those housing "conventional" drag queens, the ones that Judith Butler would say are not necessarily subversive, since they limit themselves to the reiteration of patriarchally construed norms (1993: 125).

One might ask why it is that those transvestites are the target of harassment and violence, and not Vasconcelos' overtly politically engaged ones? Could it be that authorities dismiss his performances as "theater," and thus as harmless entertainment? While homosexual themes had previously been censored, as with the 1973 adaptation of *The Boys in the Band*,[10] theatrical drag is seldom touched. An exception Vasconcelos recalls is that of a production inspired by *Maricosas* called *Lilas* in Ciudad Sahagún, State of Mexico, in a predominantly working-class area with no tradition of theater. During its premiere, some people angrily emerged from the audience and dragged the actors off the stage, an incident that led to the show's closure.

Transvestites in Mexico are considered by the state bureaucracy and the more conservative sectors of society to be a serious threat to "public morality," in part because of their gender-bending appearance, but also because they are often thought to be prostitutes. While many *travestis* do sell their sexual favors, many others limit themselves to nightclub performances; differences that the police do not bother to investigate. Another important factor determining censorship is that of class, since actors belong to an elite within the middle class, while most *travestis* have a lower-middle-class or "social outcast" status which makes them vulnerable. Tito Vasconcelos' immunity may also be attributed to his kinship association with the renowned intellectual and politician, José Vasconcelos (his great-uncle), a fact that is not widely known, but that nonetheless accords him privileged status in Mexico.

Cultural theorist Marjorie Garber argues that female impersonation is ultimately "a space of possibility" that both structures and confounds culture. According to her, the "disruptive element that intervenes, [is] not just a category crisis of male and female, but the crisis of category itself"(1993: 17). Transvestites destabilize the – in Garber's terms – "comfortable binarity" of male/female, while a theater actor's cross-dressing performance (in itself an ancient practice) can be explained away as simply "acting." Garber's take on what she calls epistemological "anxiety" is linked to her argument that cross-dressing unsettles stable holds on gender identity. It could be argued that the *travesti* prostitute – a subject position that Garber overlooks – introduces an additional *moral* anxiety to the scheme, especially in the context of predominantly Catholic Latin American societies. This anxiety could be located in the ambivalent attitude of "straight" machos who feel attracted to *travestis*. The desire/fear tensions that emerge in these exchanges often lead to violence. While *Maricosas* might have contributed to a more positive attitude towards cross-dressing in general, it left unexplored issues of oppression towards *travestis*. Indeed, the transvestite as a subject was not explicitly dealt with in the play. Rather, *Maricosas* used cross-dressing in parodic ways already popular in *carpa* and gay camp performances.

Doctora Tatiana Ilhuicamina cooks up sexual politics

The Crawford segment served, in Vasconcelos' view, as an "antipode" to the earlier sketch that featured *la doctora* Tatiana Ilhuicamina:

> She was the antipode to Joan Crawford, totally unglamorous, a cook dressed as a Sanborn's waitress, suffering the trials of live television and the stereotypes that TV imposes on certain personalities. I didn't want to make fun of women or of Sanborn's waitresses, so I made my character a very intelligent woman, more interested in sexual politics than in the cooking itself. She would complete her soup opening a Campbell's can, since it was the more practical thing to do. It was a feminist statement, without more ambitions than to oppose the stereotypical image of women.

Television's Chepina Peralta is a typical middle-class housewife, generous in her sharing of recipes and cheerfulness. Vasconcelos' Tatiana departed from Chepina in the traditional Mexican cooking utensils she used, such as clay pots and huge wooden ladles. Her last name, "Ilhuicamina," identifies her as a direct descendant of Aztec nobility (one of the early Aztec emperors was Moctezuma Ilhuicamina), as opposed to the very Spanish surname "Peralta." Another twist is having a woman with an indigenous name boast a Ph.D. in Cuisine so that everyone respectfully calls her *doctora*.

The segment begins with the theme of *Star Trek*, as we see Tatiana come on stage along with her secretary, played by Sergio Torres Cuesta. Tatiana places herself behind a table full of clay pots and vegetables, while the secretary sits to the left ready to take the viewers' calls. Tatiana greets her audience with a trademark Chepina expression: "*¿Qué tal amigas?*," a very gendered "How are you doing my (female) friends?,," now transformed into a gay pun, since her *amigas* were a predominantly male audience. She then proceeds to set the tone for the rest of the segment by asking, "*¿a cómo les amanecieron los huevos?*" She is using an *albur*, or sexual pun, a common audience-teaser in *carpa* performances. The question literally translates as: "How did you find your egg's price this morning?,," but can also be interpreted as "How are your 'balls' this morning?" The question draws a hearty laughter from the audience. Tatiana insists on the question's literal meaning, and proceeds to comment on the rising prices of eggs and of all food staples, an everyday conversation topic among housewives in times of severe inflation. She then announces that today's recipe will be a delicious *flor de calabaza* (zucchini blossom) soup, a very traditional but, more importantly, economical treat. Throughout the segment, Tatiana displays linguistic acrobatics in her lightning-speed conversation that jumps from straightforward advice to sexual puns and scolds to the callers who reveal ignorance or reactionary views.

As she is beginning to cut up the vegetables, the phone rings. The secretary passes on the call of a housewife (Sergio Cassani), who falls into uncontrollable sobs as she recalls that her son was kicked out of home by his father. She nervously explains that her son is sick. Tatiana asks her to specify and, after lamenting that "nature failed me," and that she'll be forced to send her son to a psychologist, the lady blurts "*¡es un desviado!*," or "he's a deviate," a typical euphemism, which Tatiana sarcastically takes to its literal meaning, asking if then his problem is walking sideways. In a fit of desperation, the caller exclaims: "Don't you understand anything *doctora*? He's an *homoxsexual* [sic]!!" A significant pause follows the funny mispronunciation of the taboo word. Tatiana then proceeds to tell the caller that she could very well have defended her son. She takes one of her recipe lists, and flips it over ("I always have important information on the back of these recipes; you never know when it'll come in handy in a live show like this"). She implicitly admonishes her caller by quoting Freud, "the father of psychoanalysis":

> Homosexuality is certainly no advantage [to which Tatiana remarks, "well, remember he wrote this 80 years ago"]. However, it's not a vice nor a depravation. We consider it a simple variant of sexual tendencies.

The cooking teacher is unexpectedly revealed as an advocate for homosexuals, whose recipes' flip side store authoritative information on sexual politics. Tatiana also takes issue with internalized homophobia within the gay community, when a man calls to claim that he is homosexual, but not a *joto*, or fag. The actor is turned away from the audience, wears a leather jacket, and high-heeled pink shoes that contradict his claims to macho-hood. He argues – with an exaggerated "masculine" voice – that "nature made me a man that happens to like men," but

that he is repulsed by sissies and fags. With a pedantic tone, he claims to be
activo (top), and that his homosexuality is unnoticeable. This last statement ("*a
mí no se me nota*") is marked by a slip in his voice towards an effeminate tone
that makes the audience laugh. Tatiana angrily chides the caller on his prejudices,
and on his denigrating use of labels. She flips another recipe, and reads from an
unspecified source:

> Effeminate gestures vary greatly according to each individual, and depend
> on each person's personality. Above all, they depend on the historical and
> cultural context where they take place.

She then acts out examples of men's fashions throughout the ages (including pre-
Hispanic feathered headdresses) that by today's standards are considered
effeminate. After several comical interludes in which she parodies so-called effeminate mannerisms of eighteenth century France, *doctora* Ilhuicamina concludes, in
a matter-of-fact tone, that effeminate manners are completely relative to context,
and have nothing to do with desire, or with what people do under the bedsheets.

Vasconcelos' representation of gay identity is somewhat ambiguous at this
point. The man's views are ridiculed by having him wear high heels and slipping
to an effeminate tone of voice. This might suggest the operative assumption here
is that all gay men who choose to be "masculine" are actually masking an effeminate "essence" of gay behavior. It would also seem that transvestism is presented
as an identifying mark of the homosexual, and thus that all gays are potential
drag queens, or all transvestites are gay, assumptions that are far from being true.
Within the sketch's comedic tone, however, the scene can work as a parody of
the binary poles – *macho/loca*, *activo/pasivo*, butch/femme – where the second,
oppressed term mischievously slips to the surface in spite of the subject's inten-
tions. The man's confident assumption that "nature made him" is unmade by
this ludic flash of the oppressed term.

The next caller interrupts Tatiana's vegetable-mincing and identifies herself
as a worker for the Homosexual Rehabilitation Institute. She hollers:

> Attention, Mexican families! Homosexuality is a sickness, and thus can be
> cured! I have a scientifically proven recipe that I will now share with you.
> The man suspected of being homosexual must: 1) talk to a woman, 2) kiss
> her, 3) sit her on his lap, 4) begin foreplay, 5) take her to his room,
> 6) take her clothes off, 7) penetrate her. If this doesn't work, then elec-
> trical shocks might be tried.

Horrified, Tatiana hangs up and wonders how could Nazis survive their defeat
in Europe and now thrive in Mexico. The last call is from an extremely effeminate

person wearing heavy make-up, who claims he is a gay Catholic confused because of a booklet a young priest gave him called "Does the Church Abandon Homosexuals?" Tatiana happens to have the booklet with her, takes it out from under a pot, and proceeds to thoroughly deconstruct it with a sharply ironic reading. When she reaches a question posed in the text, "Is homosexuality contagious?," Tatiana seizes the opportunity to attack the Church's hypocrisy by turning to the imaginary TV camera (where the audience is seated) and addressing the priest who authored the pamphlet: "Look my friend, if it were, the seminar from which you came, along with several others, would be closed as sources of infection." She comforts the caller by assuring him that the inquisitorial views posed in the text are completely out of order.

Throughout the segment, food, advice, and sexuality intermingle. The vegetables and their juices are sexually metaphorized, and lend a comically erotic edge to Dr. Ilhuicamina's advice. Although she is well read and sensible to sexual politics, she never adopts a pedantic stance, but rather the manner of an opinionated *comadre*, close friend, or confidant. The night I saw the show, the audience reveled in the *albures*, so characteristic of *carpa*, and adapted to the gay sensibility. A feeling of complicity developed, a bonding among the gay spectators, who would look around to see who was "getting it" and who wasn't.

With a few deft strokes of her wit and wisdom, Tatiana has tackled the reactionary institutions of patriarchal family, mental health clinics, and the Catholic Church. Using a language that's accessible to her audience, she has rendered complex psychological and gender theories as common sense. Her eclectic use of quotations is in line with what Butler calls "performative citation" (1993: 225): she lends authority to her discourse by the same means that hegemonic law conveys authority on itself. In doing so, Dr. Ilhuicamina is not reiterating a hegemonic strategy, but rather turning it around on itself. It is a power struggle that exposes the arbitrary nature of citation; how certain information can be used for oppression, and certain others can be used for resistance. Her quotation of Freud's progressive views, for example, comes after her caller's remarks on seeking a psychologist to cure her "deviate" son. If the "Father of Psychoanalysis" considers homosexuality a "variant" and not a "deviation," then why seek a cure in the clinic? Dr. Ilhuicamina is clearly aware of her citations' performative power, and uses them to confront hegemonic institutions. By drawing her quotes from the flip side of her recipes, she brings academic authority into a space that is at once domestic and mass-mediated: the TV (and theater) kitchen. With her double-sided recipes, Dr. Ilhuicamina reveals the other, *politicized*, side of the coin as she simultaneously cooks a penny-wise soup and speaks about the social construction of gender role-playing. She is aware that knowledge is power, but also – and importantly – that knowledge is best consumed when accompanied by the aroma of a *flor de calabaza* soup and the sexual innuendo of the *albur*.

On Tatiana Ilhuicamina's impact on the audience, Vasconcelos recalls:

> Something amazing happened with the character; a great following among the female audience, not necessarily gay, but heterosexual women that approached not Tito Vasconcelos, but Tatiana Ilhuicamina, in order to get advice. I think it was an identification with a progressive woman who shared the everyday drudgery of being a married señora, but also had time for social work, however unintended that activism might have been.

Vasconcelos' art was to convey the message as *como quien no quiere la cosa* (popular saying for an unintentional accomplishment). Rather than being an angry soapbox activist, *doctora* Ilhuicamina rendered politics into common sense, that is, made it palatable, as the dishes she prepared for her audience. By combining elements of camp naiveté, the sexual puns of *carpa*, and unassuming but forceful political statements uniquely hers, she became a *comadre* of homosexuals – simultaneously friend, advisor, and awareness promoter – at a time when the community was disarticulated and under attack. When asked if he considers his theater political, Vasconcelos answered "definitively yes," and added that he hoped his work "motivates my audience to read and educate itself. I'm worried that our community can be so ignorant and in diaspora."

Although *Maricosas* included no mention of AIDS – Vasconcelos said that in 1984 the crisis seemed still to be very distant – the show did much to strengthen the community's self-esteem and political awareness during the days when the media were beginning to sensationalize the "gay plague." Indeed, Vasconcelos was using his characters to give voice to a community that at the time was largely silent. Gay issues were being staged in a highly entertaining way that made them attractive to both homosexual and *buga* (straight) audience members. *Maricosas* was an empowering performance, since it articulated fears and desires that few people knew how to convey to their family and friends.

Conclusion

Mariposas y Maricosas ran for nine months, which was record-breaking for this kind of show, and developed a sort of cult following that led to its two 1988 sequels. By that time, AIDS was already taking its toll on the Mexican population, so Dr. Ilhuicamina performed a safe-sex demonstration using condoms and cucumbers.

Maricosas was a high point in Mexican gay theater. Its succession of music, dance, poetry, and comedy explored a wide scope of male homosexualities.

Cross-dressing, however, had a privileged position, and served the show in somewhat ambivalent ways. At times, it seems to have been used more for purposes of parody than for the affirmation of a particular transgendered identity, while in other instances drag was problematically presented as a symbol of *gay* identity. There prevailed an unspoken agreement that to be out of the closet is to be in drag, or acting with hyperbolic effeminacy, as in the case of *doctora* Ilhuicamina's last caller, the only one who identified himself as "gay" while wearing make-up, a wig, and speaking in a shrill voice. Therefore, while critical of certain stereotypes, the show risked reinforcing other ones. But this risk was perhaps unavoidable in a performance that sought to work against the grain of a heterosexist society that dictates masculinity for both *buga* and gay men. The privilege of effeminate attitudes confronted the audience's anxieties regarding men who don't conform to the macho stereotype, upsetting some gay people's internalized homophobia.

Mariposas y Maricosas combined camp and *carpa*, mixed American popular culture with Mexican *cultura popular*, and blended Euro-American gay sensibilities with those specific to Mexican *jotos* and *travestis*. That way, as in Dr. Tatiana Ilhuicamina's recipes, a deliciously varied performance was presented to our palate. It delighted the senses, while also managing to unexpectedly, "*como quien no quiere la cosa*," display its flip side: that of politics as common sense.

Notes

1.   I wish to thank Luis Esparza, my unfailing *compañero* with whom I've seen many of Tito Vasconcelos' plays, for his illuminating feedback on this essay. Gustavo Geirola and Coco Fusco likewise provided valuable critique.

2.   An earlier gay production was the adaptatiopn of Mat Crowley's *The Boys in the Band*, directed by Nancy Cárdenas in 1973.

3.   Tito Vasconcelos' other credits include starring in the Mexican version of Fierstein's *Torch Song Trilogy*, directed by Carlos Tellez in 1986. In 1991, he had a supporting key role as a transvestite in María Novaro's breakthrough film *Danzón*. Since the early 1990s, he has paired with Jesusa Rodríguez in a series of cabaret-like political parodies. He currently has a show called *Cabare-Tito*, in which he impersonates a different woman every Thursday at a gay bar in Mexico City's *Zona Rosa*.

4.   In Mexican society, a *comadre* or *compadre* belongs to a non-sanguineal kinship arrangement that closely links one family with another when a person is chosen to be a child's godparent. The term is also used to address special friends.

5.   The most celebrated of *carpa* comedians was Mario Moreno "Cantinflas", who inspired generations of Mexican and even Chicano performers. See Broyles-González (1994: Chapter 1) for a discussion of *carpa* as a source for early Chicano theater.

6.   All the quotes in this essay derive from a personal interview with Tito Vasconcelos in Mexico City on December 6, 1997. The translation is mine.

7.   Although homosexuality is lived and conceived differently in Mexico than in Europe or the US (see Almaguer 1995; Lumsden 1991), the idioms and behavior codes that refer to homosexuality have become more fluid and hybrid during the last decade. For example, English words like "gay" will coexist with a rich local vocabulary of words like *chichifo* (a boy who charges for his sexual services), *mayate* (heterosexual who willingly engages in active anal intercourse), and *buga* (male or female heterosexuals).

8.   I use the present tense while describing the show's segments, so as to convey a sense of immediacy. Reconstruction of the performance was aided by a video Vasconcelos gave me.

9.   In a recent essay on Afro-Mexican-American drag superstar Vaginal Creme Davis, critic José Esteban Muñoz used the term "terrorist drag" to describe the performance of "the nation's internal terrors around race, gender and sexuality" (1997: 91).

10.   The public protest of artists, intellectuals and journalists led to that play's re-staging (Monsiváis 1995: 203–04).

References

Almaguer, Tomás (1995). "Hombres Chicanos: Una Cartografía de la Identidad y del Comportamiento Homosexual," *Debate feminista*, vol. 11, April, 46–77.

Broyles-González, Yolanda (1994). *El Teatro Campesino: Theater in the Chicano Movement*. Austin, University of Texas Press.

Butler, Judith (1993). *Bodies That Matter: On the Discursive Limits of "Sex."* New York, Routledge.

Dasgupta, Gautam (1998). "Preface to the 1998 Edition." *Theater of the Ridiculous*. Ed. Bonnie Marranca and Gautam Dasgupta. Baltimore, Johns Hopkins University Press.

Garber, Marjorie (1993). *Vested Interests: Cross-Dressing and Cultural Anxiety*. New York, Harper Perennial.

Lumsden, Ian (1991). *Homosexualidad, Sociedad y Estado en México*. México, Solediciones, Canadian Gay Archive.

Monsiváis, Carlos (1995). "Ortodoxia y Heterodoxia en las Alcobas (Hacia una Crónica de Costumbres y Creencias Sexuales en México)," *Debate feminista*, vol. 11, April, 183–210.

Muñoz, José Esteban (1997). "'The White to Be Angry': Vaginal Davis's Terrorist Drag," *Social Text* 52/53, vol. 15, nos. 3 and 4, Fall/Winter, 80–103.

Sontag, Susan (1966/1990). "Notes on Camp." *Against Interpretation*. Susan Sontag. New York, Anchor Books, 275–92.

Memory performance: Luis Alfaro's "Cuerpo Politizado"

José Esteban Muñoz

Mapping downtown: the space of memory

Queer theory's early alliance with activist movements like Queer Nation and Act-Up meant that theory-making would maintain an ongoing dialogue with activism and political performance. Nonetheless, the "theory" end of the "queer theory" formulation has remained rather rigid and traditional in its meaning. In this respect the "theory" in queer theory has not been queered. In this essay I will consider performance as a site of theoretical production to enhance the body of queer theory discourse. To my mind the performance sites most worth investigating are the works by artists whose experiences are marked by multiple points of antagonism within the social.

Luis Alfaro's solo performances present us with views of the intersecting worlds that formed him as a queer, working-class, urban Chicano.[1] I will discuss his work as a theorization of the social. His memory performances help us not only image a future queer world, but also actually achieve a new counter-public formation in the present through lived performance praxis.

Alfaro's performance of "Cuerpo Politizado" (Politicized Body) opens with a song by Petula Clark – "Downtown." The song evokes a utopic urban sprawl, recalling a moment when downtowns were the hubs of excitement and progress. Today, in the age of financially depressed commercial zones, the song's lyrics and soft pop melody seem rife with irony. Then a video called "Chicanismo" is projected onto the screen.

The video begins with slow moving sweeps of downtown Los Angeles and then accelerates. The soundtrack sounds like a scratchy car stereo that jumps from station to station. The visual montage includes shots of low riders gliding down crowed city streets, a man in a mariachi outfit getting off work, Chicana homegirls with heavy make-up leaning against a street pole, homeless men with overgrown beards, and graffiti that reads, "Shy boy is crazy." The now rapid-fire editing stops four times. The montages work as transitions between sections in which Alfaro delivers brief monologues as different characters.

The four characters of "Chicanismo" are all excerpts from the rich ensemble of social types that constitute Los Angeles. The first figure, a bearded and disillusioned Chicano Studies professor, represents faded nationalism. He is followed by a teenage mother who, despite her love for her baby, stands for youth in crisis. A hyper-assimilated Gap employee inadvertently reveals the situation of young people trapped within the service industry; while an undocumented maid, who identifies with her employers and declares that the US is her home, demonstrates how the most economically vulnerable are compelled to sacrifice their own nationality. These social players map the different horizons of experience that delineate the space of contemporary Chicano LA. The four characters are bodies that do more than inhabit space – they also create space, in this case the space of Chicano Los Angeles. Elizabeth Grosz suggests that the relationship between bodies and cities is a complicated one:

> . . . there may be an isomorphism between the body and the city. But it is not a mirroring of nature in artifice. Rather, there is a two way linkage which could be defined as an interface, perhaps even a co-building. What I am suggesting is a model of relations of bodies and cities which sees them as, not as megalithic total entities, distinct identities, but as an assemblage between subject and form linkages, machines, provisional and often temporary sub- or microgroupings.[2]

Bodies and cities define each other. The bodies represented in "Chicanismos" are the city of Los Angeles, which is to say that one cannot abstract them from the social matrix of Los Angeles. This brings me back to the song "Downtown." The song's idealistic lyrics, "Downtown, it's a beautiful day . . .," are ironically invoked, in that the downtown that Alfaro describes is one of faded dreams, poverty, self-hatred, and social subordination. But Alfaro's citation of the song reads as more than simply ironic. The song is also a memory of space. For Alfaro, the song is a passionate act of remembering, a strategy to conjure the romanticized media images of a world that never really existed. Thus, a dream from the past is read in relation to a mapping of the present. Both of these temporalities are starkly juxtaposed, and a new temporality, a new moment, one of social transformation and activist politics, is called for.

As the video concludes, the house lights go up and a man sitting in front of me speaks loudly from his seat. He get ups and slowly walks toward the stage. The man is Luis Alfaro, the performer who has just appeared in the video. When he emerges from the audience, after having been one of "us" the sense of tranquil spectatorship is displaced. The leap from performances "contained" within the video and the live body of Alfaro produces a shock effect that stirs the spectator.

The house lights begin to dim as the performer reaches the stage. The monologue he has recited since he began his migration from the audience to the stage is titled "On a Street Corner." The story is about a heterosexual couple walking down Broadway in downtown Los Angeles. The man says to the woman, "Shut up bitch." She complains about the beatings he inflicts upon her and he threatens to leave her. She pleads for him to stay by saying: "Aw, no baby, you're the only thing I remember." The woman is so deeply immersed in this relationship that the man has overwhelmed her memory. Alfaro then accesses his own memory testimony as he reaches the center of the stage and says:

> Because desire is memory and I crave it like the born agains in my mama's church. But it's hard to be honest sometimes, because I live in the shadow of the Hollywood sign. Because on the street corner known as Pico and Union, my father made extra money on pool tables, my mother prayed on her knees.

The performer continues to transform downtown into a narrative series of childhood vignettes. He talks about the time that Sonia Lopez slapped him after he forced a kiss on her, and he concludes that this must have been his introduction to S/M. He recalls Bozo the clown at the May Company on Broadway, tossing presents to a throng of kids that he is part of. When a board game hits another boy in the eye, Alfaro became terrified that the clown would throw something in *his* direction.

He then slips out of the directly autobiographical register, while still performing memories laced with violence. He paces around the stage as he tells the story of the woman who dances in the projects and of the husband who beats her. We hear about the drunk from the bar who staggers home. We also listen to the story of the man who rides the Pico bus and slides his hand under women's seats. There is also the glue sniffer on Venice Boulevard who watches the world in slow motion. Alfaro's pace and voice quicken as he concludes the monologue with an incantation that summarizes the piece: "A man got slapped./A woman got slugged./A clown threw toys./A drunk staggered./An earthquake shook,/A slap./A slug./A shove. A kick." The stories condense into acts. These acts suggest bodies and the conjured bodies exist in an interface with the image of a city. These performative acts – slaps, punches, and so forth – render the social through the performative. Theatrical mimesis outlines the performances and acts the frame and punctuates everyday life. In doing so, queer theory begins to work as an embodied social theory.

Memory, as I have been suggesting, is a central theme here. It is related to the concept of affect, a key word that informs this inquiry. Memory is structured through the violence and pain that inform much of urban Latina/o reality. Memory recalls and indexes both the affective lifeworld of US Latinos and the collective

affective performances of *latinidad*. The term *"latinidad,"* which I use as a theoretical catalog of different modes of Latina/o performativity, is not about race,
region, nation, gender, language, or any other easily identifiable demarcation of
"difference." Thinking of *latinidad* as anti-normative affect engenders a model of
group identity that is not exclusionary, yet still coherent. Performed memory is
a deployment of rehearsed and theatricalized Latino affect. Through performed
memory, Alfaro negotiates two different temporal narratives of the self. The
migrant child and gay man of color – two affective registers of Latino experience
that interrogate each other through the performer's theatrical mixing.

Alfaro has described his work as series of combinations; "mixing gay life
with Chicano life, street life with Catholic life, cholo life with my life."[3] This
mixing resonates with the kind of cultural layering that queers of color often
need to enact if they wish to maintain simultaneous memberships in queer communities and communities of color. Memory is not a static thing for the queer of
color; it is an anti-normative space where self is made and remade and where
politics can be imagined. While memory is not static for anyone, its is always
"in the making" for the minoritarian subject, who cannot perform normative
citizenship and thus has no access to the standardized narratives of national
cultural memory. The memory performances I am interested in exploring are
decidedly anti-normative, which is to say that they are deployed for the purposes
of contesting affective normativities that include, but are not limited to, white
supremacy, the cultural logics of misogyny and homophobia. For the queer of
color's performances of memory transmits and broadcasts affectively charged
strategies and tactics of minoritarian survival and self-making, carving out a space
for resistance and communal self-enactment.

Performances of memory are necessitated by a dominant culture that projects
an "official" history that elides queer lives and the lives of people of color. Many
of us take periodic refuge in the past. We need to remember a time before, not
as a nostalgic escape, but as a vision of a different time and place that enables a
critique of the present. Performances of memory remember, dream, and recite
a self and reassert agency in a world that challenges and constantly attempts to
snuff out subaltern identities. Memory performances deploy affective narratives
of self, ways of being from the past, in the service of questioning the future, a
future without annihilating epidemics, either viral or ideological. Alfaro's work
demonstrates the importance of memory for the politics of the present and the
future. His memory performances are the dreams of a subject who falls out of
the narrow confines prescribed by the state, the law, and other normative grids.
They are the dreams of subjects whose affect is deemed excessive, wrong, or
simply off. Such performances amplify and transmit these recitations of dreams

and contribute to a project of setting up counter-publics – communities and relational chains of resistance that contest the dominant public sphere.

Between two virgins

Alfaro walks into a circle of light after "On a Street Corner" as he prepares to tell a family story called "Virgin Mary." He commences by explaining that "We used to have this Virgin Mary doll. Every time you connected her to an outlet she would turn and bless all sides of the room." The cylinder of light around him contains him, as though he, too, were in a glass case. The performer goes on to recount the story of the Virgin Mary's origin, how she was purchased during one of his father's surprise drunken trips to Tijuana, when he would come home from the racetrack at about midnight and load the entire family into the station wagon. Young Luis offers the Virgin as a gift to his Tia Ofelia when she was suffering from breast cancer.

Tia Ofelia, like everyone else in the family was a grape-picker from Delano, California. She lived on the top floor of a two-storey wooden home that was flanked by high-rise projects. The bottom floor was occupied by cholos from the 18th Street Gang. After his aunt passes away, their rivals, the Crips, come looking for them and they firebomb the house, killing the cholos and destroying the house, along with the Virgin Mary.

Years later, as a young man, Alfaro recounts that he meets a man who will become his first love. He owns a rotating Virgin Mary doll that he bought in Mexico. Alfaro describes him as having white skin, eating broccoli, and talking like characters on a TV series. He was "every *Partridge Family/Brady Bunch* episode rolled into one." This white man teaches the young Alfaro how to French-kiss, lick an earlobe, and dance in the dark. The young Alfaro's fascination for this man has much to do with the way in which he is the embodiment of a normative imprint that dominates North American culture. In part Alfaro desires his whiteness, which is also his normative affect, his way of being in the world, and the man's performances of affect – which include a taste for broccoli, a certain way of dancing in the dark, and a general affective register that is reminiscent of situation comedies about normative white families. Alfaro is crushed when this lover leaves him and he once again finds himself surrounded by family, who let him know that "The Virgin Mary, that old Virgin Mary, she watches over all of us."

Alfaro uses this rotating deity to forge a connection between these different layers of experience and affect. The life Alfaro describes, positioned between a straight ethnic past and a predominantly white queer present, is the kind of reality that queers of color often negotiate. One way of managing such an identity is to forsake the past, to let go of it altogether. But for Alfaro the cost is too high. The enactment of self via the routes of memory performance is the mode of managing identity that Alfaro calls upon. More precisely, he invents a theater of memory. While the coherent self is most certainly an exhausted fiction, what I will call a "self effect" is necessary to make interventions in the social. Minority, diasporic, and exiled subjects recalibrate the protocols of selfhood by insisting on the radical hybridity of the self, the fact that the self is not a normative citizen or even coherent whole, but instead a hybrid that contains disparate and even contradicting associations, identifications, and disidentifications. Alfaro historicizes the self through theatricalizations of Latino affect that index the personal memory of a family of migrant grape pickers from Delano and the collective and spatialized memory of Chicano Los Angeles.

The Moo-Moo of history

In the segment titled "A Moo-Moo Approaches/A Story about Mamas and Mexico," Alfaro focuses on the figure of his mother. Moo-Moo is meant to connote his mother's large colorful dresses and her fat body. Alfaro himself foregrounds his own body image as a fat man through this meditation on his mother. The performer begins by walking up to a table of Twinkies and eating them one by one. As he literally gorges himself on dozens of Twinkies, a tape plays the story of the Moo-Moo, a story I want to read alongside Benjamin's angel of history. In order to do so, I would like to refer to a valuable reading of Benjamin's angel fable by Jonathan Boyarian, a Judaic scholar of memory and ethnography.

> This reading of the storm from paradise, which emphasizes the howling gap between us and the past and the past's proximity to us, suggests the need for a "double gesture" toward our past. We need constantly to be interrogating and recuperating the past, without pretending for long that we can recoup its plenitude. This double gesture, this contradictory movement of new recognitions and new distances between the present and the past, may be most easily articulated in a juxtaposition of explicit traditional and postmodern figures of multiplicity, rather than modern identity.[4]

Boyarian's concept of a "double gesture," which recognizes the need to reclaim a past while resisting the temptation to succumb to a nostalgic and essentialized concept of the past, is especially useful with respect to Luis Alfaro's memory performances. The double gesture of remembering and not being lost to memory, for the minority subject, leads to a powerful emergence into politics, the social, and the real. Memory is a catalyst, it assists in the shoring up anti-normative

Latino/a affect and enables performances of the self that contest the affective normativity of dominant culture.

With this notion of the double gesture in mind, let us now return to Moo-Moo. The tape-recorded voice in this section of Alfaro's performance explains that when Alfaro's father first came to this country there simply wasn't enough for him. This is why he married Alfaro's mother, the Moo-Moo. He describes her as having "hips as wide as a river. She was abundance personified." The Moo-Moo's function was to signify their accruing wealth and to hide their actual poverty. But the children were embarrassed by the Moo-Moo, who attended every PTA meeting and boy scout outing, as well as inserting herself in altar-boy affairs at church. She threatened to kill a neighborhood woman who called her precious son effeminate. The Moo-Moo fended off burglars with a baseball bat; she chased the man who stole the family's small television set down to the corner of Pico and Union. The performer summarizes his mother during this period by saying that, "The Moo-Moo was serious, girl."

As time went on and Alfaro's father felt compelled to become "American," he decided that the Moo-Moo was too much. The Moo-Moo who once represented an abundant future now "was no longer desirable. The Moo-Moo of Mexico represented all the problems and setbacks we had endured in America. The Moo-Moo of Mexico was too big, too fat, too much. Too much for our new American sensibility." The Moo-Moo then also, like Tia Ofelia, lost a breast. She gave up her brightly colored moo-moos and began wearing simple dark dresses that she sewed on an old-fashioned sewing machine from the Deardens store on 5th and Main.

By this time Alfaro has eaten at least thirty Twinkies. He continues to stuff them down his throat in a violent fashion. The tape continues with the story of the Moo-Moo's slow suicide, courtesy of "Hostess Manufacturing." The family home is overrun with cupcakes, sno-balls, lemon pies, donuts, and ho-ho's. This image inhabits Alfaro's imagination. He reports that at night, "far from the breast of The Moo-Moo, the nightmare that is the Mexico that I do not know haunts me. I clear the kitchen of all traces of my bicultural history; the Mexican tele-novela and a sweetener called America. The nightmare continues, a Moo-Moo approaches."

The Moo-Moo is the angel of history. Her face is turned to a past that is Mexico. The Moo-Moo would like to awaken the dead from a past life, another place and time, and make whole what has been shattered through relocation and migration. The forces that call the Alfaro family to assimilate are a storm blowing from paradise, which is also coded as progress. Her back is turned to this paradise, her eyes are focused on a past that is being debased by those around her. She is

tragic, like history's angel, insofar as she has lost control of herself. She is coming towards Alfaro like a house lifted by a tornado. She represents the nightmare that is his history and his bicultural queer body shakes at the thought of her. He performs a ritual re-enactment of his mother's slow suicide by consuming the table full of Twinkies. By doing so, he inhabits her abjected form. This effeminate queer son who was once protected by this Moo-Moo mother becomes her in an effort to rehabilitate a body and an image that has been battered by progress and assimilation. By doing so, Alfaro finds a place for himself in this nightmare. He identifies with this tragic Moo-Moo and with his father's will towards assimilation. His performance is an attempt to redeem what has been lost.

"Primitive Latino First Aid": the double gesture of memory performance

The double gesture described by Boyarian is evident in another moment in Alfaro's performance. Standing behind a podium, as though he were giving a lecture, he holds one small finger up in the air. Alfaro recalls having cut his finger jumping through his mother's rose bush when he was 11 years old. He reveals that he has jumped through the rose bush to avoid his grandmother. The first half of the piece explains how he despises his grandmother more than his fifth-grade teacher. The poem expresses the shame this second-generation Latino feels because of his grandmother's refusal to assimilate into North American culture.

After emerging from the bush Alfaro discovers a wound:

> I rise out of the rose bush
> and immediately plunge into
> the other Latino dramatic effect,
> the painful
> ay yai yai.
>
> There's a gash on my finger
> and it starts to bleed
> pretty badly.

13. Luis Alfaro
"Cuerpo Politizado" (Politicized Body), 1996
Los Angeles, California
Photo courtesy of Luis Alfaro
Alfaro evokes memories by dancing in drag in "Cuerpo Politizado."

Abuelita turns on the hose
and runs my hand
under the water.
Inspecting my finger she laughs,
pinches my cheek,
Thanks the *Virgen*
for the minor miracle,
does a sign of the cross, and applies
Primitive Latino First Aid,

She looks at me,
smiles, raises a bloody finger
to her face.
Closely inspecting
my afflicted digit,
she brings it up close
to her eyes.

I can't tell
what she is looking for.
As if holding it up close
she might find
some truth,
some small lesson
or parable
about the world
and its workings.

Her eyes canvass the finger,
probing her vision
slowly and carefully.
And then quickly
and without warning,
she sticks it
inside her mouth
and begins
to suck on it.

I feel the inside of her mouth,
wet and warm,
her teeth

lightly pulling
equally discomforting
and disgusting
at the same time.

Being in that womb
feels as if I am being eaten alive
on one of those
late-night
Thriller Chiller movies
Vampira, Senior Citizen Bloodsucker.

But it isn't that at all.
This is the only way
that *abuelita*
knows how to stop the bleeding.

The narrative then shifts from the past to the present.

See this finger?
Cut it at work.
Making another pamphlet
critical of those
who would like
to see us dead.

The long gasp.
Four Gay Latinos
in one room
Four long gasps.

Afraid to touch my wound.
Would prefer
to see it bleed
and gush
than to question
mortality
and fate.

Could go on
about being tested,
but it seems

so futile.
As if we
don't know
that one little test
could have been wrong.

Hold the finger
in front of me
Stick it
close to mouth
Drip, drip, drip
all over the desktop
from Ikea.

Hold it close
to face.
Quickly
and without
warning,
stick it in my mouth
and I begin to
suck.

Tears roll down.
Salty wet
tears.
Down my face.
Can feel my teeth
lightly pulling
and I wish,

I wish for an *abuelita*
in this time.
This time of plague.
This time of loss.
This time of sorrow.
This time of mourning.
This time of shame.

And I
heal myself.
I heal myself

> with *abuelita's*
> Primitive Latino First Aid.

The politics of Alfaro's memory performance brings into view the importance of the past to our immediate political present. The first half of the text is transfixed upon the artist's conflicted relationship to the past, to his grandmother, and his own 11-year-old Chicano self. The prevailing tone of the poem's first section is that of shame. But the double gesture of interrogating the past while not collapsing under the gravitational pull of nostalgia helps us grasp its importance to the formulation of a politicized self in the here and now.

We also see a deep desire for a space of identity-formation here. What is imagined is a rehabilitated and reimagined Latino family, one that is necessary in the face of a devastating and alienating pandemic. Memory performance reinvents the space of familia. It is a hub of identity consolidation. This hub is reinhabited through the auspices of memory performance.

Family has been much criticized in contemporary queer theory as an oppressive totality. I want to argue that such a characterization, from the perspective of queers of color, is deeply reductive. On the one hand it is true that not all families of color affirm their queer sons and daughters. On the other hand, the generalized gay community often feels like a sea of whiteness to queers of color and, thus, the imagined ethnic family is often a refuge. It is a space where all those elements of the self that are fetishized, ignored, and rejected in the larger queer world are suddenly revalorized. Alfaro's memory performance attunes us to those enabling characteristics.

Queer theater and social theory

In Michael Warner's introduction to his collection *Fear of a Queer Planet*, he produces a sharp critique of social theory's "heteronormativity," and calls upon queer studies to engage with the social. He notes that "the energies of queer studies have come more from rethinking the subjective meaning of sexuality than from thinking the social."[5] Warner contrasts ethnos and eros, arguing that, as experiences of identity, sexuality, and ethnicity are fundamentally distinct, "People tend not to encounter queerness in the same way as ethnic identity. Often the disparity between racial and sexual imperatives can be registered as dissonance." In "Cuerpo Politizado," Alfaro theatricalizes this dissonance, considering it as part of queer experience.

Warner takes pains to show the way in which ethnicity and race are not corresponding experiences. While I agree that these categories need to be differentiated, I would suggest that his reading of the differences between queers and people of color in relation to the familial sign requires more elaboration. His reading of the role of family is organized by a particularly white queer experience. He writes:

> Familial language deployed to describe sociability in race- or gender-based movements (sisterhood, brotherhood, fatherland, mother tongue, etc.) can either be a language of exile or a resource of irony (in voguing houses, for example, one queen acts as "mother").[6]

In Alfaro's work, the family is more than just a site to run from or a source of irony. Alfaro's work returns to the space of an ethnic past in order to formulate his identity as a queer of color. In the Moo-Moo sequence and the Abuelita sequence, he specifically turns to maternal and grandmaternal sites to draw an energy and critical force. While the majority of white queers can more easily fashion a break (an exile) from their childhood in heteronormative culture, since the queer community is a white normative one and they would therefore not be dislocated from their cultural formation as white people, the queer of color who cuts ties with his familial past is often also cutting ties with his ethnicity and/or race.

In the performance's final section, "Orphan of Aztlan," Alfaro literally preaches this last monologue, taking on the voice of a charismatic minister, one who might be preaching at his mother's church. He stands behind a music stand as if it were a pulpit. Aztlan is the imaginary homeland that is a central organizing principle of Chicano nationalism. Alfaro's status as orphan (or exile) from this nationalist community foregrounds Chicano nationalism's inability to claim queer sons and daughters. But Alfaro expounds a more nuanced political position at this point in his performance. He sounds a militant political note in relation to liberal queer politics:

> There has been no power-sharing
> so we are power-taking
> empowered
> to march with a million
> because I am
> sick and tired
> of seeing straight people
> kiss and hold hands
> in public
>
> while I am
> relegated to

> a T-dance
> at Rage
>
> Fuck that shit!

Alfaro calls on queers to take power and insert themselves within the national body as opposed to waiting for liberal inclusion. For the performer, Rage is not a T-dance, but a politics.

After speaking in general terms about queer politics, Alfaro locates himself within the terrain of Chicano politics. He reintroduces the biography that we are familiar with from his memory performances:

> I am a Queer Chicano
> A native in no land
> An orphan of Aztlan
> The pocho son of farm worker parents
>
> The Mexicans only want me
> when they want me to
> talk about Mexico
> But what about
> Mexican Queers in LA?
>
> The Queers only want me
> when they need
> to add color
> add spice
> like salsa picante
> on the side
>
> With one foot
> on each side
> of the border
> not the border
> between Mexico
> and the United States
> but the border between
> Nationality and Sexuality
> I search for a home in both
> yet neither one believes
> that I exist.

These lines from the performance poem beautifully delineate the situation of queers of color. The borderland he writes of is not the geographical one between Mexico and the United States; it is a zone that is located at an intersection between sexuality and nation, between queerness and ethnicity. This is the liminality that characterizes the experience of being queer and of color. Alfaro's work brings these concerns into the foreground but does not stop there. He calls for social change in relation to these politics:

> Blur the line
> take the journey
> play with the unknown
> deal with the whole enchilada
> Race
> Class
> Sex
> Gender
> Privilege
>
> Arrive at the place called possibility
> Try once again to create a language
> a sense of what it means
> to be in community
>
> I am fast-forwarding
> past the reruns *ese*
> and riding the big wave
> called future
> making myself
> fabulous
> as I disentangle
> from the wreck of this
> cultural collision.

Alfaro's memory performance, with its focus on the production of hybrid selves and space, is in and of itself a mode of queer theory-making that also functions as social theory. Alfaro's work explores wishes and struggles that inform a transformative politics. In the course of the piece, the audience witnessed Alfaro's migration from Tia Ofelia's burned-out lot to the performance space. Spectators feasted on a "delicious spectacle," a performance that engenders queer Latino possibility where it could not flourish before. Queer Latino selves are called into existence through "Cuerpo Politizado." Social space is reterritorialized as queer theater demands change.

Notes

1.   Luis Alfaro grew up in the Pico–Union district of Central Los Angeles, as the son of farm workers. While working as a custodian at a theater where LAPD, the Los Angeles Poverty Department, worked, Alfaro met director Scott Kelman, who became his mentor. He later went on to study with playwrights Maria Irenes Fornes and Tony Kushner. Alfaro has worked as a member of different artist collectives and as a solo artist.

2.   Elizabath Grosz, *Space Time and Perversion: Essays on the Politics of Bodies* (New York: Routledge, 1995), p. 108.

3.   Quoted in Doug Sadownick, "Two Different Worlds: Luis Alfaro Bridges the Gap Between Gay Fantasies and Latino Reality," *Advocate*, Issue 568, January 15, 1991, pp. 6–63.

4.   Jonathan Boyarian, *The Storm from Paradise: The Politics of Jewish Memory* (Minneapolis: University of Minnesota Press, 1992), p. xvi.

5.   Michael Warner, "Introduction," *Fear of a Queer Planet: Queer Politics and Social Theory* (Minneapolis: University of Minnesota Press, 1993), p. x.

6.   *Ibid.*, p. xix.

"The Adventures of Connie Chancla," 1997–98

María Elena Gaitán

Los Angeles, California
Photo: Gina Roland
Gaitán was active in radical Chicano politics and trained as a classical cellist before turning to performance in the 1980s. Her lastest solo work features her griot character Connie Chancla (slang for "slipper"), who combines acerbic social commentary on Chicano realities with musical interludes blending European classical and traditional Mexican music.

Architectures of Seeing

May Joseph

Pastoral kitsch

To the strains of Santana's "Samba Pa Ti," the show opens with two figures, one clad in kitschy urban renderings of the Brazilian Baiana, a "Latin Bombshell" with white tulle, fake pearls, and campy pink heels, and the other, a long-haired "naked savage," wander through the audience towards the stage.[1] The experience is at once hilarious, surreal, familiar, and surprising. With self-conscious giggles, the audience adjusts to the blurring in expectation and genre.

A collaboration between Patricia Hoffbauer and George Emilio Sanchez, "The Architecture of Seeing: A Performance Piece for the New Millennium on the Nature of Identity," involves elements of theater, the sideshow, vaudeville, dance-theater, acrobatics, and music-hall routines. Sanchez, a New York writer and performer born and raised in Los Angeles, and Hoffbauer, a New York choreographer and dancer/performer born in Rio de Janeiro, collaboratively choreographed and scripted the work. According to Sanchez, it is an excursion into how we see, how we are taught, and how we perceive ourselves and others. The performance unfolds as a series of montage sequences entitled: "The Dream," "The Intellectual," "The Native," "Linda Rivera and Chief Half-breed," "Ricky and Lucy." Its stylized *mélange* of dance, theater, and movement brings together the multilingual text, the expressive body, the costumed inhabitants, and the intersecting conflicting histories of unnatural citizens.

In the opening sequence, two performers, the Intellectual (Hoffbauer) and the Native (Sanchez), meander through the audience. They are named the "Intellectual" and the "Native," and they startle the audience with their bizarre dress and their jarring proximity. At once seductive and eccentric, these performers play with the conventional ideal of the classical dancer's body framed by the proscenium. They disrupt the field of identification by drawing the audience into the muscularity of their moving pedestrian bodies. Instead of posing in framed gestures staged for the viewer, they invoke a stylized everyday banality as they walk in slow, deliberate, and exaggerated movements. Their languorous journey through the audience suggestively draws our attention to the way architecture frames the movement of physical bodies. This moving spectacle prompts us to question our assumptions about the relationship of certain types of bodies to particular logics of space.

As the Intellectual and the Native wander through the audience during the opening sequence, spectators are tempted to laugh and touch the semi-naked man as his skin beckons, and to feel the body of the provocatively attired woman as she teases our desire for tactility and passive submission as spectators in an event of our choosing, though not of our staging. The living space, Richard Schechner reminds us, includes all the space in the theater, not just what is called the stage. There are actual relationships between the body and the spaces that the body moves through.[2] Hoffbauer and Sanchez draw us into the circle of performance by walking through the audience at the beginning of the show, blurring the role of spectator and performer.

Space becomes the fluid medium for unraveling historical periods which impinge upon the individual's interiority. Burlesque figures such as Chief Half-breed, Ricky and Lucy, the Intellectual and the Native, buffoons and storytellers, offer glimpses into the conjunction of performance art, anthropology, cultural studies, and globalization processes. A cascade of soundbites from the colonial imaginary accosts the audience in this opening, as the Intellectual is seized by the excess of words:

> The rhythm
> the syncopation . . .
> the manner in which he moves
> the rolling of the muscles as it tingles down the spine
> the look in his eyes
> the unknown territory that lies within its glint
> the mystery
> the unintelligible sounds emanating from his hips
> the nameless fruits
> the unnamed flowers . . .
> the unknown jungles . . .
> the unblemished sands
> the virgin lands of paradise
> the faceless existence of history.[3]

Beginning with the metaphor of the dream as the landscape of the urban unconscious, the Intellectual recites a long list of different images, which evoke a generic native. She displays the Native as if in an ethnographic exhibit, and then proceeds to civilize him by dressing him in a skirt/tutu, Peruvian vest, and braiding his hair while reciting from a storehouse of colonial imagery.

The entrance of the Intellectual and the Native confronts the audience with the historic commodification of non-European bodies. As the Intellectual declares, the "power of mapping" the body and its territory onto our dreams, as well as our everyday lives, structures our perceptual lenses. Western societies' machines of knowing, such as science, the law, and technology, deploy representational systems in their efforts to manage their heterogeneous populace. In response to this larger civilizing machine, the body in "Architecture" is presented as mobile and dynamic, filling the room with agency and presence.

"Architecture" disrupts the proscenium frame as it involves the audience in a fictive re-enactment of museum viewing and exhibition of colonial specimens, intermingling the ethnographically strange with the performatively disorienting. The proximity of the Intellectual and the Native convey in one image the extremes of our prefabricated civilization, the civilized and the savage, the known and the unknown, the beauty and the beast, the oppressor and the oppressed.

"Architecture" invokes different urban histories framing the public display of colonial bodies as viewed event. Exhibition. Slave auction. Performance art. The performers invert the theme of savages in the city, and startle the audience with the contradictory image of post-industrial natives. Both Hoffbauer and Sanchez are clad in anachronistic and citationally ethnographic costumes, though the language evokes the multicultural topography of New York City. These urban primitives are in a sense ethnographers of New York. Their site is the city, and their savages are urban citizenry. The Intellectual and the Native are not innocent peasants on the periphery of modernity. They attack the notion that modernity is something separate and inaccessible to them with postmodern paroxysm of horror and laughter. For the two protagonists, there is no "elsewhere" to be traveled to and written about. The natives are embroiled in an ongoing present history that is manifest as their own urban dreams of where they are going and what kinds of action they will continue to enact. "I love the island of Manhattan!" mimics the Intellectual invoking Anita in *West Side Story*. She declares the city to be the starting-point from which this post-imperial tale can be told as a collection of multiple colliding stories that compose urban reality.

15. Patricia Hoffbauer and George Emilio Sanchez
"Architectures of Seeing," 1997
New York
Photo: Albert Sanchez
Hoffbauer as The Intellectual discourses on Sanchez The Native.

Architectonics of seeing

For Hoffbauer, the process of formulating a complex politics of belonging as an immigrant performer in New York is deeply intertwined with former histories and multiple spheres of belonging at a local, national, and transnational level. Hoffbauer's own struggles to forge political affiliations within postmodern dance in the US as a Brazilian immigrant artist is a contemporary tale of desire, ambivalence, and arrival. She stages her own history through an interrogation of US Latino identity in her creative work.

According to Hoffbauer, in the 1960s and 1970s theater became harnessed to the cause of freedom for Brazilians working under the censorship of the dictatorship from 1964 to 1980. It was a forum for addressing political ideas in coded message, pushing further the ideals of emancipation *vis-à-vis* the dictatorship. At one point, breaking the fourth wall and directly addressing audiences was the most popular form of political art. That gradually changed and direct address lost its impact as political strategy, as it did in other third world states, and became largely relegated to theater for education. Didactic performance gave way to Humanism, and an interest in "universal man," with the individual at the center of the universe. This shift was expressed by an interest in European modernism, Abstract Minimalism, ritual, and improvisation. By the early 1980s, the political theater of practitioners like Augusto Boal had given way to a rising interest in other theatrical forms, as well as more eclectic approaches to content.[4]

For Hoffbauer, concerns of form and content assumed a greater complexity through her work with Graciela Figueroa in Brazil, and her exposure to Merce Cunningham, Yvonne Rainer, Twyla Tharp, and Sara Rudner in New York. Pina Bausch and Oswald de Andrade were other major influences on her. Ideologies of form and content also impacted Sanchez's approach to the moving body, particularly through the work of the Brazilian director Paulo Freire. Merging these performance histories, Sanchez and Hoffbauer began to experiment with form, and to combine American, Brazilian, and other Latin American traditions that contributed to the New York cultural scene. They refuse the logic of modernization and aesthetic theory that sets third world and US minority cultures on the periphery of the history of modernity, viewing them instead as an integral part of postmodernity. Hoffbauer asserts that her work was always postmodern in its historical and aesthetic situatedness: "Being who I am and coming from where I come from, I never thought of declaring myself as Latino and postmodern because the concept of postmodernism did not strike me as belonging only to the territory of white artists, historians, and performing-arts scholars."[5] On the contrary, suggests Hoffbauer, the confluence of international and local political cultures that shaped her own political consciousness as a Latina artist in New York City is an expression of that very same postmodernity.

"Architecture" critiques periodizing narratives that separate the modern and the postmodern. Sanchez and Hoffbauer's choreographed text philosophically breaks the available categories of identity and aesthetics, such as "Latino and postmodern" by deploying multilingual and heterotopic frames of community and conflict. Their self-reflexive approach to inventing forms of community is expressed through the piece's resistance to categorization in singular terms as theater or dance. Using minimalist *mise-en-scène*, flanked by a podium covered with an Argentinian poncho stage left and a chair stage right, their performance unfolds as a series of poetic vignettes, critically interrogating the facile versions of multiculturalism. Instead of a programmatic sequence of folkloristic scenes staged realistically, Sanchez and Hoffbauer combine everyday gesture, postmodern choreography, vaudeville, revue sketches, and theater. Their performance reworks history in public ways, by placing specific kinds of bodies in fictionally compressed contexts. While these techniques are not unique in their particular deployment, since such format is used in much downtown New York performance, it does at the same time challenge the embedded pressures for minority artists to explain one's culture through the vehicle of structured linear narratives.

One important influence in their work is the aesthetic of Anthropophago. With its antecedents in the notion put forth by Oswald de Andrade during Brazil's Modernismo period of the 1920s, *anthropophago* means to devour homogeneity and spew out syncretism, referring to the cannibalizing of Europe to produce the heterogeneity of Brazil. Anthropophago has become an influential term for rethinking New World syncretism and postmodernity as a process. Sanchez and Hoffbauer's techniques are enmeshed in anthropophagic expressions, drawing upon modern dance, vaudevillian minstrelsy, capoeira, social dance, dance theater, *Commedia dell'Arte*, the Grotesque, and Teatro de Revista, to create a playful, referential, fragmented, and non-linear movement spectacle in cultural drag.[6]

In anthropophagic fashion, the vignettes of "Architecture" draw attention to the territorial issues of sovereignty, to space's implication in aesthetic practice, and spatialization as a means of negotiating history. Names of indigenous nations and places compress the material and imagined losses of native peoples in the Americas. Naming at once brings forth the visceral body and the poetic trace, a matrix of the architectural, the legal, and the sensorial. Naming invokes the vastness of historical erasure while concretizing its disappearance through sound, incantation, and writing. Like skin on the surface of the body, it opens up the cavernous interiorities of public memories.

In the third vignette, the Native condenses different genealogies of violence, which are invoked through a list of the names of dispossessed native tribes. This section of the performance stages a different history of belonging that is incomplete, partial, irretrievable. The legal spaces of territorial sovereignty and the polylingual traces of US history become markers of this conflicting spatiality, at once etched out of history and reinscribed through performance:

> The Native:
> Djinjujua tupi o not tupi arapahoe
> Arapahoe jicarilla lakota ute
> Lakota ute mochica nazca toltec
> Mochica nazca toltec huancavilca
> Huancavilca chimu kayapo.[7]

Naming disrupts the forgotten memories of erased communities, throws up shards of ruined cities, and allows the unconscious to take up home in strange quarters. Naming opens up cities within the city, "Architecture" suggests.

"Architecture" builds upon the dialogue among ethnology, performance, display, syncretism, Latin cabaret, and primitivist critique engaged with by other Latino performers and artists such as Guillermo Gómez-Peña, Carmelita Tropicana, Pepon Osorio, Merian Soto, Evelyn Velez, and Culture Clash. Guillermo Gómez-Peña and Coco Fusco's groundbreaking itinerant performance, "Two Undiscovered Amerindians Visit the West," was influential, although Sanchez and Hoffbauer experiment with movement and text in ways that are conceptually different. Paulo Freire was also an inspiration in the creation of "Architecture," providing a lexicon of pedagogy through which "Architecture"'s educational import is furthered. "We fully integrate into our performance texts/language our rejection of essentialist identity and a constant exploration into how to mirror our performance collaboration with a philosophical and aesthetic belief in hybrid identities and culture," says Sanchez.[8]

Tactility and the urban body

In the conjunction between the moving urban body and the history of architecture, the body as a muscular, three-dimensional, unstable entity capable of the unexpected and the involuntary has tenuously remained visible, often overwhelmed, by the sheer verticality of modernity's visual frames. Writing at the turn of the nineteenth century, Georg Simmel speculated on the implications of the increasing impact of freedom of movement in the modern metropolis. For Simmel, the individual's mental life is profoundly shaped by the rapidity, shifts, and contradictions in events, leading to a certain blasé mental attitude toward the unexpected. The concept of the blasé attitude proposed by Simmel suggests a distracted, indifferent but lucid approach to the new needs and experiences posed by a changing modernity. This blasé attitude is, however, occasionally shocked into new perceptions by the unexpected sensations of the sensuous that can be encountered in the metropole.[9] In "Architecture," tightly knit segments of architectural vignettes surprise us into rethinking how we see, are viewed, are made visible, and forcefully make our presence felt in the world.

In these vignettes, seeing is not just ocular – it is a way of being in the world that is tactile, sensorial, olfactory, aural, and muscular. Seeing involves the mechanical and phenomenological reproduction of life through everyday art in these choreographed gestures. Walking, standing still, grimacing, convulsing, hiding, dancing, contorting – all build a lexicon of daily movement that forces the audience out of the sensorial apathy that Simmel calls the blasé attitude.

"Architecture" offers tactility as the fascia of social interaction. Through interaction and participation, the artists thus propose, urban civic identity can be learned and shared. The city draws individuals into modules of experience. But the architecture of experience is a contingent and embodied one. It is messy and contradictory. It is also extraordinary and seductive, vivacious and lethargic. Tactility in the city is the structuring logic of communality and avoidance, sociability and individualism. "Architecture" incorporates the past as an evocative tool, articulating differences between past and present through contrasts in sound and sight. Bits of music by Carlos Santana, Burt Bacharach, Los Lobos, and Hermanos Castro form the retro ambience of the late 1970s. That era is thus juxtaposed to a present that is marked by a sense felt by some minorities in the post-civil rights era that history has betrayed them; rather than being able to reap the benefits of social change, some perceive more elaborate forms of containment and tokenism as dominating their experience. In an era in which many of the goals of the civil rights movement and of multiculturalism are being thrown into question, tactility has legal implications. Relating to the sphere of infection, illegality, and uncivicness, tacitility has implications for the realm of the social and the legal, as Hoffbauer's Linda Rivera the talk-show host belts out to Sanchez's Chief Half-breed in a Surrealist sequence:

> Linda Rivera: (As she introduces her show we see The Native get dressed into Chief Half-breed. She speaks with a strong accent.) Buenas tardes, amigos, or should I say buenas noches, here we are in the town of La Mezcla on the border of Bolivia and us, I mean the U.S. I want to welcome you to our alternative television program "Despiertate Americ – Wake Up and Smell that Coffee." We discuss and elaborate local, national, and global

news of the day and we broadcast to both sides of the border because today there are more North Americans living in Cochabamba, Machu Picchu, and Pirasununga due to NAFTA and to the building of retirement colonies. And there are more Argentinos, Brasileros, and Mexicanos living in North America due to NAFTA and to the land lost to the developers building those retirement colonies. Today our guest is Chief Half-breed. He's an expert, first-hand, on the Latino experience within the current scholarship of Multicultism and the Post-mortem Gaze.[10]

As Linda Rivera babbles the past as a pastiche of border-lingo and global talk in vignette four, she invokes Guillermo Gómez-Peña's early work but with a ribald physicality that offers a new dimension of garrulity and farce to ethnographic parody. Linda Rivera and Chief Half-breed embark on their raucuous journey through Latino kitsch identity at once unreal, exotic, grotesque, comic, and poetic, disrupting easy spatial configurations of first and third worlds, as Chief Half-breed turns out to be a US-born native with a repressed history to reclaim.

"Architecture" plays with urban spatiality by drawing upon the partial and incomplete ways in which communities can be imagined today, as the above dialogue enacts. Its choreography is self-consciously inclusive, as it plays with issues of bilingualism and the changing demographics of audiences between locations. The piece reworks urban space through its tactile imagery. The audience is the *mise-en-scène*; the actors are the spectators; the city is the stage. Physical space and the momentum of the performers through gymnastics, variety show, revue sketch, marionette, Brechtian distanciation, dance theater, and Freirian consciousness-raising merge in a *mélange* of form, style, movement, and content.

Space in "Architecture" works simultaneously at conceptual, metaphorical, and literal levels. The artists open the work to the particularities of each site, allow the piece to shift in relation to space as a kind of political statement. According to George Sanchez, different sections offer varying insights into the architecture of language. The street, the classroom, the downtown club, and the corporate meeting room all serve as possible venues where questions of subjectivity and pedagogy are raised and reworked. The rhythm of space in conjunction with the spatiality of movement opens up ways of knowing.[11] Urban context such as the bus stop, the laundromat, the grocery store, the Department of Motor Vehicles, church basements, museums, airports, and lost cities spatially inform the piece.

Conceived as an odyssey on Latino identity, "Architecture" examines the mechanisms of cultural representation. It is composed of discrete, intertwining sections with the themes of jungle, anthropology, folklore, and pop culture structuring the narrative. For Hoffbauer and Sanchez, the official history of minority bodies in public spaces is a troubled and uneasy one as they implicitly bear the burden of this legacy This burden of representation is exacerbated by the mainstream media, which offers an amusement park of minority archetypes even as people of color struggle to re-present their turbulent histories within public discourse. The precariousness of their visual and aural presence is enmeshed in contradicting cultural stereotypes. Hence "The serape-clad peasant, the cultural impresario, the naked savage, the slick talk-show hostess, the smooth Latin lover in black tie, and the Latina bombshell" in "Architecture" juxtapose Hollywood's version of Latino stereotypes and the multiple histories that constitute Latino experience.[12] In light of this cultural baggage, "Architecture" suggests that a fundamental realignment of audience expectations, viewing practices, performance philosophies, and spatial configurations need be made. This can only begin to happen through mutual dialogue and a more fluid reworking of urban spaces for human-scale interaction.

Defamiliarizing the urban

As the Latina talk-show hostess, Linda Rivera emphasizes, the political use of muscularity and laughter is crucial to the piece. Much minority performance work in the 1980s was politically astute, comic, and acerbic, but the body itself was often hidden behind the weight of the political message at hand. Narrating the tale often superseded the dexterity and versatility of the bodies staging the story. At the time, the sheer presence and historic import of the work being produced merited attention. Hoffbauer's choreography foregrounds the body of the performer as much as the text, and stretches the imaginative lexicon of mimicry, clowning, danger, lightness, buffonery, and graveness towards corporeality and embodiment. Says Hoffbauer,

> Humour is a weapon. If people think you're funny, you push that a lot further, creating almost an uneasy, disconcerting moment where what I think they think of me gets played out in a freakish way, exposing oneself as a methodology of surviving and attacking. In this performance we use gestural movement, and play with awkwardness and the idea of the bad lounge act. We use splits, trash, pop american music and vaudevillian minstrelsy to heighten this effect.[13]

The function of laughter and the use of the muscular body in "Architecture" delves into the phenomenology of sensation and humor in new ways. The artists draw on the traditions of garrulity and clowning from the Commedia and Grotesque, and mix them with Latin American, US Latino, pop-cultural and cabaret comedic strategies. Old and New World cultural references collide in a satire that is exasperating, delightful, and unpredictable.

> I ask myself sometimes if I could create pieces dealing with the body and its relationship to itself and to others in space. Or if I could make dances that investigate the references of the body in relationship to other bodies. Or am I interested in creating dances that deal with the very issue of translating my movement into the dancer's bodies? . . . I am fascinated with the body and its infinity of coordination. The coordinations that automatically happen once you juxtapose real-life dialogue/situation with pure abstract movements. I am fascinated with anything that propels bodies into motion – and propeling into motion for me could be someone standing still. And I love comedy and I love politics . . .[14]

"Architecture" plays with the notion of architectural spaces as discursive, tactile, man-made, and urban figurations of physicality. It draws attention to the built as well as empty spaces of the city, at once malleable and dynamic, made concrete by the moving body. Space in "Architecture" is foregrounded as the condition of play between built environments and human movement, opening up new ways of reading the urban.

Public spaces and partial communities

At the heart of this project is the open-ended question about the relationship of the city to its citizens, and to the management of specific bodies in the national imaginary. It revisits the urban issue of how to address the city's multiple communities in ways that allow for a shared sense of the civic. Sally Banes points out that the idea of inventing community is one of the founding concerns for the New York experimental avant-garde. During the 1960s and 1970s, different kinds of alternative communities were experimented with by the New York avant-garde in their search for democratic performance. Writes Banes:

> The rhetoric of community – the desire for community – is everywhere evident in the artworks and institutions of the Sixties avant-garde. This potentially nostalgic desire marks the group's affiliation with the modernist project of recuperating the loss of wholeness. But their resolutions were often subversive, proposing new social roles and institutions.

Banes underscores the point that the kinds of communities that were envisioned during this time were radically different from conventional notions of bourgeois society.[15]

From the utilitarian communities theorized by Buckminster Fuller, to notions of countercultural utopian communes of the late 1960s and early 1970s, to the proletarian communities invoked by Augusto Boal, Paulo Freire, and Ngugi Wa Thiongo, the notion of non-authoritarian collectives opened up older sociological models of "community" and "society" onto new territories of social interaction during this time. In New York City during this period, entrenched ethnic community or *Gemeinschaft* coexisted with the elaborate networks of artistic communities that arose through social practices such as direct involvement with participatory theater as well as the various cooperatives and alternative institutions that turned artmaking itself into a community-building process. But older notions of ethnic community have been continually disrupted in New York by new waves of immigration and more recently by the reworking of notions of affinity based on sexuality and lifestyle.[16]

The anti-hierarchicalism of the 1960s' avant-garde offers a legacy of strategies in communal possibilities from the vantage-point of our current anti-utopic moment. However, ideas about *communitas* have been dramatically fractured within the local and national imaginary in the US today. A shrinking economy and the declining role of the state under globalization have exacerbated the rifts between the economically disempowered and those who have. This increasing gap between those who demand state intervention and those invested in the economics of privatization has shifted the attention of *communitas* away from that of civil society and concomitant notions of the public towards the spheres of private property, consumption, and ownership. Hence, the question of what notions of community we can possibly work towards in the era of dispersed, fragmented, migrant, and contingent affiliations is a constructive and urgent one in "The Architecture of Seeing." According to Hoffbauer and Sanchez, we can begin to address this continuing search for a provisionally shared context by prioritizing the local urban milieu. The specific experience of sharing public citizenship in the city is a way to begin a conversation offering other frameworks for *communitas* outside the narrow categories of identity. Such a process can be initiated through translocal experiments between neighborhoods and individuals, between communities within the same city, and between individuals and ommunities across regions.

Hoffbauer and Sanchez's collaborative choreography and text envision such a conjunction of politics and community. One could argue that the implications of "Architecture" are utopic, far-sighted, and hopeful, as it extends the fluidity of space between architecture and social interaction to a different realm of encounter and exchange. Hoffbauer's conviction that it "is necessary to nurture a community of inclusion" informs their collaboration as a certain amount of improvisatory open-endedness leaves room for reworking the performance according to context.[17]

By marking different performance venues of the city with their collaborative experimental project, Hoffbauer and Sanchez imaginatively offer ways of thinking about community and urban space through the notion of translocal community work as a possible model, as it alters and reinvents itself through its encounters with different contexts and viewing communities in the city.

Sanchez and Hoffbauer explore the liminal boundaries of the aesthetic, political, and cultural concerns of urban life as they open up the idea of collaborative spectatorship as a creative forum. Their work implicitly raises the institutional agendas within arts funding over the last fifteen years that have made it difficult to separate the institutional pressures leading artists to work with different communities from their political interests in doing so. The strategy on the part of art centers to make monies available in connection with workshops and residencies, and certain grants for intercultural performance, demanded that artists work this way. For Sanchez and Hoffbauer, however, their pedagogical philosophy towards performance as a possibility for social transformatin demands a kind of commitment to the possibility for multiple-sited community involvements that is important for rethinking the future of urban, community-based cultural work, despite the institutional pressures driving such impetus.

The concept "translocal" makes it possible to talk about blocks or areas within the city. Such engagement includes exchanges between communities that take place when performers move from venue to venue within a given city or between cities. The distance covered could be small, from SoHo to the East Village, or it could be linked across other networks like the Downtown Dance venues, or the Latino theater networks, but all these connecting matrices demand a practice and theoretical orientation that can include new situations and audiences into a performance. This sort of openness to possibility shifts the configuration of performance spatiality onto different premises of mobility and audience. It coerces new communities of encounter, and often links younger, marginalized, frequently minority, artists working within the margins to more formalized institutions of experimental innovations in temporary but important ways. In spirit with the New York avant-garde's resistance to encrusted aesthetic categories, "Architecture" deploys space in creative ways. Economic necessity generated by changes in arts funding policies, combined with political commitment, has demanded new ways of producing democratic work on the margins of New York's performance circuits.

"Architecture" reflects upon the logics of its own making, deconstructing classical ballet and ironically commenting on the Broadway predilection for tap, jazz and other song-and-dance routines driving performances like *Rent*, *Bring in da Noise*, *Riverdance* and *Stomp*. Such citational humor makes "Architecture" a barometer of the times, provoking audiences into a critical engagement with their role as consumers of culture. At the center of the pedagogical process is the gritty urban context that infuses their script and movement even as they question our views of the world.

Notes

1. Patricia Hoffbauer, "Report from In Between," in *FYI*, Spring 1997, vol. 13, no. 1: 3.

2. Richard Schechner, "Environmental Theater," in *Environmental Theater* (New York: Applause Books, 1994), 2.

3. George Emilio Sanchez, *The Architecture of Seeing*, (unpublished).

4. Patricia Hoffbauer, interview, June 9, 1998, New York City.

5. Patricia Hoffbauer, "The War at Home," in *Movement Research Performance Journal* 9, Fall/Winter 1994/5: 3.

6. Ella Shohat and Bob Stam, *Unthinking Eurocentrism: Multiculturalism and the Media* (London: Routledge, 1994), 309.

7. George Sanchez, *The Architecture of Seeing*.

8. George Sanchez, interview, July 31, 1998, New York City.

9. Georg Simmel, *On Individuality and Social Forms* (Chicago: University of Chicago Press, 1971), 330.

10. George Emilio Sanchez, *The Architecture of Seeing*.

11. George Sanchez, interview, January 26, 1996, New York City.

12. Patricia Hoffbauer, "Report from In Between," in *FYI*, Spring 1997, vol. 13, no 1: 3.

13. Patricia Hoffbauer, interview, June 9, 1998, New York City.

14. Patricia Hoffbauer, "The War at Home," in *Movement Research Performance Journal* 9, Fall/Winter 1994/5: 3.

15. Sally Banes, "The Reinvention of Community," *Greenwich Village 1963: Avant-Garde Performance and the Effervescent Body* (Durham: Duke University Press, 1993), 36–37.

16. *Ibid*. See also John Cage, *For the Birds* (Boston: Marion Boyars, 1995), 6, and Ferdinand Tonnies, *Community and Society* (Gemeinschaft and Gesselschaft) (New Brunswick: Transaction Books, 1988).

17. Patricia Hoffbauer, "The War at Home," in *Movement Research Performance Journal* 9, Fall/Winter 1994/5: 3.

PART II

Ritualizing the body politic

Henny-Penny Piano Destruction Concert, 1967

Raphael Montañez Ortiz

New York

Montañez Ortiz was one of the leading figures of the Destructivist art movement of the late 1950s and early 1960s. He participated in the now legendary Destruction Art Symposia held in London in 1966 and at the Judson Memorial Church in 1968, two key events that brought together avant-garde artists associated with Fluxus and with happenings. Ortiz's view of destruction posited it as a quasi-ritualistic sacrificial process in which artefacts and human beings could be released from the logical form and self of Western culture. In addition to his artistic activities in the late 1960s and 1970s, Montañez Ortiz engaged in arts-related activism. He founded the Museo del Barrio, the first Latino art museum in the UK, in 1969, and was an active member of the Artist Workers' Coalition in the early 1970s.

From Inscription to Dissolution

An essay on expenditure in the work of Ana Mendieta
Charles Merewether

From 1972 until her untimely death in 1985, Ana Mendieta created Super-8 films and videos, performances, actions and site-specific installations, drawings, prints, objects, and sculpture. Throughout her career, she produced an art whose fugitive appearance contains the disembodied trace of the real, of the remains of life amongst the ruins of modern culture. Two critical approaches to the making of art appear central to Mendieta's concern: the question of the performative having to do with issues of the body, authorship, and the self, and the work of art as a trace. That is, the work displaces the location of meaning and identity from the fixity of the image or place onto the performative and the marks of inscription. In these terms, the work emerges as a profound critique of the social sphere, and an attempt to think the outside, the heterogeneous as a site of restitution and dissolution.

Performing the self

In the autumn of 1969 when Mendieta enrolled in graduate studies in painting at the University of Iowa, the school was undergoing a change that would have a profound influence in shaping the course of Mendieta's future studies and ultimately her art. During the spring of 1969, four teachers from the university – musician William Hibbard, the visual artist Hans Breder, the filmmaker Ted Perry, and Bob Gilbert, a theater professor – had staged a multimedia performance called *Interplay*. The success of this performance became the inspiration for the founding the New Center for the Performing Arts and, at the same time, under the direction of Hans Breder, a Multimedia and Video Art program in the School of Art and Art History. Mendieta was one of the first to enroll.

In his own multimedia pieces or "Body Sculpture," Breder worked closely with his women students as "performers" of his work. Mendieta was one of those who performed. Holding mirrors, they intertwined their naked bodies to create a dazzling fragmentation and multiplicity of images. Producing a confusion as to where the bodies began and ended, Breder was able to create a living sculptural form. Breder wrote that with such work he sought to produce a "new ordering of the elements," that entailed treating the performers" bodies as objects.[1]

This kind of work provided Mendieta with a conceptual framework with which to begin her own projects and by 1972 Mendieta had abandoned painting. Moreover, the influence of the sociologist Erving Goffman's ideas at this time was considerable, and provided a theoretical basis for performance art and the idea of the public dimension to art as providing the site of exchange or encounter.[2] Goffman described human interaction as theatrical, an encounter in which people established "performance areas." The subject was located within the locus of relationship, of social exchange; and, therefore, identity was not innate but socially constructed and product of the circulation of representations in society.

Mendieta began exploring representations of herself by assuming and mimicking different identities. Between January and March of 1972, she produced a series later referred to as "facial hair transplants" and "facial cosmetic variations," intimating that the human face was on loan to her from society. The first in the series, which became her M.A. thesis, entailed masquerading as a man with beard and mustache. The power of hair fascinated her, so she asked a friend to cut off his beard for her own use. Gluing it on her face, what struck her was the power of the image to take over the real. No longer did it appear as a disguise, but had "become a part of myself and not at all unnatural to my appearance."[3] It was a homage to Duchamp's *Mona Lisa* of 1919. Duchamp had drawn a beard and mustache on a reproduction of Leonardo da Vinci's portrait of Mona Lisa, declaring that: "The curious thing about that mustache and goatee is that when you look at it the Mona Lisa becomes a man. It is not a woman disguised as a man. It is a real man, and that was my discovery, without realizing it at the time."[4] This was also Mendieta's discovery, whereby the idea of being able to assume another identity through the reimaging of oneself as an/other.

Over the next three years, Mendieta produced a startling series of experimental "actions" and performance works which drew upon Goffman's concept of social exchange, but as a confrontational encounter regarding social taboo and violence. And from this perspective, it was the work of Foucault and Marcuse who, in their critique of the repressive conventions of society, provided Mendieta an important theoretical and political armature for her work. In their terms, modernism could serve as a critical aesthetics of emancipation from the symbolic order.

During 1972, Mendieta made several short Super-8 and video pieces in which the repetition of simple gestures constitute the subject of the work itself. Some of the actions were nothing but a series of mundane and reiterative events – events, that is – which are part of the repetitive structure of human activity. By restaging, Mendieta exposed such gestures as virtual rituals of everyday life. The pieces also suggest the transformative power of ritual and repetition.

Other pieces from this period deploy, each time more emphatically, devices of disguise or shrouding (masquerade), the body as an object of violation or distortion in order to displace a recognition of it as woman, as a fixed identity that one can read off its surface. Mendieta sought to critically reflect and re-present the surface construction of femininity. She was less concerned with the formation of identity through experience than with the violence of experience which the social formation of identity entails. Like her contemporaries, Vito Acconci, Chris Burden, or Dennis Oppenheim, Mendieta's work concerned a subjection of the body to physical stress or exertion in order that, as a closed system or boundary, it is forced to its limits.[5] In a series from 1972, for example, she pressed a piece of glass (and sometimes clear acetate) against different parts of her naked body and face. The effect was not only a distortion of form, but a sensation of pain and infliction of violence against the body, a brutal forcing of the body against itself.[6]

The scene of a crime

From the period of November 1972 until late 1973 Mendieta began to push even further Goffman's notion of the performative and ritual character of every social exchange by focusing on the subject of sacrifice and crime around the body as woman.

One of the first of these works was an untitled performance of November 1972 in which she presented herself standing naked against a wall holding a white beheaded chicken.[7] In the beginning of a short Super-8 film she made of the performance, the audience sees the head of the chicken being cut off and the remaining body handed to Mendieta.[8] As Mendieta takes the beheaded chicken by the legs, it jerks about uncontrollably. Mendieta holds the chicken tightly, away from her body, but upside down by the legs in front of her at the height where its neck dangles in front of her pubis.[9] Closing her eyes momentarily, the death throes of the chicken reverberate through her body and the blood spurts across her own body.

Mendieta's subjection of herself to this scene suggests an identification of woman's body with that of the animal.[10] We as spectators are taken to what anthropologist Victor Turner would define as a point of liminality, a threshold state of exchange between the dying body and that of the living. In staging the act of animal sacrifice, Mendieta's performance invokes what a Western audience would associate to be a "primitive custom."[11] While the action appears as a trans-gression of everyday civility, the fact that Mendieta refused to mark it as the custom or ritual of another culture suggests that the site of such sacrificial violence lies within the profane world in which we live.[12]

This was the first work in which Mendieta used blood, and, commenting on it later, she remarked that she "started immediately using blood, I guess because I think it's a very powerful magic thing. I don't see it as a negative force." She then added, "I really would get it because I was working with blood and with my body. The men were into conceptual art and doing things that were very clean."[13]

In April 1973, she performed what was the first and most confrontational of three actions around the subject of rape.[14] This followed an incident on the Iowa University campus where a fellow student had been raped and murdered the month before. The first piece was performed in her own apartment in Moffitt Street, Iowa City. Mendieta had invited friends and fellow students to visit her and, leaving the apartment door slightly open, they entered to find themselves in a darkened room except for one light over a table, where Mendieta lay stretched out and bound, and stripped from the waist down and smeared in blood. On the floor around her lay broken plates and blood.[15] In an interview in 1980, Mendieta related how the incident had "moved and frightened" her. Referring to the work, she added: "I think all my work has been like that – a personal response to a situation . . . I can't see being theoretical about an issue like that."[16] The issue was about naming rape; that is, of not only breaking the code of silence surrounding it, but its anonymity and generality.

The subject of rape was not new to the field of art. During these years an emerging feminist movement had influenced women working in performance art, happenings and dance, to address the subject not only in terms of its violence, but also as a process of gendering woman as feminine.[17] In Mendieta's staging the incident herself, the performance intervened upon the event. That is, by the act of repetition, of its reiteration, an audience was constructed as participant. The focus is not then only on the victim, but on the witnessing, of the event-taking-place.[18]

The demand to participate, to be witness, became central to Mendieta's work during this period. In these months of 1973, she also produced another series of actions in downtown Iowa City. The first entailed leaving a small suitcase filled with blood and bones on a street corner. The following month she presented two further "scenarios" of blood seeping out from beneath the doorway of her apartment building onto the pavement, and another, "Clinton St: Dead on Street," where Mendieta lay in the middle of a street as if dead. The fourth in October was a *mise-en-scène* of an apartment violently destroyed, mattresses strewn and torn, stained with blood, and again leaving the door open so that the passerby might chance across the scene. In each case she had a camera set up in order to photograph the reactions of people as they passed. Each of these actions demanded that the public become an audience and bear witness to an event about which they had no real knowledge. All that was left was the evidence of a crime: the severed body, the spilled blood. The scene of the crime is not only the object to which they are witness, but, insofar as the actions acquire meaning through their public reception, the public is itself transformed into a participant in the crime.

By symbolically restaging the act of crime, Mendieta was also making a link between art and crime and defining the potentially transgressive function of art and her role as an artist. For Mendieta, the relation between art and criminality was its position of exteriority or heterogeneity to society. In a 1983 interview, Mendieta referred to the anger she had felt and still did growing up in an orphanage and as a Latina in the US. Art was, she said, her "salvation."

> I know if I had not discovered art, I would have been a criminal. Theodore Adorno has said, "all works of art are uncommitted crimes." My art comes out of rage and displacement. Although the image may not be a very rageful image, I think that all art comes out of sublimated rage . . . .[19]

Sacrificial violence

In a period of two years between her first visit to Mexico in 1971 and her next in the summer of 1973, Mendieta began to read what had become for many a kind of handbook to Mexican culture, Octavio Paz's *The Labyrinth of Solitude*.[20] The impact of the book on Mendieta was profound and its ideas would remain with her throughout her life.

Paz's book contains an extended reflection on the theme of sacrifice and relation between man, the sacred, and nature.[21] For Paz, the two dominant religious traditions of Mexico, Catholicism and Aztec culture, had been both founded on economies that entail death through sacrifice as a means of releasing a surplus vital energy and the possibility of community.[22] In these terms, Paz's book was indebted to the work of the French anthropologist Marcel Mauss and, in turn, to both Bataille and Caillois, whose elaboration of a theory of sacrifice was based on a concept of excess or *dépense* (expenditure).

Caillois also noted that, just as with festival where waste and destruction "are rightfully part of the festival's excess, so death by sacrifice is a ceremony of renewal or generation of the socius."[23] Such a connection between the economy of sacrifice and that of festival, resonated strongly in Paz's conception of Mexico, and was reflected in the following words:

> Everything merges, loses shape and individuality and returns to primordial mass. Ritual death promotes a rebirth; . . . the orgy, sterile in itself, renews the

> fertility of the mother or of the earth. The fiesta is a return to a remote and
> undifferentiated state, prenatal or presocial. It is a return that is also a begin-
> ning, in accordance with the dialectic that is inherent in social processes . . .
> The group emerges purified and strengthened from this plunge into chaos. It
> has immersed itself in its own origins, in the womb from which it came.24

Paz invokes violence as a necessary passage to obtain transcendence, a transcendence empowered by a dialectic of love for, and aggression against, the maternal.
Paz's fascination with Mexican culture was to understand how modern and ancient
Mexico resolved "man's eternal solitude." Under the influence of Catholicism
and the impact of postwar existentialism, Paz argued that in a modern society
dominated by individualism it is only through "expiation and redemption" that
the "solitary or isolated individual transcends his solitude, accepting it as a proof
or promise of communion."

For Paz poetry could resolve the conflict between the local or contingent and
the universal by appealing to a language whose source is prior to and outside history,
in a realm of myth. Poetry offered the possibility of returning to a kind of communion, of oneness with the self and environment, which religion once provided. Such
an appeal could be made because this place outside of history provided the source
of moral order. Paz suggests that modern culture was based on its denial and an
estrangement from the natural world on which ancient myth had been founded. Paz
viewed myth as a universal model of communion, which could offer a way towards
integration and wholeness. To him modernity could be realized through the primitivist construction of Mexico as Other, and woman as the womb of the earth;
woman, that is, as the telos and origin of man's desire and redemption, her sacrifice
as the foundation of representation and his promise of continuity.

Such ideas offered an extraordinarily direct account for Mendieta's sense of
herself and experience of exile from her country and detachment from the United
States. Mendieta copied and integrated directly into her artistic statements whole
passages and phrases from Paz. The following statement by Mendieta reveals the
profound movement which generated her work.

> All detachment or separation provokes a wound. A rupture, whether it is
> with ourselves or what surrounds us or with the past or present produces
> a feeling of aloneness. In my case where I was separated from my parents
> and my country at the age of 12 . . . this feeling of aloneness identified
> itself as a form of orphanhood. And it manifested itself as consciousness
> of sin. The penalties and shame of separation caused me necessary sacri-
> fices and solitude as a way of purifying myself. You live it, like proof and
> promise of communion.[25]

Instead of reaching the point of overcoming exile and the idea of redemption resolving itself in communion, Mendieta remains with the idea of the necessity of living a life of sacrifice and solitude.

In the summer of 1973 Mendieta returned to Mexico, this time to Oaxaca with her companion Breder. Each morning they went to the market and she would plan her work for the day. On one occasion she lay covered by a white sheet on the parapet of Hotel Principal, placed an animal's heart over her stomach and poured blood over the body, between her legs, and on the ground beside her. On another occasion, after returning from the market with white flowers, she drove to a place she had been to before, an ancient Zapotec site with court-yards, a crypt, and open tomb. Taking the flowers, she lay naked in the tomb with branches of white flowers laid over her body, so that they appeared to be growing out of her. Named "El Yaagul" after the site, she later spoke of it in these terms: "The analogy was that I was covered by time and history."

Although her performance work, at this time, appears close to Paz's conception of death and renewal, what was of equal importance to Mendieta in Paz's account was that the unstated, but necessary, sacrificial object was woman. This was something she had also discovered in Frida Kahlo's work – which she had had the opporunity to see in Mexico City – and for Mendieta this relationship was critical. Not only did it expose the subject of society's repressive violence but it revealed that the relation between death and nature was the constitutive condition given to woman, in order to keep her always outside the social, displaced, in a state of exile.

The sacred imprint

Between late 1973 and February 1974, Mendieta performed and filmed a series in which she returned to the use of blood. The first Super-8 film was entitled "Sweating Blood." With her eyes closed, blood begins to trickle down from her hairline over her face, and then runs freely, covering her face completely. She then made a series she would call "Blood Writing," followed by "Blood Sign 1" and "Blood Sign 2." "Blood Writing" (March 1974) comprised a series of "action paintings," applying blood directly onto the wall with her body. In the first of these, Mendieta appears half-clothed, pushing herself against the wall, dragging

17. Ana Mendieta
Death of a Chicken, 1972
Iowa City, Iowa
Photo courtesy of the Estate of Ana Mendieta and Galerie Lelong

it down to leave the mark of her breasts and a silhouette of the body.[26] This was followed by another series of actions, but with her clothing on. Covering her hands and arms in red liquid, then stretching them out or holding them high over her head, she pulled herself down against the wall to a crouching position, leaving different curving lines suggestive of the body.[27] In "Blood Sign" she dipped her hand in bucket of blood to spell out on the wall "SHE GOT LOVE," and in another action she painted an arch with her outstretched arms, then the words "there is a devil inside me."

It was during this time that Mendieta wrote:

> I was looked at by the people in the midwest as a erotic being (myth of the hot Latin), aggressive, and sort of evil. This created a very rebellious attitude in me until it sort of exploded inside me and I became aware of my own being, my own existence as a very particular and singular being. This discovery was a form of seeing myself separate from others, alone.[28]

What Mendieta emphasizes in the work is the body as woman, and as an instrument and material for the production of art. Art becomes both a form of expenditure and transgressive form of reinscription. The work appears as a form of signature trace, which both issues from within the interior of the body and yet is also its textual exterior. Not only does it release woman as the eroticized subject of defilement but, by reference to menstrual blood, symbolizes, as Kristeva notes, "a danger issuing from within the identity (social or sexual)."[29]

During this period, Mendieta's art reveals a fascination with the idea of a symbiotic relation between eroticism and death. In an interview some years later, she stated: 'I don't think you can separate death and life. All of my work is about those two things ... it's about Eros and life/death."[30] Sometime between 1973 and 1975, Mendieta had copied out the words of Octavio Paz beneath her own artistic statement:

> Our cult of death is also a cult of life in the same way that love is a hunger for life and a longing for death. Our fondness for self-destruction derives not from our masochistic tendencies but also from a certain variety of religious emotion.[31]

Incorporating this observation into one of her artistic statements suggests Mendieta's interest is not simply the subject of death, but the relation of "self-destruction" to "religious emotion." Mendieta, in her series "Blood Writing," appears as if possessed, in a state of intoxication. From this perspective, it can be likened to what Kristeva defines as the masochistic economy of the Christian mystic, a "fount of infinite jouissance," which far from being for the benefit of symbolic or institutional power . . . displaces it indefinitely . . . within a discourse where the subject is reabsorbed . . . into communication with the Other and with others."[32] Masochism, like crime, was a form of gathering power through self-loss, an unbinding of subjectivity that dissolves the boundaries in Otherness.

While in Mexico, during the summer of 1974, Mendieta began to experiment with the idea of the stain and shroud. This included:

- a series of *mises-en-scène* of a figure covered in a white sheet standing a niche, suggesting the Catholic custom of covering sacred statuary at Easter
- a white sheet on which she had imprinted herself in red blood and paint, which was then held up, as if to make visible the act of sacrifice
- her imprint as a silhouette on the ground filled by red blood/paint that slowly spreads out to suggest the bleeding body
- a silhouette with red liquid poured onto the ground in an open tomb.

In December Mendieta drew a number of these actions together, as if to produce the final staging of the scene of the crime, the shrouded corpse, and its corporeal remains, the stain. Covering herself in blood and paint, she lay on the ground, had herself covered over with a black sheet and then a white one. The first recalls her Mexican parapet piece (1973), while the second, comprising only the "body prints," more dramatically marks the disappearance of the body.

Death enables representation to take place, the disappearance of the body marks its appearance as an image. The stain is an "index of the absent wound," the sheet, a funereal shroud. And, in using her own body and the cloth, Mendieta refigures the direct reference to the body of Christ and the shroud in terms of woman. The sheet serves not only as a support, like a canvas, but the work itself. Mendieta's work makes evident again that this advent of the visible is achieved only through the death of the Other. The violent erasure which she performs on her work constitutes an attempt to critically distance the work from the possibility of recuperation, a recuperation which rationalized the outside as heterogeneous or other than cultural.

Becoming other than oneself

The work of this period represents the beginning of a new phase in Mendieta's art. She made two decisive shifts. The first was in removing herself as the material object of her art and in its place replicating herself; and the second was to work directly within the landscape, that is, the land. One of Mendieta's favorite stories, a story she refers to many times in her notes and statements, was of a custom amongst the people of Kimberly.

> The men from Kimberly go outside their village to seek their brides. When a man brings his new wife home, the woman brings with her a sack of earth from her homeland and every night she eats a little bit of that earth. The earth will help her make the transition between her homeland and her new home.

After citing this, Mendieta notes:

> In other words that little bit of earth will make possible the transition between the two homes. By the same token making earth–body sculptures is not the final stage of a ritual for me but a way and a means of asserting my emotional ties with nature and conceptualizing religion and culture.[33]

The earth itself is disinterred in the woman's body as a gesture of depatriation. This figure of utter submission is an abandoning of oneself. The woman transforms herself into the earth. The significance of the Kimberly story was that, for Mendieta, it represented a poignant example of her own exploration of the relation between the interiorization of the foreign and exteriorization of the self. Furthermore, the idea of being taken outside of oneself to that of becoming Other, as characterized by the story, symbolized the relation between her homeland, exile, and her place of adoption. Exile meant for Mendieta both a "discovery within the self of a capacity to survive and grow in the new environment, and transcendence" of her condition of exile.[34] Art became a refuge, a means, the only means, of forging a link to her culture, but also engaging with her new-found environment and culture. In this sense, art becomes a discourse of desire to recuperate and return. As she writes:

> My exploration through my art of the relationship between myself and nature has been a clear result of my having been torn from my homeland during my adolescence. The making of my silueta in nature keeps (make) the transition between my homeland and my new home. It is a way of reclaiming my roots and becoming one with nature. Although the culture in which I live is part of me, my roots and cultural identity are a result of my Cuban heritage.[35]

In the early summer of 1975 Mendieta made her first major autonomous silhouette piece entitled "Silueta de Yemaya." She returned to her favorite site of Old Man's Creek on the outskirts of Iowa City, where she constructed a wooden raft and covered it with dark, red velvet and a silhouette of herself made of white flowers.[36] Setting it afloat the river, she then filmed, over a period of six minutes, the raft drifting downstream, caught in the flows and eddies of the current, bobbing in and out, and slowly merging as its form becomes one with the water. Similarly, the year before Mendieta had worked directly with water, filming herself floating in the water. Using a fixed camera, there is nothing more than this, nothing but the surrounding silence and stillness except for the constant movement of the water streaming over her body. The immersion in nature achieves the quality of an erotic encounter, suggesting a flowing back or return to the source.

While Mendieta's raft of flowers, "Silueta de Yemaya," symbolized an offering of this kind, the figure also suggests iconographically that of the *ánima sola*. With the arms upraised and legs pinned together, the image of the *ánima sola* symbolizes the wandering soul and, appropriately for Mendieta, is represented by the figure of woman. Cast outside of society, she is standing in the flames of purgatory with her hands held up towards the heavens, seeking redemption.[37] However, Mendieta has laid the figure down as if the figure returns to, or is buried within, the earth.

In these terms, Mendieta's work articulates what may be called the negative dialectics of exile. It occupies a borderland, homelessness, wandering, a solitude that yearns for an imagined community, yet yields to living out a community of absence. The land of exile becomes both a spectral land of absence and a place of a certain freedom. Rather than the association of women with the home and with the "earthbound mother," associations that contain woman, the place of exile is defined by what is missing, not by what it contains.

While the concept of the shroud pieces had elaborated the idea of her imprint, the silhouette form now formalized a further step. By creating a template replicating the contour and scale of her own body, Mendieta was able to remove herself as the object of the work, and work directly on a form that could be used alternatively as a surface of inscription, transformed, or be destroyed leaving only a residue or trace. It is evident from the work of this time that Mendieta recognized the power that could be achieved both through the process of the body's replication and its direct interaction with materials and the environment.[38]

Ashes to ashes

After her return from Mexico in 1975, Mendieta produced a series of works that represent a stark contrast to her floating silhouette. Deciding to work on a new piece, Mendieta chose again a place alongside the Iowa River. Carving a concave silhouette into the earth, Mendieta recorded four actions on Super-8 film. In the first, "Corazon de Roca con Sangre" (Heart of Rock with Blood), she knelt beside the open form, laying an animal heart at the corresponding place on the figure. She then poured blood over it from a bowl, lay naked and face down in the silhouette. The second action, "Genesis Buried in Mud," of October is the most dramatic of all these pieces. Focusing the fixed camera on the ground, the viewer is aware of little else but the landscape with the rich dark earth, occasional stones, and falling autumn leaves. Time passes, then suddenly we are witness to the earth moving before us. We watch, the earth appears almost as if it is palpitating, breathing, rising and falling more and more quickly. We continue to watch, as slowly the earth itself falls away to reveal the outline of a body – Mendieta herself.

While the possibility of return becomes more and more prominent in the work of this period, the very image of burial haunts each piece. The image of the silhouette appears as much a shallow grave as an image of a nurturing womb. However much we think of these pieces as a return to nature, to the earth as a way of regenerating life, the idea of being literally buried alive as much as symbolically being buried dead and returning, overwhelms the image. The focus on burial and the site of burial, notably the tomb or crypt, marks a liminal site of sacrifice and fertility, death, and rebirth.

The third action, in the following month, "Silueta Sangrienta" (Bleeding Silhouette), opens onto her lying naked face up in the silhouette. It then cuts to an empty silhouette, then another cut to it filled with red blood, and then again to her lying face down. The last of the four filmed actions was "Alma Silueta en Fuego" (Soul Silhouette in Fire), produced also in November. The film begins with the burning of a silhouette made of a white sheet. The white sheet that had wrapped and covered her as a shroud in a earlier work is now burned and destroyed. Nothing is left but a darkened, scorched form of burning ashes in a hollowed-out form, her former self. There is no corpse, symbolic or otherwise; nothing but an empty grave or ashes. What is pointed to is the disappearance and absence of the body through what remains, a trace. While the silhouette produced the idea of disembodiment, the ashes marked the trace of the body. In this sense, Mendieta's work posed the question of the trace – that is, what is constitutive of the trace is its erasure, a lack of origin or originary presence, because the trace never refers back to an original marking.

With the disappearance of the work itself, Mendieta decided to exhibit only one photographic image. Simply called "Silueta de Cenizas" (Silhouette of Ashes), the image is of the burned ashes of a silhouette form in the hollowed-out image. Although the photographic image had always played an important role in Mendieta's work, its reproduction now displaces the real altogether. These performances and actions were never seen by a public, nor did they remain. They disappeared, reappropriated by the landscape. The photograph marks a play of rupture and repetition, a space between experience and representation, between the materiality of the body and the work. And yet the photographs also carry something above and beyond the distancing, bearing a sense of an "after life" lived out through the appearance of the image.

Mendieta becomes her muse, rather than the material or matrix of another's creation. Her cultural displacement from her homeland Cuba inscribes itself in her work as a haunting estrangement of herself from herself. It is as if her art is the only way she can construct a memory that otherwise cannot be recalled. Rather than re-enacting an endless series of origin stories, as if to cover loss through an appeal to the paternal model (of Oedipus) of authorship, Mendieta's work evokes Eurydice as the muse, whose disappearance is the advent of inspiration, of poetry, of art. The destination of woman, in exile, dead, this is the beginning point. In Mendieta as in other women artists and authors, the idea of death as always, already, perpetually present in life. Death is not left outside, although we need to go there in order that art and culture begin.

A longer version of this essay was originally published in the catalog of the 1996 retrospective of Ana Mendieta's work organized by the Centro Galego de Arte Contemporánea in Spain.

Notes

1.   Hans Breder, "Constructivist Tendencies," 1970. Reprinted in Hans Breder *Threshold States*, (Hachmeister Verlag: Munster, 1992), 17. Later Breder organized a performance along these lines entitled "Hybrids" at the Center for New Performing Arts, University of Iowa, and then presented at Max Hutchinson Gallery in New York City in November 1972.

2.   See Erving Goffman, *The Presentation of the Self in Everyday Life* (Garden City, New York: Doubleday, 1959); and *Interaction Ritual* (Garden City, New York: Anchor Books, 1967). See also Kate Linker for a discussion of Goffman's influence on the work of Vito Acconci, *Vito Acconci* (New York: Rizzoli, 1994).

3.   Mendieta, unpublished M.A. thesis statement, University of Iowa, May 1972.

4.   Marcel Duchamp, cited in Mendieta, M.A. Thesis.

5.   See Kate Linker, op. cit., 26.

6.   Other experimental actions included a photodocumented series in which men's hands made from latex were placed over different parts of her body, a series of photographs of a naked woman tied and bound on the floor, and another of black shrouded forms.

7.   Enrique Sosa Rodriguez in his commentary on animal sacrifice in the Cuban secret society of the Abakua notes, amongst other things, that blood on the head of the devotee purifies and bestows power. See *The Nanigos* (La Habana: Ediciones Casa de las Americas,

1982). This relation is referred to also in Mary Jane Jacob, *The "Silueta" Series 1973–1980*, exhibition catalog (New York: Lelong Gallery, New York, 1991), 10. This relation to the spilling and presence of blood corresponds with Mendieta's idea of blood as a positive rather than negative force.

8.   Mendieta's interest in the sacrifice or death of animals was intimated earlier in February when she photographed a series of dead animals (chickens, birds, snakes, squirrels) on the street and the environs in which she worked.

9.   The positioning of the chicken so that the decapitated head corresponds with the sex of woman suggests also a correspondence with Bataille's use of the image of the chrysalis as framing the operation of interdiction/transgression. The chrysalis represents an erotic animal and is also defined as the small lips of the vulva.

10.   In this sense, Mendieta's purpose distinguishes itself from the Viennese Actionists', whose incorporation of animal sacrifice into their work exemplifies the critique by Bataille and Caillois of the constitution of male virility through sacrifice and violence. For a commentary regarding this, see the foreword by Denis Hollier in *The College of Sociology, 1937–39*, ed. Denis Hollier (Minneapolis: University of Minnesota Press, 1988).

11.   It is at this point also that her work introduces references to other cultural traditions, notably Mexican and Afro-Cuban.

12.   The naming of the action to be other in advance serves to displace its inherent critical power. The question of naming has afflicted the scholarship and reception of Mendieta's work insofar as by naming it as Afro-Cuban, Mexican, even feminist, her work has been marginalized as peripheral to modernism, rather than at the central to the constitution of modernism itself. This marginalization itself constitutes a form of sacrificial economy at the heart of modernism.

13.   Artist statement, undated. It includes a further sentence: "I decided that for the images to have magic qualities I had to work directly with nature. I had to go to the source of life, to mother earth." See Mendieta, "A Selection of Statements and Notes," in *Sulphur*, (no. 22, spring, 1988) 70. Although Mendieta suggests that she had begun to work "with nature" in 1972, it was not until the following year that she actually produced work in the landscape.

14.   The second and third actions were produced outside on the perimeters of the campus as tableaux that were photographed. Both face up and down, she was seen lying semi-naked with blood splattered across her body. She also produced another "incident" as part of this series in which she placed the cast of a severed foot and bones, splattered by blood on the ground.

15.   Later in an interview, Mendieta recalled of the people who came to the apartment that: "They all sat down, and started talking about it. I didn't move. I stayed in position about an hour. It really jolted them." Cited in Kittredge Cherry: "Mendieta incorporates herself, earth and art," *Daily Iowan*, (December 1977), 7.

16.   Cited in Judith Wilson, "Ana Mendieta Plants her Garden," *Village Voice* (August 13–19, 1980), 71.

17.   In 1972 Judy Chicago, Suzanne Lacey, Aviva Rahmani, and Sandra Orgel had staged a performance "Ablution" in a studio in Venice, California. While one woman was being bound naked in gauze and a group of nude women submerged themselves in tubs filled with blood and animal intestines, eggshells, blood, and clay, an audiotape played back testimonies of women who experienced rape. Later, in 1977, Suzanne Lacy presented "Three Weeks in May," where she recorded daily rape reports. In her piece "She Who Would Fly," a flayed lamb hung over the viewers' heads while above the door entered, crouched, four nude blood-stained women. Cited in Mary Jane Jacob, op. cit., p.10, n. 9.

18.   Lippard referred to the piece as a "shocking, bloody 'rape tableaux' performed by Ana Mendieta with herself as a victim ... [among] a growing number of artworks by women with the self as subject matter." Lucy Lippard, "Transformation Art", Ms. 4, No.4 (October 1975), 33. In a recent discussion of this work, Hannah Kruse has argued that Mendieta's "identification" with the victim barred the stereotyped notion of "victim" by negating her status as an anonymous object. See Hannah Kruse, "A Shift in Strategies: Depicting Rape in Feminist Art," in *The Subject of Rape* (New York: Whitney Museum of American Art, June 23–August 29, 1993), 56.

19.   Eva Cockcroft, "Culture and Survival: Interview with Mendieta, Willie Birch and Juan Sanchez," *Art and Artists* (February 1984), 16, in association with the exhibition "Ritual and Rhythm: Visual Forces For Survival" (New York: Kenkeleba House, 1982).

20.   Octavio Paz, *The Labyrinth of Solitude* (New York: Grove Press), 1961.

21.   Within the Aztec society, each person has "tonalli," or an energy source, that gives them a vital autonomy. Christian Duverger, "The Meaning of Sacrifice" in *Fragments for a History of the Human Body*, vol. 3, (New York: Zone 5, 1989), 367–85. "Tonalli" could be understood as an equivalent to Afro-Cuban concept of "ashe."

22.   Paz, op. cit. 50ff. and 332. See also Bataille's discussion of this concept in "The Notion of Expenditure" in *Visions of Excess: Selected Writings 1927–39* (ed. Allan Soekl, University of Minnesota Press: Minneapolis, 1985, 116–29. Moreover, Bataille's theories drew on ethnographic studies of "primitive" cultures, including Aztec sacrifice and Haitian voodoo, sacrifice was understood as holding a structural relation to festival's economy of excess and metamorphosis. For both Bataille and Caillois, sacrifice, as with festival, make evident repression through overturning the law of prohibition, therefore blurring the boundaries between the profane and sacred.

23.   Roger Caillois, "Festival," in Hollier, op. cit., 281.

24.   Octavio Paz, *Las Peras del Olmo* (Universidad Autonoma Nacional de Mexico: Mexico, 1965), 24.

25.   Mendieta, unpublished notes, written sometime between 1973 and 1975. Paz writes in *The Labyrinth of Solitude* the following: "Now every separation causes a wound. Without stopping to investigate how and when the separation is brought about, I want to point out that any break (with ourselves or those around us, with the past or present) creates a feeling of solitude. In extreme cases – separation from one's parents, matrix of native land, the death of the gods or a painful self-consciousness – solitude is identified with orphanhood.

And both of them generally manifest themselves as a sense of sin. The penalties and guilty feelings can be considered, thanks to the ideas of expiation and redemption, as necessary sacrifices, or pledges or promise of a future communion that will put an end to the long exile. The guilt can vanish, the wound can heal over, the separation resolve itself in communion. Solitude thus assumes a purgative, purifying character. The solitary or isolated individual transcends his solitude, accepting it as a proof and promise of communion," 64.

26.   Earlier Mendieta had shot a film of painting with blood/paint directly onto her body rather than the wall. In a studio barely lit and with a bowl of blood/paint beside her on a table, she stood naked before the camera and performed with slow deliberation three actions. In the first she marks her torso, forehead, and eyes with crosses, then lifts her arms and hands up as if in a gesture of declaration. In the second, she draws with the red liquid a heart shape around the breasts with the word "BESAME" (Kiss me) in between; and in the third, she draws a skeletal form down the body. See Tape #6, 66–81N, Filmworks, 1974.

27.   This became a prototype for a series of three works, "Blood Tracks," produced on paper at Franklin Furnace in 1982. This was part of an exhibition by Mendieta called "Isla and other works." See Tape 1–18, undated, 1974–75. By late 1974 she repeated these actions on different-colored material and titled them "Blood Writing."

28.   Mendieta, excerpt from unpublished notes, undated.

29.   Julia Kristeva, *Powers of Horror: An Essay on Abjection*, trans. Leon S. Roudiez (New York: Columbia University Press, 1982), 71.

30.   Interview with Linda Montano, in *Sulphur* (no. 22, spring, 1988), 67.

31.   Paz, op. cit., 23, cited in Mendieta, unpublished notes, undated.

32.   Kristeva, op. cit. p. 127. Writing on feminine masochism, Jessica Benjamin suggests that "The torture and outrage to which [the masochist] submits is a kind of martyrdom ... her desire to be known is like that of the sinner who wants to be known by God." See Jessica Benjamin, *The Bonds of Love: Psychoanalysis Feminism, and the Problem of Domination* (New York: Pantheon, 1988), 60.

33.   Cited in Mendieta, unpublished notes, undated. She refers to this African custom as analogous to her work.

34.   *Ibid.*

35.   *Ibid.*

36.   Yemaya is the Afro-Atlantic deity of love. Water is her sacred domain and devotees place flowers and other objects in the water as a form of offering. Mendieta, too, had been raised by an Afro-Cuban nanny who was a daughter of Yemaya and, like all Cubans and people of the Caribbean, water had always held a significance for her. In Brazil, on Yemaya's Day, women initiated into the religion of Umbanda dress in white and enter the sea, holding hands and throwing flowers into the sea as an offering.

37.   Sometimes the *ánima sola* appears alone and in other instances surrounded by others seeking the divine intervention of the Virgin who appears above. These images circulate throughout Spanish-speaking countries as popular postcard-size color prints.

38.   In making a copy of herself, she was also able to introduce Afro-Cuban religious beliefs and practices that she had not only been aware of in her childhood, but had begun to read about through the writings of contemporary anthropologists, such as the work of Lydia Cabrera. Interview with Hans Breder by author, November 1993. According to Afro-Cuban religious principles, the replication of the body could be, through its mediation with the human form, imbued with a deity or spirit's power, and therefore reunited with the forces of nature. In *The Golden Bough*, James Frazer delineates what he perceives as two principles of "sympathetic magic," the "law of imitation or similarity" and the "law of contagion." Frazer suggests that, while the principle of similarity suggests the importance of copying, of re-presentation (the actual process of making a copy in the likeness of one), the principle of contagion emphasizes the importance of materials.

18. Tania Bruguera
"The Burden of Guilt," 1997
Museum of Fine Arts, Caracas
Photo: Grandal
One of Bruguera's early artistic projects involved the re-enactment and then the contin-
uation of the oeuvre of Ana Mendieta, as a way of marking the importance of Mendieta's
work for Cubans living on the island. Bruguera also published *Memoria de la Posguerra*
(Memory of the Post-war), one of only a few independent artists' magazines of the
1990s that included works by Cubans outside the country. An active participant in
the small network of non-official artist-run spaces that sprang up in Havana in the
1990s, Bruguera uses part of her apartment as a performance space.

The Burden Of Guilt

Tania Bruguera

There are events that are talked about in whispers; it's not known if their purpose is to serve as testimony or if these stories are created because somebody needs to hear them.

That was the uncertainty I felt when someone told me that the Indians in Cuba – at least a group of them – chose to rebel against their Spanish conquerors by eating dirt, and only dirt, so that their deaths would mark their resolve.

The practice of eating dirt is found primarily in Africa and Latin America, where it is used as a means to be close to the place where you are from as you travel to a new destination, to supplement necessary vitamins and proteins in the diet, to feed (physically and metaphorically) the fetus that is about to be born.

But the Cuban Indians, however, ate dirt as a weapon of resistance. They ate from earth where they had been born, which is to say, they ate their ancestors, themselves, their history, their memory, as if they were committing a cultural suicide.

"The Burden of Guilt" is the recovery and realignment of this story. The burden is really the slaughtered lamb that hangs from the neck like a shield, like an open wound that reveals what's inside. The lamb is the weight that is carried as a consequence, as well as a symbolic attitude; the emotion, saltwater which drops like tears and washes the earth, which is the guilt, before it is digested.

19. María Teresa Hincapié
Una Cosa es una Cosa (A Thing is a Thing), 1990
33rd National Artists' Salon, Bogota, Colombia
Photo: Isidro Medina
Colombian artist María Teresa Hincapié worked as an actress in an experimental theater group in her country for several years before turning to solo work. Over the past ten years, she has created several durational performances that often incorporate everyday domestic tasks, the details of which are rendered more visible via repetitive structures or by their being carried out in slow motion. She has also carried out several performance peregrinations in South America, some of which have lasted weeks. Often implicit in her work are subtle calls for renewed appreciation of the environment and the sanctity of human existence.

Una Cosa es una Cosa (A Thing is a Thing) (1990)

María Teresa Hincapié

movement here. then. in the corner. in the center. to oneside. near him. hers. very far. further. very far. very, very far. here are the handbags. here the pocket. here the bag. here the box. there the handbags. here the bag and over it the pocket. at one side the box. in the corner the pocket and the bag, in the center the paper bags and very near the box. leakage, dispersion, everything getting empty. everything disappears. everything scatters. disseminates. blends. stops. organize themselves in a cue in a random way. they mark a space. they separate in groups. one beside the other. common groups. where they are similar. because they are white, because they are made up of fabric. because they are dresses because they are made up of fabric. because they are dresses. because they are made up of plastic. because they are large. because they are covered. because they are ceramics. because they are jars. because they need one another as the toothbrush and toothpaste. but also because the paste is by itself and the toothbrush is with other toothbrushes. or by itself. all the flowers here. the dresses are extended. the black ones are near me. the pink ones here, the towels by themselves, the coverlet by itself. the blankets by themselves, the handbags by themselves. the pencils by themselves, the dresses by themselves. the colors by themselves. the broom by itself. the onions by themselves. the carrots by themselves. the corn by itself, the sugar by itself. the onions by themselves, the carrots by themselves. the corn by itself. the sugar by itself. the wheat by itself the plastic by itself. the handbag by itself, the bag by itself. the box by itself and empty. the mirror by itself. the shoes by themselves. the socks by themselves. I, alone. he alone, she, alone, we, alone, they, alone. a space alone. a place alone. a line alone. one sock only. one shoe only. everything is alone. all of us are alone. a mass of rice. a mass of sugar. a mass of salt. a mass of wheat. a mass of coffee. a mass of different things.

Lygia Clark and Hélio Oiticica

A legacy of interactivity and participation for a telematic future

Simone Osthoff

The rapid development of the Internet since 1994 and the increasing number of artists working with digital communications technology has brought new attention to the role of interactivity in electronic media and in emerging digital culture. Interactivity in art, however, is not simply the result of the presence and accessibility of personal computers; rather, it must be regarded as part of contemporary art's natural development toward immateriality, a phenomenon that is evidenced, for example, in the works of Brazilian artists Lygia Clark and Hélio Oiticica. Concerning itself with the circulation of ideas among artists working in vastly different cultures, this article explores visual and conceptual parallels between Clark's and Oiticica's sensorial creations from the 1960s and 1970s – masks, goggles, hoods, suits, gloves, capes, and immersive environments – and early virtual-reality experiments from the 1960s and 1970s, such as Ivan Sutherland's head-mounted display and the Sayre Glove. Although not technologically based, Clark's and Oiticica's works are also related conceptually to those of artists pushing interactivity in art into new territories. Both in Brazil and elsewhere, Clark's and Oiticica's participatory creations continue to yield new meanings.[1]

With the exception of a period spanning the 1970s, when Oiticica resided in New York and Clark in Paris, both artists spent their lives in Rio de Janeiro, where they shared a common theoretical ground based in the Brazilian Neoconcrete Art movement.[2] They also shared a fertile artistic dialogue that lasted throughout their careers. Their complementary trajectories were unique and, in both cases, radical. From different perspectives, they contributed to the development of an original vocabulary of interactivity. Clark, merging the body/mind duality, focused primarily on the subjective and psychological dimensions of sensorial experimentation, while Oiticica engaged in sensorial explorations involving social, cultural, architectural, and environmental spaces.

Translating geometric abstraction into a language of the body

Clark and Oiticica questioned representation in art by examining ideas inherited from modern avant-garde movements – Neoplasticism, Constructivism, Suprematism, and Concrete Art – that broke with mimesis and assumptions of realism. In the late 1950s, they reframed modernist notions of universal aesthetics by translating them directly into life and the body. Weaving a web of relationships around the body's internal and external spaces, they relayed a modern European geometric abstract tradition to Brazilian vernacular culture. This syncretic process fused two very different traditions – a Western aesthetic canon that privileges vision and metaphysical knowledge, and Afro-Indigenous oral traditions in which knowledge and history are encoded in the body and ritual is profoundly concrete.[3] It must be noted that, in a true syncretic spirit, both traditions have always coexisted in Brazilian society at large, but it was not until Oiticica began working that this syncretism was methodically investigated in the visual arts.

In spite of affinities with late 1950s' and 1960s' countercultural movements that were also subversive of the modernist aesthetic canon, Clark and Oiticica's works – resisting the labels of body art, conceptual art, performance, and happening – stressed the meaning of participation as opposed to its form. Their emphasis on meaning stressed the experiential aspect of viewer participation. Their resistance to assimilation within mainstream art movements was perhaps less a matter of conceptual incompatibility than a way of emphasizing their original development at the margins of cultural centers, independent of international trends.[4]

Their rich and complex legacies were not only plastic, but also conceptual and existential, expressed in not easily classifiable oeuvres that embraced hybrid, contingent, and often immaterial forms. De-emphasizing visuality, Clark and Oiticica centered their work on the body, exploring haptic space through tactile, auditory, olfactory, and kinetic propositions. Their contributions to contemporary art are relevant not only because of their original development in the context of Brazilian art, but also because of the unique universal interactive vocabularies they created and explored with their manipulable objects, immersive environments, and experiential propositions based on wearable works.

Probing a language of the body and signifying processes through concrete operations that explored touch, sound, smell, and movement, Clark and Oiticica worked with life's energy and simple matter, merging perceptual and conceptual knowledge in ever-changing forms. In his 1968 book *Kinetic Art*, London-based critic Guy Brett compared Clark's work with Takis's kinetic sculptures, which introduced the magnet in sculpture as the presence of energy:

> Actual energy is the subject of both their work . . . Lygia Clark encourages the spectator to use his own energy to become aware of himself. This is something very unusual, and it seems to be a specifically Brazilian contribution to art, a kind of kineticism of the body.[5]

Clark's and Oiticica's creations, as they changed the traditional role of the viewer and the status of the artistic object, confronting in the process the function of artistic institutions, redefined the identity of the artist and the idea of authorship. Emphasizing viewer participation and material precariousness, their works continue to resist being frozen in museum displays as relics of past actions. Their move from hard to soft and ephemeral materials clearly establishes a historical link to the current immaterial and software-based practices of electronic art. Stressing relational actions, they focused on immaterial exchanges that did not conform to traditional curatorial practices. The challenges still presented by the preservation and presentation of their work relate the issues they explored to those of artists working with new forms of communication through global computer networks.

Lygia Clark's trajectory: from form to experience

In their development from purely optical-formal concerns to participatory and body-based work, Clark and Oiticica explored the body's multidimensional aspects. Once Clark left one phase of her work, she never returned to it, taking the experience forward into a form that was ever more immaterial than the last. The artistic residue acquired in one phase was always carried into the next, in a process described by Maria Alice Milliet as "traveling with baggage."[6]

In his 1975 book *Art – Action and Participation*, Frank Popper pointed to the new forms of spectator participation as partially responsible for the disappearance of the art object. He named Moholy-Nagy and three others – Israeli artist Yaacov Agam, Roy Ascott, and Lygia Clark – as pioneers of the viewer-participation movement. Popper described Clark's work as "perhaps the most telling example of the way in which the discipline of optical/plastic research has led to multi-sensorial participation and a type of aesthetic behavior which reconciles the problem of individual and group activity."[7]

Clark's participatory creations spanned nearly three decades. The rich interactive vocabulary she developed with objects made from very simple materials began with a series of Neoconcrete geometric sculptures dating from 1960 to 1964. These demanded the spectator's manipulation to yield their organic meaning. These sculptures developed into a second series of interactive works centered on the body, roughly divided into two parts: *Nostalgia of the Body*, and *Organic or Ephemeral Architectures*. Dating from 1964 to 1968, *Nostalgia of the Body* consists of hoods, goggles, masks, suits, gloves, and other objects used by the viewer/participant in individual or two-person sensorial explorations. In these works, viewer participation becomes the focus of attention, while the object remains secondary, existing only in order to promote a sensorial or relational experience. After 1968, these works developed into collective body works Clark titled "Organic or Ephemeral Architectures." In the last phase of her work, lasting from approximately 1979 until her death in 1988, Clark moved even further from traditional definitions of art and artist, employing the whole range of her interactive vocabulary in a form of synesthetic therapy used for emotional healing.

Clark derived the basic defining qualities of her early work from Concrete Art's emphasis on non-representational space and rigorous explorations of line, plane, color, and structure. Her reductive black, white, and gray paintings from the 1950s explored the complementary aspects of positive and negative space and the boundaries between virtual and literal planes. In the development of her work from painting to interactive sculpture, the issue of edges between painterly illusion and literal space, or between the canvas and the frame, had a kind of primary importance that was similar to the role that color played for Oiticica. Clark moved into three-dimensional space by way of folding the plane into hinged sculptures that combined geometric shapes and organic movements. This development away from Concrete paintings resulted in a series of Neoconcrete sculptures titled "Bichos" (Animals, or Beasts) from 1959 and 1960.

Clark's geometric Bichos needed to be manipulated by the viewer to reveal their organic nature and unfold their multiple configurations. When people asked her how many movements the Bicho had, she answered: "I don't know, and you don't know but it knows . . ."[8] Despite their interactive aspect, which also introduced time and movement into the work, the Bichos remain formally beautiful objects, and many are displayed today with the attached label "do not touch." Clark, however, emphasizing the importance of viewer's experience, abandoned the production of art objects altogether to enter a sensorial phase of her work with *Nostalgia of the Body*, starting around 1964. When Clark abandoned the production of the art object, she used the Möbius strip as a metaphor for a new start – a new start that was paradoxically without beginning or end, inside or outside, front or back. Shared by other Concrete artists, her interest in the reversible, continuous, limitless space of the Möbius strip expressed her attraction to non-Euclidian geometry.[9] Clark's new works dissolved the hard edges of the Bichos into soft, almost immaterial actions that had no value in themselves, but only in their relation with the participant. She referred to these action-based works as "propositions." The endless fluid space of the Möbius strip symbolized the path she would pursue for the rest of her career.

Clark's work with the Möbius strip contrasts sharply with Max Bill's sculptures employing the same form. Bill pursued the visualization of non-Euclidean ideas using traditional techniques as well as permanent materials with noble associations – marble, stone, and bronze – in Möbius-strip sculptures to be contemplated by the viewer. Clark, by contrast, defined the concept of endless space as a succession of paradoxical relationships to be directly experienced in the body. Her propositions acknowledged the coexistence of opposites within the same space: internal and external, subjective and objective, metaphorical and literal, male and female. For Clark, the radical new space of the Möbius strip called for new forms of production and communication impossible to explore within traditional artistic categories and practices. For "Caminhando" (Trailings, or going), dating from 1964, Clark simply invited the spectator to take a pair of scissors, twist a strip of paper, join it to form a Möbius strip, and cut continuously along the unending plane. *Hand Dialogue*, from 1966, is an elastic band in the form of a Möbius strip that two people use to connect their hands in a tactile dialogue.

Head-mounted and sensorial works: hoods, masks, goggles, gloves, body suits

The relational aspect of Clark's work in the series *Bichos* became even more apparent in *Nostalgia of the Body*. Brett describes some of Clark's masks from this period:

> Clark produced many devices to dissolve the visual sense into an aware-
> ness of the body. The *Máscara Sensorial* (Sensorial Hoods), 1967,
> incorporate eyepieces, ear coverings and a small nose bag, fusing optical,
> aural and olfactory sensations. A number of helmets hold small movable
> mirrors in front of the eyes: one can either look out into the world or
> back into oneself, or any fractured combination of both. *Máscara-Abismo*
> (Abyss-Masks), 1967, often blindfolds the eyes. Large air-bags weighted
> down with stones can be touched, producing the sensation of an imagi-
> nary empty space inside the body, and so on.[10]

Clark's hoods, masks, goggles, gloves, suits, and other relational objects made of cheap materials, provide viewers with experiences that sometimes constrain and sometimes enhance the various senses to activate new connections between them. Clark's gloves, for instance, are made in various materials, sizes, and textures. The gloves aim at a rediscovery of touch. Participants use the many combina-tions of gloves and balls of different sizes, textures, and weights, and then hold the balls again with their bare hands.

Clark's experiences tend to merge the body's interior and exterior spaces, stressing the direct connection between the body's physical and psychological dimensions. The pure optical emphasis of her geometric abstract paintings from the 1950s are transformed by *Nostalgia of the Body* into sensory explorations

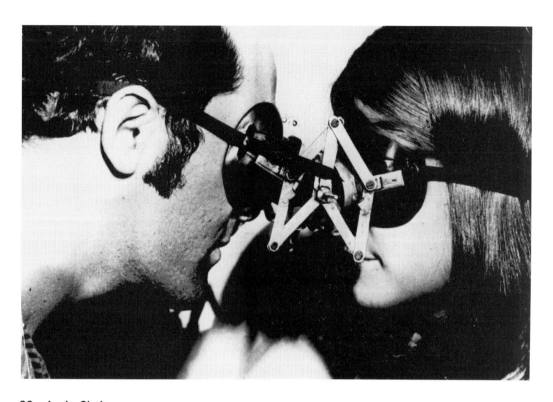

20. Lygia Clark
"Diálogo," (Dialogue), 1968
Photo courtesy of the Museum of Modern Art, Rio de Janeiro
Clark's "Diálogo" is part of the *Nostalgia of the Body* series which began in 1964 with self- and two-person sensorial explorations, and developed, after 1968, into collective creations she titled *Organic* or *Ephemeral Architectures*. The "Diálogo" goggles restrict the visual field of the two participants to an eye to eye exchange, merging interactivity and dialogism, two central concerns in Clark's work.

of texture, weight, scale, temperature, sound, and movement. These sensations are the basis of a non-verbal language employed both in processes of self-discovery and collective explorations among a group of participants. There is a significant conceptual link between these collective explorations and the characteristic of telecommunications art that Roy Ascott calls "distributed authorship." Clark's collective creations became her main focus during the period she lived in Paris.

Collective and participatory works

In 1968, as a result of the traumatized public space created in Brazil,[11] Clark moved to Paris. From 1970 to 1975 she taught at the Sorbonne, returning to

Rio in 1977. During this period she developed with her students collective body works that she referred to as *Organic or Ephemeral Architecture*. She called these events "rites without myths." She titled one of them *Baba Antropofágica* (translated in English as "Dribble"), meaning literally "Anthropophagic Drool" or "Cannibal Spit".[12] For this work, participants placed in their mouths a small spool of colored thread that they unwound directly from their mouths onto another of the participants, who lay stretched out on the ground. The body of the latter was gradually buried under a mottled web of regurgitations. This event was inspired by Clark's dream of an unknown material endlessly flowing from her mouth to create the loss of her own inner substance. The collective vomiting experienced by the group was described by her as the exchange among the participants of psychological content. She also mentions that this exchange was not pleasurable and that it was about the vomiting of lived experience, which was then swallowed by others.[13]

In the last phase of her work, Clark employed a vocabulary of "relational objects" for the purposes of emotional healing. Objects made of simple materials such as plastic bags, stones, air, shells, water, sand, styrofoam, fabric, and nylon stockings acquired meaning only in their relation to the participant. Continuing to approach art experimentally, Clark made no attempt to establish boundaries between therapeutic practice and artistic experience, and was even less concerned with preserving her status as an artist. The physical sensations caused by the relational objects as she used them on the patient's body, communicated primarily through touch, stimulated connections among the senses and awakened the body's memory. Clark's use of relational objects in a therapeutic context aimed at the promotion of emotional balance.

The material simplicity of Clark's propositions confront viewers, however, with very complex issues about art, perception, and body/mind relations. Considering participants as subjects-in-process, Clark's work concerns the restructuring of the self through preverbal language preceding the enunciation of sentences. Stressing both the present moment and the flux of time, the work is constantly redefined by each participant. Clark's apparently simple creations are, in fact, demanding propositions that ask viewers to infuse the work with their lives and energy. Clark was never concerned with self-expression in art, but instead with the possibility of self-discovery, experimentation, invention, and transformation. She began with formalist problems about the exhaustion of representation in painting and ended, three decades later, in a form of synesthetic therapy. In its unique development, Clark's trajectory shows an original inventiveness, a conceptual cohesion and a critical rigor rarely seen in Brazilian art.

Hélio Oiticica's 1960s' aesthetic of subversion and cultural contamination

In the late 1950s, in a process both analogous and complementary to Clark's, Oiticica moved away from optical/pictorial investigations by incorporating time and movement as an active element of his work. His participatory strategies, however, contrast with Clark's in their engagement of the viewer's cultural, social, architectural, and environmental space. Color had, in Oiticica's early development, the same importance that edges had for Clark in her transit from pictorial to three-dimensional space. As he explored the relations between color, time, structure, and space, Oiticica stated that color frees itself from the rectangle and from representation and "it tends to 'in-corporate' itself; it becomes temporal, creates its own structure, so the work then becomes the 'body of color'."[14]

Oiticica's creations, like Clark's, became increasingly interactive as he moved from object-based to body-centered works in which viewer participation became the central focus. His Neoconcrete works, *Spatial Reliefs* and *Nucleus* (1959–60) – painted wood constructions suspended away from the wall – expanded ideas inherited from Modernist avant-garde movements, particularly the ideas of Mondrian and Malevich. These works incorporated color, hue, and value in geometrically shaped constructions to be observed from various points as viewers walked around them.

Continuing to expand color, structure, and the act of seeing in space and time, Oiticica surrounded the viewer's body with color in a series of immersive, labyrinth-like painted constructions entered by the spectator, which were titled *Penetráveis* (Penetrables). His series of object-containers, *Bólides* (the Portuguese word for "fireball" or "flaming meteor"), are also concerned with the essence of color. The first *Bólides* were glass containers and brightly painted boxes with unexpected openings and drawers filled with pure pigments to be opened by the viewers. The *Bólides* developed from the earliest boxes and glass containers full of pigment, their number expanding throughout the 1960s to reach a total of approximately fifty around 1969. As the *Bólides* evolved, they varied greatly in scale, form, medium, and function. They were both constructed and appropriated: some include words or images, some are olfactory, others are homages to people, and some are large structures to be entered and inhabited by the spectator. They all invite perceptual explorations combining, as do many of Oiticica's creations, conceptual sophistication with a raw physicality.

Although *Spatial Reliefs*, *Nucleus*, *Penetráveis*, and *Bólides* increasingly invited the active participation of the viewer in the perception of the works, it was with his series of wearable creations, titled "Parangolés," and later on with two installations – *Tropicália* and *Eden* – that Oiticica's work became centered on the body, promoting through interactivity radically new sensorial experiences. From his colorful painted structures, Oiticica derived his first *Parangolé*, created in 1964. It transformed hard-edged geometric planes into folds of wearable materials made specifically to be danced with. The *Parangolés* were types of capes inspired conceptually by the Mangueira Samba School[15] to which Oiticica belonged, and they were often made for particular performers. They were, according to Oiticica, "proposals for behavior" and "sensuality tests." Communicating through experience, the *Parangolés* emphasize the fluidity of life in opposition to any attempt to fix and systematize the world. With this series of uncanny wearable creations made of cheap and ephemeral materials often found on the streets, work and body merge into a hybrid of geometric and organic forms. The participant wearing the *Parangolé* dances with it, exploring kinetically its multiple possibilities.

Expanding the *Parangolés'* architectural origins, Oiticica made two large installations in the late 1960s that he referred to as "experiences." Entitled *Tropicália* and *Eden*, these environments gave a new spatial context to his previous works – *Bólides*, *Penetráveis*, and *Parangolés* – by placing them among natural elements such as water, sand, pebbles, straw, and plants. Oiticica invited viewers to take off their shoes and inhabit the spaces through leisure activities (such as the simple activity of lying down). The first of these environmental installations, *Tropicália*, was mounted at the Museum of Modern Art in Rio de Janeiro in 1967. *Tropicália* and the *Parangolés* series are seminal works within the history of Brazilian art.

Addressing the possibility of the creation of a "Brazilian image," *Tropicália* gave name to the emerging Tropicalist movement and opened a cultural discussion that is still far from exhausted.[16] Among the many complex issues raised was Oiticica's notion that the myth of "tropicality" is much more than parrots and banana trees: it is the consciousness of not being conditioned by established structures, hence highly revolutionary in its entirety. Any conformity, be it intellectual, social, or existential, is contrary to its principal idea.[17]

Tropicália was the product of an aesthetic of cultural contamination that Oiticica expressed by the writing on one of his *Penetráveis*: "A Pureza é um Mito" (Purity is a Myth). In *Tropicália*, Oiticica made an important reference to the role of the media by placing at the center of his tropical environment a TV set. In 1968, he wrote,

> Entering the main *Penetrable*, undergoing several tactile-sensorial experiences . . . one arrives at the end of the labyrinth, in the dark, where a TV set is permanently switched on: it is the image which then devours the participants, because it is more active than their sensorial creations.[18]

In this text, also titled "Tropicália", and in others, Oiticica called attention to the dangers of a superficial, folkloric consumption of an image of a tropical Brazil, stressing the existential life-experience that escapes this consumption.[19] This concern also informed his second large installation, *Eden*, exhibited at the Whitechapel Gallery in London in 1969.

Eden, like *Tropicália*, contained different areas for participants to explore in a leisurely way. "Eden" was, however, more abstract in its architectural references than was *Tropicália's* direct allusion to the *favela* of Mangueira. Avoiding the notion of representation in art, as well as the construction of a tropical image for exportation, the *Eden* experience, similar to the rebirth of the senses enabled by Clark's objects, invited viewers to rediscover pleasurable ways of inhabiting space. In 1970, Oiticica received a Guggenheim fellowship and built for the Information show at the Museum of Modern Art (MOMA) in New York twenty-eight *Ninhos* (Nests) that also invited viewer participation in the exploration of space and behavior.

Oiticica's leisure strategies: crelazer and the supra-sensorial

Oiticica's contribution to a vocabulary of interactivity expanded upon Clark's paradoxical explorations of aspects of the body's internal/external space. He created interrelations around the sensual body and the many spatial forms it interacts with. His participatory creations were based on two key concepts that he named *Crelazer* and the *Supra-Sensorial*. *Crelazer*, one of Oiticica's neologisms, meaning "to believe in leisure," was for him a condition for the existence of creativity and is based on joy, pleasure, and phenomenological knowledge. The second concept, the *Supra-Sensorial*, promotes the expansion of the individual's normal sensory capacities in order to discover his/her internal creative center. The *Supra-Sensorial* could be represented by hallucinogenic states (induced with or without the use of drugs), religious trance, and other alternate states of consciousness such as the ecstasy and delirium facilitated by the samba dance. For Oiticica, the *Supra-Sensorial* created a complete de-aestheticization of art underscoring transformative processes. In his words:

> This entire experience into which art flows, the issue of liberty itself, of the expansion of the individual's consciousness, of the return to myth, the rediscovery of rhythm, dance, the body, the senses, which finally are what we have as weapons of direct, perceptual, participatory knowledge ... is revolutionary in the total sense of behavior.[20]

Oiticica's work fused formal investigation with leisure activities, inviting viewer participation in the creation of "unconditioned behavior".[21] In the cultural context of "the country where all free wills seem to be repressed or castrated,"[22] the concepts of *Crelazer* and the *Supra-Sensorial* directly defied a pleasure-denying productivist work ethic, subverting it through activities that embraced pleasure, humor, leisure, and carnivalesque strategies. Reverie and revolt were never far apart in Oiticica's work, as Brett has pointed out. Leisure for him was first and foremost a revolutionary anti-colonialist strategy.

Parangolés: samba and interactive art

Among the many implications emerging from Oiticica's fusion of geometric abstraction and samba culture is the return to the mythical, primordial structure of art; a recreation of the self through an initiatory ritual. Oiticica described his relation to the popular samba, making reference to the intense experience provoked by dance:

> The rehearsals themselves are the whole activity, and the participation in it is not really what Westerners would call participation because the people bring inside themselves the "samba fever" as I call it, for I became ill of it too, impregnated completely, and I am sure that from that disease no one recovers, because it is the revelation of mythical activity. . . . Samba sessions all through the night revealed to me that myth is indispensable in life, something more important than intellectual activity or rational thought when these become exaggerated and distorted.[23]

For Oiticica, samba was a conduit for the flow of energy and desire. Samba was a relay, a connector. In an article from 1965 entitled "Ambiental Art, Post-modern Art, Hélio Oiticica," critic Mario Pedrosa traced Oiticica's trajectory from purely plastic concerns to the existential, the culturally based and the postmodern. In this process of development from modern to postmodern art, Pedrosa noticed that Brazilian artists participated "this time, not as modest followers but in a leading role."[24] According to Pedrosa, Oiticica's aesthetic nonconformism merged with his social/individual nonconformism due to his Mangueira experience. It was the artist's initiation into samba that dissolved dualisms and expanded his work from being object-based to environmentally based, incorporating in this process the kinetic knowledge of the body, the structures of popular architecture, and the cultural environment in which they existed. In Pedrosa's words,

> It was during his initiation to samba that the artist went from the visual experience in all its purity to an experience that was tactile, kinetic, based on the sensual fruition of materials, where the whole body, which in the

previous phase was centered on the distant aristocracy of the visual, became the total source of sensoriality.[25]

Oiticica's premature death at the age of 43 left as loose ends the many threads he explored, both as an artist and a thinker, in a meteoric career. His experimental creations assumed a range of forms that have conceptual rather than formal coherence. Ranging from paintings to writings, from sculptures and objects to public actions and events, from constructed immersive environments to found and appropriated objects, and from wearable works to ambulatory experiences through Rio's bohemian, marginal, and poor neighborhoods, his creations emphasized sensorial expansion through leisure activities. Oiticica took playfulness seriously, infusing interactivity with what Pedrosa termed "the experimental exercise of liberty."[26]

Body/machine hybrids, interfaces, and networks: interactivity into new realms

In general, Neoconcrete artists, among them Clark and Oiticica, did not explore the possibilities of technology for artmaking. Their trajectory from object-based works to body-centered experiences, from material to immaterial, and from hard to soft processes, however, opened conceptual ground for practices similar to those of electronic performance and telecommunications art, with their emphasis on fluid, intangible exchanges.

The masks, hoods, and goggles Clark made between 1965 and 1970, which altered binocular perception, can be compared, for instance, with the helmets and goggles made by Australian artist Stelarc from 1968 to 1972 – the starting point for his relentless investigation of the limits and possibilities of the body. Clark's works are connected stylistically to virtual-reality head-mounted displays and can be perceived as radical parallels to early prototypes of the new immersive technology, exemplified by Sutherland's well-known stereoscopic headset.[27]

Contrary to the suggestions of many advocates of virtual reality and related technologies, that virtual reality promotes a disembodied mind, Stelarc, who has been exploring body–machine relations for three decades, is concerned, as was Clark, with blurring the body/mind dichotomy. Developing his work through direct actions on the body, Stelarc celebrates a fusion of the body and technology – the cyborg hybrid of "wet" and "hard" ware. His explorations of the body's limitations have included sensory-deprivation performances; twenty-four body-suspension performances with insertions into the skin (in different situations and locations); amplified brain waves, heartbeat, blood-flow and muscle signals; and films made inside his lungs, stomach, and colon. His strategies to enhance the body's capabilities have included prosthetics – such as an artificial hand activated by electromyograph signals of the abdominal and leg muscles – and computer technologies promoting body/machine interfacing. In his latest performances involving the Internet, his body became a host for interactions with remote agents. Stelarc's remote explorations with the body both contrast with and recall Clark's collective works, in which the body was a host for interaction with local agents.

The affinities between Oiticica's creations and the participatory paradigm in telematic art are evidenced in the *cyber Parangolé* created by the New York-based X-Art Foundation, a non-profit artmaking organization that involves individuals and groups at the intersections of art, cultural studies, and information technologies. The *Parangolé* (after Oiticica) was presented as part of *Bioinformatica*, issue 4 of *Blast* named after a corresponding exhibition that showed at Sandra Gering Gallery in New York in December 1994.[28] The X-Art Foundation created new, colorful *Parangolés* worn by participants both at the physical space of the gallery and in the virtual space of their MOO (Multi-User Object-Oriented Dimension) on the Internet. In the *Parangolés*' "pockets," both in the gallery and on the Internet, participants could find fragments of texts and maps that were assembled and reassembled through body movement. Participants accessed these texts and maps in different ways in both virtual and real spaces. In the MOO, the user produces action by means of a typed set of codes in order to "reach" into a pocket. Keyboard commands locate a virtual body in telecommunicational space, while in the gallery the body sitting at the computer terminal finds texts, maps, and computer diskettes in the pockets of the *Parangolé* he or she was invited to wear. A double play was produced between the movements of the virtual body and the experiences of the "real" body visiting the gallery. The ambiguity between bodies and *Parangolés* and between material and immaterial exchanges added new meanings to Oiticica's work by expanding the *Parangolés*' interactive nature in analogy to digital interfaces. The *Parangolés* recreated for the *Bioinformatica* show regained the conceptual fertility they once had by virtue of their direct involvement with viewers, who were invited to wear the brilliantly colored cloaks. Expanding the meaning of these works across cultures and disciplines, the X-Art Foundation revisited the radical, subversive experience of the *Parangolés* created by the samba dancers at Mangueira in the mid-1960s.

The abandonment of an aesthetic of closure and completion for one that stresses relations across different modalities, disciplines, and dimensions, privileging what is relative and dialogical rather than absolute, identical, and monological, opens multiple connections across heterogeneous forms, spaces, and cultures. These concepts are, however, not related exclusively to technological approaches. They are tied viscerally to the continuing development of a new aesthetics beyond the fixed immutable object. As Clark's and Oiticica's interactive legacies so poignantly illustrate, a participatory art endlessly merges conceptual and perceptual, material and immaterial, embodied and disembodied experiences.

A longer version of this essay originally appeared in Leonardo, *vol. 30, no. 4, 1997.*

Notes

1.   Although Clark and Oiticica did not focus on technology as a medium for artmaking, they ventured into it either conceptually (Clark's Four Propositions of the late 1960s) or experimentally (Oiticica's explorations with drugs and audiovisual media in the mid-1970s). Clark's Four Propositions, two involving film and two involving magnets, remained unrealized. See Lygia Clark, *Lygia Clark* (Rio de Janeiro: Funarte, 1980) p. 32; and Lygia Clark, "Nostalgia of the Body," *October 69* (Summer 1994) pp. 107–08. Her film proposition "Man at the Center of Events" is very similar to Gary Hill's video work *Crux* (1983–87), in which five cameras were attached to a walking man and the recorded images shown simultaneously in a room in the shape of a cross. Clark's second film proposition, "Invitation to a Voyage," involved the relation between real and virtual events that were to take place on the screen and in front of it, in an early form of virtual reality. The project is analogous to Jeffrey Shaw's *The Legible City* (1988–189), in which a stationary bicycle is placed in front of a large screen that projects the roads the cyclist explores. Oiticica's experimentation with Super-8 film and other audiovisual media in the mid-1970s, when he lived in New York, mixed art and life in an even more radical way, further enhancing his leisure strategies. See Ligia Canongia, *Quase Cinema* (Rio de Janeiro: Funarte, 1981) pp. 20–23.

On Lygia Clark, see also Guy Brett, "The Proposal of Lygia Clark," in M. Catherine de Zegher, ed., *Inside the Visible* (Cambridge, MA: MIT Press, 1996); Guy Brett, "Lygia Clark: In Search of the Body," *Art in America* (July 1994); Maria Alice Milliet, *Lygia Clark: Obra-trajeto* (São Paulo: Edusp, 1992); Guy Brett, "A Radical Leap," in Dawn Ades, ed., *Art in Latin America* (New Haven, CT: Yale Univ. Press, 1989). Lygia Clark's works and archives can be seen at the Museum of Modern Art of Rio de Janeiro, Centro de Documentação Museu de Arte Moderna do Rio de Janeiro. Av. Infante Dom Henrique 188, Parque do Flamengo, Rio de Janeiro, RJ, Brazil, CEP 20021–140, tel: (021) 210–2188 extension 212, fax: (021) 240–6351; contact: Anna Maria Innecco.

On Hélio Oiticica, see also Waly Salomão, *Hélio Oiticica: Qual é o Parangolé?* (Rio de Janeiro: Relume Dumará, 1996); Celso Favaretto, *A Invenção de Hélio Oiticica* (São Paulo: Edusp, 1992); Guy Brett, "Hélio Oiticica: Reverie and Revolt," *Art in America* (January 1989); Lucilla Saccá *Hélio Oiticica: La Sperimentazione Della Libertà* (Udine: Campanotto Editore, 1995); and Guy Brett, Catherine David, Chris Dercon, Luciano Figueiredo, and Lygia Pape, eds., *Hélio Oiticica* (Minneapolis, MN: Walker Art Center and Rotterdam: Witte de With Center for Contemporary Art, 1993). This comprehensive catalog accompanied Oiticica's international traveling retrospective from February 1992 to February 1994 (Rotterdam: Witte de With Center for Contemporary Art; Paris: Galerie Nationale du Jeu de Paume; Barcelona: Fundación Antoni Tapies; Lisbon: Fundação Calouste Gulbenkian; and

Minneapolis, MN: Walker Art Center). It contains a large part of Hélio Oiticica's writings as well as essays by Catherine David, Guy Brett, and Waly Salomão. Hélio Oiticica's works and archives can be seen at the Centro de Arte Hélio Oiticica, Rua Luis de Camões 68, Centro, Rio de Janeiro, RJ, Brazil, CEP 20060–040, tel: (021) 232–2213, 232–1104, 232–4213, fax: (021) 232–1401. Curator: Luciano Figueiredo.

2.   Concrete Art movements were formed in Rio de Janeiro (Frente, formed in 1953) and in São Paulo (Ruptura, formed in 1952) as part of the artistic explosion created by rapid industrialization in Brazil during the postwar era. In the visual arts, the theoretical polarization between a "functionalist" tendency in São Paulo and a "vitalist" tendency in Rio de Janeiro resulted in the creation in 1959 of the Neoconcrete Art movement in Rio. Clark and Oiticica were the two most original artists to come out of the Neoconcrete movement. See the Neoconcrete manifesto in October 69 (Summer 1994) pp. 91–95 and also in Dawn Ades, *Art in Latin America* (New Haven, CT: Yale University. Press, 1989) pp. 335–37.

3.   For a discussion on the concreteness of thought and ritual in oral-based traditions, see Marilyn Houlberg, "Magique Marasa," in Donald Cosentino, ed., *Sacred Arts of Haitian Vodou* (Los Angeles: UCLA Fowler Museum, 1995) pp. 273–74. Holberg's observations about the physicality of ritual in many Afro-American religious ceremonies can illuminate this discussion on the concreteness of Oiticica's and Clark's notion of the body. The artistic traditions of Haitian Vodou have also been recently examined in the light of a postmodern aesthetic by M. A. Greenstein, "The Delirium of Faith," *World Art*, No. 3 (1996) pp. 30–35.

4.   In a discussion between Chilean Nelly Richard and Briton Guy Brett, Brett illustrated the traditional hierarchical gap between South American and Euro-American artists that Clark and Oiticica struggled to overcome:

> There was an interesting comparison to be made between the exhibition of Hélio Oiticica, a Brazilian artist, which took place in London at the Whitechapel Gallery in 1969, and an exhibition of Robert Morris, the American minimalist, which took place at roughly the same time at the Tate Gallery. Both exhibitions had a participatory element for the public, and the differences between the two approaches were very fascinating ... but it was very unlikely at the time that such comparisons would be made because of the immensely greater prestige enjoyed by American artists in London. To have suggested a comparison on equal terms between a famous American and an unknown Brazilian artist would have been somehow "improper," to borrow Nelly Richard's use of the notion of propriety. For a Brazilian writer to have made claims for Oiticica in direct comparison with Morris would have seemed the height of naive nationalism, and even for a non-Brazilian it would have been difficult. The same naiveté on the part of the British or North Americans, went, well, unnoticed here.

See *Witte de With Cahier* No. 2 (June 1994) p. 90. For further discussion, see Nelly Richard, "The International Mise-en-scène of Latin American Art," *Witte de With Cahier*, no. 2 (June 1994) p. 83; Nelly Richard, "Postmodern Disalignments and Realignments of the Center/Periphery," *Art Journal*, No. 51 (Winter 1992); Mari Carmen Ramirrez, "Beyond "the Fantastic': Framing Identity in U.S. Exhibitions of Latin American Art," *Art Journal* no. 51 (Winter 1992); Simone Osthoff, "Orson Welles in Brazil and Carmen Miranda in Hollywood: Mixing Chiclets with Bananas," *Blimp* 33 (Spring 1996)

5.   Guy Brett, *Kinetic Art* (London: Studio Vista/Reinhold Art, 1968) p. 65. In another article entitled "In Search of the Body," Brett further emphasized Clark's and Oiticica's roots in Brazilian culture, underscoring a special dimension of the body in Brazil: "Like most such generalizations about national character, perhaps, the 'popular culture of the body' exists both as a stereotype and a truth. It is what makes it possible to read a phrase 'Brazilian elasticity of body and mind' in both a football report and an article on Lygia Clark!" This special dimension of sensuality in Brazil poses theoretical challenges both within and without the culture. On one hand, within the Western metaphysical tradition, it reinforces the stereotype of sensuality in opposition to logos along with other related antinomies such as nature/culture and primitive/civilized. On the other hand, as a source of body knowledge inherited from oral traditions, it dissolves the body/mind duality, which was precisely what Clark and Oiticica strove to accomplish. For further discussion, see Simone Osthoff, "Lygia Clark and Hélio Oiticica: Translating Geometric Abstraction into a Language of the Body," thesis, Department of Art History, Theory and Criticism (Chicago, IL: School of the Art Institute of Chicago, 1996).

6.   See Milliet, *Lygia* Clark p. 179; and also Maria Alice Milliet, "A Obra É O Trajeto," MAC Revista, no. 1 (Museu de Arte Contemporânea da Universidade de São Paulo, April 1992) p. 37.

7.   Frank Popper, *Art – Action and Participation* (New York: New York University Press, 1975) p. 13.

8.   Lygia Clark, as quoted by Lula Vanderlei and Luciano Figueiredo, in *Hélio Oiticica and Lygia Clark Salas Especiais*, 22 Bienal Internacional de São Paulo (Rio de Janeiro: Museum of Modern Art of Rio de Janeiro and Museum of Modern Art of Bahia) n.p.

9.   Max Bill, "The Mathematical Way of Thinking in the Visual Art of Our Time," in Michele Emmer, ed., *The Visual Mind: Art and Mathematics* (Cambridge, MA: MIT Press, 1993) p. 8. Originally published in *Werk* 3 (1949).

10.   Brett, "Lygia Clark: In Search of the Body", pp. 61–62.

11.   The year 1968, a historic milestone in many Western countries, marks in Brazil the beginning of an era of state terrorism. The military government in power since 1964 issued the AI-5 (Fifth Institutional Act) signed by military President General Costa e Silva on December 13 1968. The AI-5 closed Congress and suspended all political and constitutional rights, initiating a period of political oppression and persecution, youth revolt movements and counterculture. The period is the darkest one in the history of the Brazilian military dictatorship. The suspension of human rights opened the way to political persecution, torture, and censorship, making it extremely difficult for artists to work. According to Zuenir Ventura, ten years after the AI-5 was declared, approximately 500 films, 450 plays, 200 books, dozens of radio programs, and more than 500 music lyrics, along with a dozen soap opera episodes, had been censored. See Ventura, *1968 O Ano que Não Terminou* (Rio de Janeiro: Nova Fronteira, 1988) p. 285. The AI-5 was responsible for an artistic and intellectual diaspora (Oiticica and Clark included) and for the fragmentation and isolation

of artistic production in Brazil. Cultural production in the 1970s became mostly marginal, isolated from the public and hermetic, communicating only to a small elite. During the 1980s, the country slowly returned to democracy, and little of the irreverent experimentalism of the 1960s survived.

12.   *Anthropophagia* literally means "cannibalism." As employed by the Brazilian avant-garde of the 1920s (the "Anthropophagic Manifesto," by Oswald de Andrade, was published in 1928), anthropophagy called for a cannibalization of European culture in Brazil. It highlighted Afro-Indigenous myths and traditions as superior to the Christian ones, for they were without the double standards of morality and repressed sexuality that artists saw in the patriarchical Catholic behavior. The Anthropophagic movement pointed to the "out of placeness" of European ideas in Brazil using inversion, humor, and parody as subversive anti-colonialist strategies.

13.   Lygia Clark as quoted by Brett, "In Search of the Body," p. 62.

14.   Hélio Oiticica, in Brett et al., *Hélio Oiticica*, p. 33.

15.   Mangueira is the name of one of the oldest and most famous *favelas* (hillside slums) in Rio de Janeiro. The Mangueira Samba school is among the most popular in Rio. See Alma Guillermoprieto, *Samba* (New York: Vintage Departures, 1990). Guillermoprieto lived for a year in the *favela* of Mangueira. In *Samba*, she gives an account of this experience while examining the history and culture of black Brazilians and the social and spiritual energies that inform the rhythms of samba. For a complete history of Rio de Janeiro's samba schools, see Sergio Cabral, *As Escolas de Samba do Rio de Janeiro* (Rio de Janeiro: Lumiar Editora, 1996).

16.   Adopting an aesthetic of mixing and contamination, the Tropicalist movement of the late 1960s aggressively combined high and low and industrial and rural cultures, merging political nationalism with aesthetic internationalism and rock and roll with samba. It included all the arts – theater, cinema, poetry, visual arts, and popular Brazilian music (especially the works of Caetano Veloso, Gilberto Gil, Gal Costa, and the group OS MUTANTES). It also inaugurated the "aesthetic of garbage," explored by the second phase of Cinema Novo. It represented a return to cannibalist strategies in the arts, leaving behind the more austere "aesthetic of hunger," with its simplistic Manichean opposition between pure popular nationalism and the alienation of international mass culture. An interesting parallel between Oiticica and the Brazilian filmmaker Glauber Rocha, who became the spokesperson for the New Latin American Cinema, is made by Katherine David in "The Great Labyrinth," in Brett et al., *Hélio Oiticica* pp. 248–59.

17.   Oiticica, "Tropicália" (March 4 1968), in Brett et al., *Hélio Oiticica,* p. 126.

18.   Ibid., p.124

19.   Oiticica's critical views of Brazilian art and culture were condensed in his 1973 article "Brazil Diarrhea," reprinted in Brett et al., *Hélio Oiticica*, pp. 17–20.

20.   Oiticica, "Appearance of the Supra-Sensorial" (November/December 1967), in Brett et al., *Hélio Oiticica*, p. 130.

21.   Oiticica, untitled text, in Kynaston L. McShine, ed., *Information* (New York: Museum of Modern Art, Summer 1970) p. 103. See also Oiticica's "Appearance of the Supra-Sensorial," pp. 127–30.

22.   Oiticica, untitled text, in McShine, *Information*, p. 103.

23.   Oiticica quoted by Brett in "Hélio Oiticica: Reverie and Revolt," p. 120.

24.   Mario Pedrosa, "Ambiental Art, Post-Modern Art, Hélio Oiticica," introduction to *Hélio Oiticica, Aspiro ao Grande Labirinto* (Rio de Janeiro: Rocco, 1986) pp. 9–13. Translation mine.

25.   *Ibid. P.* 9. Translation mine.

26.   The "experimental exercise of liberty" is a phrase created by Mario Pedrosa and quoted often by Oiticica in his writings. See, for example, Hélio Oiticica, "Experimentar o Experimental," *Arte em Revista* No. 5 (São Paulo: Centro de Estudos de Arte Contemporânea, ed. Kairós, 1981) p. 50. See also Oiticica, "The Appearance of the Supra-sensorial," p. 127.

27.   Ivan Sutherland, "The Ultimate Display," Proceedings of the IFIP Congress (1965) pp. 506–08. (IFIP stands for "International Federation for Information Processing.") Ivan Sutherland, "A Head-Mounted Three-Dimensional Display," Proceedings of the Fall Joint Computer Conference (1968) pp. 757–64.

28.   See Margot Lovejoy, *Postmodern Currents, Art and Artists in the Age of Electronic Media*, 2nd ed. (Englewood Cliffs, NJ: Prentice Hall, 1997) p. 235.

Todos Mis Muertos (All My Dead Ones) (1996)

Merián Soto

Conjuring the spirit

Some dances are gifts. The directives for the dance simply reveal themselves to me. I follow unquestioningly. This was the process of *Todos Mis Muertos*. In searching for a practice of Day of the Dead traditions, my approach was to focus on personal encounters with death.

I decided to create a piece in homage to Mamita, my beloved grandmother, long gone. In the studio as I invoked her memory I felt surrounded and filled by a yellow light. Yellow. I would be yellow, yellow costume, yellow body, yellow flowers. What better *ofrenda* than myself? I became the offering.

I later learned that yellow is the Soul light. I knew Mamita in her late years. She had lost her eyesight to cataracts. Loss of one sense heightens the others, they say. In order to feel closer to her I blindfolded myself. Touching my own fingertips I immediately connected to my childhood memory of Mamita's wrinkled fingers gently exploring my hands and face. Her electric, seeing touch. Touching my own fingertips closed an energetic circuit. I moved swiftly into an internal universe and I felt an inner awareness open up and expand.

The performance would focus on the body and its actions as *ofrendas*, offerings. I would enter the altar/performance space through the audience. I would bring with me all the objects and elements needed for the ritual. Blindfolded, balancing a large basket of flowers on my head, I would let the audience guide me to the performance space with their hands. I would feel their hands as Mamita had felt mine, conjuring her spirit.

I have been interested in the exchange of energy between performer and audience for a long time. The vulnerability of my position (blindfolded, balancing a large basket on my head, loaded down with offerings), coupled by the touch of seeing hands, created an immediate and individual connection with audience members who assume the responsibility of participants/guardians of the performance ritual as they lead me to the performance area. Being touched and touching. We have shared a moment of intimacy and presence.

Todos Mis Muertos reminds me that we are all travelers through the cycle of life and death. The piece has the nomadic quality (present in many burial rituals) of carrying everything one needs: all sorts of *ofrendas – escapularios*, bells, photos, the yellow chair hanging from one shoulder, the yellow cloth pack containing dirt, earth, hanging from the other, the large skeleton child attached to my back, the basket of yellow flowers on my head; pockets filled with more offerings – rum, food (cornmeal, bread), more flowers, candles, matches. Actions include saluting and invoking the four directions, honoring the earth, caressing/eating the soil, dancing with the dead (the skeleton figure), mourning, conjuring, eating, drinking, dancing, communing, and finally resting in the dirt.

It has been a challenge to find ways to recreate the altar experience in a context foreign to communal Day of the Dead experiences. Irene Sosa created a video altar for me. On one screen, the image of hands digging, digging up soil, an archaeology of the dead. On another screen, the same hands dig up human bones, then photographs of the deceased, and flowers. The third screen documents the Day of the Dead altar, detailing the multiple objects and offerings. The three images form a triangle and complete a simple physical altar containing photos, candles, flowers, water, and food offerings for the dead. The triangle configuration evokes multiple levels of experience: the realm of tradition in the physical/objective, the contemporary electronic realm of video, bridging time and space; the ephemeral/energetic/spiritual reflected in the performance.

Embodying Venezuela

María Elena Ramos

Translated by Eduardo Aparicio

Venezuelan visual artists gained international acclaim in the 1950s because of their investigations of abstraction and kineticism. The 1960s were a period of transition in which new forms of figuration emerged. From the end of the 1960s to the beginning of the 1980s, there was intense activity in the experimental arena of body art. Performance was influenced by a way of being Venezuelan that is very open to international influence and Western ideas of universality, and by the great national traditions of twentieth century art – that is, abstraction, constructivism, kineticism, on the one hand, and the figurative and organicist tradition on the other. Added to these influences at the end of the 1970s was another twentieth-century tradition, that of conceptual art.

Several performance artists had studied or exhibited or engaged in street actions in England, France, Italy, and Austria. Others had studied dance and theater in New York.[1] However, while the aesthetic concerns of European and American performance are important to these artists, performance art in Venezuela, as well as in other parts of Latin America, evidences a particularly critical interest in social, idiosyncratic, and political processes. These artists incorporate into their body actions such local themes as Venezuelan oil production, the myth of El Dorado, the country's beauty queen industry, the recovery of traditional saint-day celebrations and popular games, *santería* and other syncretisms. Events taken from the daily press are transformed into *informational actions*.

The great majority of performances were made for secluded spots, garages, rivers, or small parks, an art even to be made below the ground of the urban space. And although almost invariably their pieces would end up being presented at museums, many artists preferred an open urban culture over a restricted artistic culture. In this sense, Venezuelan artists were maintaining their principles with the respect to the avant-garde notion of privileging life over art. In our context, what was privileged were "spaces of everyday life" over "spaces of art." In many cases these artists' preference for marginal spaces was more of an ideal or a postulate than a reality to be fulfilled, because in the end, almost invariably, the only spaces available were the sacred spaces of the museum.

Artists experimented not only with their bodies, the spaces, and the media, but also with labeling. They called their works action poems, informational events, information-actions, situations, body ritual, ceremonies, infiltrations, no-performance, live action, body gesturing, environment-sculpture, living sculpture, body poetry, non-verbal languages. In this article, I will analyze the work done by a number of artists who have left their mark in Venezuelan body art.

Pedro Terán

From 1970 through 1985, Pedro Terán (b. 1943) was one of the most significant figures in Venezuelan performance art. He studied in Italy (1964–66) and England (1967–75 and 78–79). Terán began his performances in London in 1970. In 1969 he received the second-place award (The Multiple Competition, Ikon Gallery, Birmingham) for his piece *Levitate* (Levitate). "Terán relates the title of the piece not only to matter in suspension, but also to the spiritual states of levitation."[2] This would become one of his primary obsessions, a means by which he could relate weight and levity, body and mind, visible object and symbolic power.

Terán's work also deals with spaces, forms, and myths of the Americas. He combined his interest in levitation with the mental powers of an American shaman in such performances as *Nubes para Colombia* (Clouds for Colombia) (1981). He dealt with the myth of El Dorado, which mobilized Europeans to the Americas and which gives color, texture, and patina to the body of the artist in his actions; and the eternal search for Manoa in *Mapas, Suelos y Relaciones de Manoa* (Maps, Terrains, and Relations of Manoa) (1988), *Reino de Manoa en La Habana* (The Kingdom of Manoa in Havana) (IV Bienal de la Habana, 1991). In the *Universo de Manoa* (Reverse of Manoa), Terán inverts heaviness and lightness and finds in the stones and soil of the Americas the lightness of a spiritual force that imposes itself.

In *Estudio de Torso No 1–1 No Torso de Estudio* (Torso Study Number 1–1 Study Torso) (1980–81) a performance created in allusion to the piece *Estudio de Torso* (Torso Study) by Venezuelan master Cristóbal Rojas, Terán positioned himself between two rooms, at the dividing line between art from the Colonial period and Venezuelan art since the Republic, thus questioning the breakdown of history into periods. For this piece he was gagged and his hands were tied, as if to signal the difficulties in communication encountered by new artforms.

Using Polaroid photographs, which have been loyal companions in his events, and with his Shamanic Maracca, and, above all, with his ironic humor, he presented his *Cuerpo de Premios* (Body of Awards) (1981), a performance piece critical of exhibition awards and the idea of art as object of consumption, an event for which not only was he awarded First Place in Nonobjective Art, but he accepted the award.

22. Carlos Zerpa
Ceremonia con Armas Blancas (Ceremony with Knives), 1981
Caracas, Venezuela
Photo: Abel Naim

Carlos Zerpa

Carlos Zerpa (b. 1950) is a body artist with a passion for the syncretic cultures of
Latin America. He has produced work that has spanned religious themes, popular
hybridity between Catholicism and parallel religions, patriotic values and nationalism, political violence, and erotic violence. In his *Ceremonia con Armas Blancas*
(Ceremony with Sharp-Edged Weapons), Zerpa assumed the position of many
men who live between machismo, mawkishness, fetishism, and violence. In other
events, where the nation is the theme, he leads us into a reflection of other false
way of being. *Yo Soy la Patria* (I Am the Fatherland), *Tres Tiempos para la Patria*
(Three Times for the Fatherland), *Patriamorfosis* (Fatherlandmorphosis), *Señora
Patria, Sea Usted Bienvenida* (Welcome, Mrs. Motherland), and *Caliente-Caliente:
Cuatro Momentos en la Vida de la Patria* (Hot, Hot: Three Moments in the Life
of a Nation), present to us what Elsa Flores calls,

> Counter-rituals. These take advantage of the ritual structure, even with
> an attitude somewhere in between that of a priest and a shaman, to exert
> a strong critique of the idols of patriotism and Venezuelan jingoism, the
> institutions, the prejudices, and above all, the injustices that the notion of
> motherland allows and encourages.[3]

Zerpa's work points to the absence of essential truths, and the constant coverup
of such absence; a covering which is always sensorially excessive, in order to hide
the absence of a true center, presenting under the guise of love for our motherland what is so often a lack of true commitment. Zerpa stages characters that he
critiques. He uses boxes and display cases that he turns into "counter-altars," thus
subverting their religious meaning. His boxes and body actions of the 1970s,
which deal with fetishized religious objects indicate that he was not an atheist or
free thinker, or a conceptual artist who simply reflected on the discourse of religion, and its trivialization and commercialization. Zerpa sought to be sacrilegious,
and to provoke to the point that members of the community and of the Church
confronted him.

Diego Barboza

The *action* poems by Diego Barboza (b. 1945) express the harmony of a man
with his neighbors, as well as that of man with nature and history. A prominent
painter and draughtsman, Barboza was part of several avant-garde artist groups
in the 1960s. As a promoter of *mailart*, he created action poems of the 1970s
and 1980s about encounters among people. He has referred to his pieces as
"Acontecimientos de Arte como gente – gente como arte" (Events of Art as

People, People as Art). Traditional celebrations in our towns, or those remaining from more peaceful times in our cities, such as *retretas* (open-air band concerts), religious celebrations, carnival, *bambalinas* (scenes), and *piñatas* in children's parties, provide a strong basis for his body art and conceptual art done with his own body, such as *Pro-testas* (Pro-tests) (Fundarte, 1981) or *De la Escuela de Atenas a la Nueva Escuela de Caracas* (From the School of Athens to the New School of Caracas) (1985). In the 1970s, Barboza also created several performances in London. Of his work there, Frank Popper writes:

> A typical example of the attempt to involve the public on the streets, is the activity of the New London Arts Lab in both London and Paris in 1970. Diego Barboza organizes what he calls "Expressions" in the street . . . They are . . . a way of triggering off a particular kind of psychological behavior. They act upon the public, that is to say upon individuals, forming more or less ephemeral groups. It is in this sense that we must take such demonstrations as the "Expressions", "Art tamed and wild", "Art and life" and nowadays "Actions". The role of the artist in these projects is strictly limited to the type and intensity of the "pretext" which he provides in the hope of arousing psychological reactions in the public."[4]

Marco Antonio Ettedgui

Marco Antonio Ettedgui (1958–81) was above all a communicator: "What is art in a petroleum based culture and society?" the artist would ask. He has a profound sense of being in the world, especially of being in Caracas, which made him into an artist whose body-art principles became part of his sense of personal commitment and experience. Influenced by a the spirit of the period that posited life as being more important than art, he approached life as divided into two realms: that which was lived in his community, and that which was presented and represented in the media. One of his primary sources of material for his work was the press: "The work is based on a real event that occurred or is occurring in the life of the city," he would say. He saw art as an efficient way of transforming reality. Titles of his pieces include *Harmony, Conflict and Tension in My Work Relations* and *Encounters with Traffic to Find a Solution to My Personal Problems*. Ettedgui also celebrated his twenty-second birthday in a performance at the National Art Gallery with a piece called *Happy Birthday Marco Antonio*. He died shortly thereafter in an accident on stage in 1981.

23. Diego Rísquez
A Propósito del Hombre de Maíz (Regarding the Man of Corn), 1979
Caracas, Venezuela

Diego Rísquez

The video performances, living sculptures, and *Naturalezas Vivas* (Unstill Lives) of Diego Rísquez (b. 1949) are informed by his experience with Super-8 film and his early work as a stage actor. His films are probably among the most personal expressions of *body actions* in Latin America. In his films, which are a rare synthesis of performance, living sculpture, historical cinema, and conceptual art, Rísquez focuses on the great themes, locations, and personalities of our national history, while simultaneously showing a loving respect for traditional Venezuelan visual culture and an unprejudiced transgression of our national myths.

Between 1981 and 1988, Rísquez produced his trilogy: *Bolívar, Sinfonía Tropikal* (Bolívar, A Tropical Symphony), *Orinoko Nuevo Mundo* (Orinoco New World), and *Amerika, Terra Incognita* (America, Terra Incognita). These films are *mises-en-scène*, using cinematic language, of living tableaux taken from Venezuelan painting in the historic genre. Rísquez returns to the time of the conquest and the colony, to the time of Bolívar´s revolution and liberation, and to his heroes, showing the myths that have been constructed in our willful search for identity, as well as those myths that Europeans have shaped in their bewildered gaze upon the Americas.

It is also interesting that his is a reflexive look at history, since Rísquez bases his work on very well-known paintings by nineteenth-century Venezuelan artists, such as Arturo Michelena or Juan Lovera. He is thus able to approach the sensibility of the average Venezuelan, since we have all studied our national history with textbooks illustrated with these paradigmatic images, which are part of our childhood memories and are current symbols in our visual imaginary.

Finally, it should be noted that Rísquez also succeeded in two other syntheses: that of visual art of the past with the art of the present (historical paintings and contemporary body art), and that of historical social and political figures from past centuries represented by known figures in Venezuelan cultural circles of the 1970s and 1980s, (Rísquez among them), who lent their bodies and gestures for these peculiar cinematic body actions, unique in contemporary Latin American art.

Rolando Peña

If petroleum has become so generalized and all-encompassing in Venezuela to the point that we no longer perceive it, Rolando Peña (b. 1942) succeeds in giving it back its materiality and presence, making us aware of its supremacy. He successfully chooses some very basic objects (oil barrel, derrick, crane, rocker arm) taken not only from the oil industry, but also from the *rhetoric* of language about oil.

Significantly, the barrel that his work refers to no longer exists. It is a symbol and a code. Peña draws out the resemblance between this and a society in which locations retain the names of town squares that no longer exist, in a country where the homes of the heroes and our national monuments have given way to skyscrapers.

In some of his performances, in addition to incorporating petroleum as an axis, and time as a central structure in body action, Peña seems to welcome rejection and even tedium. This is how, in the Caracas of his videos, time passes while nothing appears to be happening, leaving on the viewer a sense of criticism and emptiness, of both tension and sleepiness.

Peña studied at the Martha Graham Dance School (1963 and 1966), the Alwin Nikolai School (1967 and 1970), and Merce Cuningham Dance Studio (1971). While living in New York, he staged *Shows Sicodélicos* (Psychedelic Shows) with Allen Ginsberg and Timothy Leary. Befriended by Andy Warhol, he was nurtured in the New York avant-garde movements of the 1960s. His happenings on the streets of New York City earned him the name of Príncipe Negro (Black Prince), a name that is still with him, about which John Stringer wrote:

> Black could be associated with an endless variety of topics: Satanism, formal attire, evil, fanaticism, formality, darkness, infinity, in contrast with Prince, which is a word that has a more specific meaning in Peña's recent work with petroleum: a black substance that symbolizes wealth and power. The expression "black gold" finds a literal representation in Peña's recent tableaux, since in our times, petroleum has become a standard measure of the economy, in much the same way as gold bars used to be.[5]

In the 1980s, Peña started to create works dealing with oil, central to the Venezuelan economy and the modern symbol of our nationality. The elements of oil exploitation and distribution – the rigs, the barrels, the towers – were transformed by Peña into elements of a visual arts language which he used in installations, performances, drawings, sculptures, and prints. Oil became a focus in his work as a representation of identity and a point of departure for critique. Peña made several works in the 1980s about petroleum, including *Crude Oil* (New York, 1980); *Oil* (New York, 1981); *Este Petróleo es Mío* (This Oil is Mine), *The Tower* (1981); *Mene, Devotional Object* (1982); *El Petróleo Soy Yo* (I Am Petroleum) (1985); *Llévense una Venezuela Suya* (Take Your Own Venezuela with You), and *Totem of Our Time*, which was reviewed in *High Performance*:

> The artist stood up grabbing an iron pick with which he punctured the three full barrels hanging from the ceiling. From the first barrel, crude oil started

to flow down to help . . . plexiglass container. From the second barrel metallic gold paint was poured until the barrel was empty. From the third, red paint, in a quite obvious reference to blood, was being poured . . . The artist grabbed, then, a fog machine, making it work in the direction of the audience . . . which caused the audience to leave the place. The sound track . . . actually recorded at an oil refinery in Venezuela . . . included sounds of oil pumps and the blowing of the wind at the Lake Maracaibo.[6]

Rolando Peña presents a wide range of images of himself as jester and charlatan, as unstable and superficial, as experimenter and creator. His language, which is a reflection of our nation and the ways in which it is constructed and perceived, reproduces the contradictions of a Venezuelan way of being that is critical and complacent, accusatory, and indifferent, mythifying, and irreverent. At the same time disbelieving of himself and in need of finding himself, Peña approaches those languages that the nation uses to communicate with us and that we in turn use to communicate with it.

Antonieta Sosa

Antonieta Sosa (b. 1940) accomplishes a synthesis of the abstract-constructivist heritage she received from Venezuelan art and the organic and sensorial freedom of her body in process. In *Del Cuerpo al Vacío* (From the Body into the Void), a situation in three acts (1985), three of her early abstract paintings of grids and illusory geometric cubical forms are placed on the wall. In front of them stands a large scaffolding, which draws out a possible interpretation of the paintings as a place for existing and vibrating like scaffolding.

Sosa moved on the scaffolding the way the sloth, a slow-moving animal, moves through trees in town squares throughout Venezuela. Space is also constructed here with the sounds that emanate from the stomach of the artist, her chest, her throat, her nose, and her head. Thus, the body became a vocal instrument. Of this performance, the artist stated:

By learning about Grotowsky's techniques with voice resonators, I was able to use these techniques in my personal expression. These sounds are not necessarily screams, they are much more subtle than that. They can be tainted with tenderness, with rage, or resemble the sounds made by birds, insects, or other animals. This is not something that I can control with my mind. It's something that happens once I'm able to connect.[7]

In the same way that her abstract painting transformed into the scaffolding of the world, Sosa's abstract sculpture opens up, transforming itself into a chair, the support for the live body. The abstraction also unfolds in the world of the senses. And the idea unfolds as an object, so that the body can express itself and be. Sosa suggests that some ideas need volume and a space that open up to the body in movement. Her series of chairs represents a kind of sculptural language that can only be understood as a permanent intermediary zone-always present in her work – between the most abstract, organizing reason and the most lively body action.

Yeni and Nan

Nature lovers Yeni and Nan worked under the assumption that the persistent core of performance art is the persistence of time itself: the passing of time and the metamorphosis that takes place within it, the observation of what only time allows: the cycles of life, of nature, of all that exists and is capable of transformation. From 1978 to 1986 they visited the cycles of life with their births and transformations, and the cycles of matter, with their interventions in water, saline solution, air, or earth.

Their approach to nature began with a self-reflection on their own natural process: they projected their bodies from gestation to adulthood, and death. *Nacimiento* (Birth) (1979); *Arte Artista* (Artist Art) (1980); and *Acción Divisoria del Espacio* (Dividing Action of Space) (1981) are some of the performances from their first period. In juxtaposition to those artists who armed themselves with a denunciation of the urban environment and thematic violence, Yeni and Nan brought to the art scene a sense of recuperating the body as a poetic support. In their work, necessarily elliptical, they succeeded in symbolizing in just a half-hour of performance, one or several of the major life cycles.

In *Integraciones en Agua* (Integrations in Water) (1981) they presented their submerged bodies, maximizing contact with the water and with the walls of the small, clear plastic container. The water in this case was in relation to the natural cycle of rivers and evaporation, snow and glaciers, rains and cascades, and the ocean from which it originated at the beginning of life. Water served to integrate symbols of origin and survival, such as psychic integrity, transformations of space, going through the stages of being full, empty, desiccated, in a self-referential use of language related to body actions: gestures for submerging, gestures for emerging, gestures for waiting for the void.

They later worked with rock salt, going to salt pits known as Salinas de Araya in *Simbolismo de la Cristalización. Hombre-Sal II* (Symbolism of Crystallization: Man-Salt II) (1986), a natural and aesthetic sanctuary in Venezuela, where what is liquid becomes solid, crystallizing and consolidating, but retaining its traits, such as surface shine, transparency or translucency, change of color under the light, light conductivity. In Araya, they transformed salt into image. The natural crystals were re-spatialized into a rectangle. The performance incorporated a reflection on the abstract, and the contact of body and salt became a body action.

In *Transfiguración Elemento Tierra* (Transfiguration, Earth Element) (1983), during the performance the loss of water is associated with diminished vitality or elasticity. A part of the face, covered with earth that was progressively dried (as shown in Polaroid or video close-ups), could be read as a metaphor for aging or a poetic reference to an arid, abandoned zone in the geography closest to us: a cracked rock or a fragment of desert. Nature is thus represented to us in a threefold process of distancing: as concept, metaphor, and audiovisual medium.

Roberto Obregón

Roberto Obregón (b. 1946) has dedicated himself to a limited range of themes (the rose, the mountain) to which he responds with different media. He observes both real, primary nature, as well as the secondary nature (art), with the dedication of a fine bibliophile of rare books. A patient record keeper, faithful and loving in his documentary passion, Obregón plants a rose bush in the garden of the museum. In *Acción No 5. Für Elisa Oder Elisa Nimm Deine Rose* (Action No. 5. For Elisa, or Elisa Take Your Rose) (1980), the artist follows the process of development of a rose bush from planting to blooming, and cutting. The artist participates with his body as agent of the acts of birth and existence. A vegetable life is transformed throughout its natural stages, and at the end the artist makes a photographic record of the process. Then, in *Alternativa I* (Alternative I), (Galería de Arte Nacional – Ateneo de Caracas, 1983), Obregón slowly constructed a paper flower, approaching the rose as an artifice and, thus, its cultivation as a form of culture.

As he plants, waters, follows, or nurtures a rose, when he picks it up after it falls, when he pulls out its petals, Obregón also keeps an hourly record, a chronicle of the various forms throughout time: waiting, growing, blooming, reaching fullness, maturing, falling, dying, possibly becoming extinct as a species. His action is a silent witnessing of nature's processes and of the transfigurations of nature into culture.

Teowald D'Arago

Teowald D'Arago (b. 1947) has divided his work into theoretical reflections, which he pursues as a university philosophy professor, and his participation in conceptual and action art. *Infiltrations* is the general term he uses to refer to his performances. According to D'Arago, "art is not a question of shaping shapes." In his *Infiltración No 2: Una Limosna para el Arte* (Infiltration No. 2: An Alm for Art) (Caracas, 1981) he circulated wearing placards on his chest or back, or distributing photocopies of paper money on days of major museum openings. These languages were still not understood or were underestimated in the 1970s and 1980s. D'Arago himself has presented a completely dematerialized art, by proposing philosophical ideas as pieces with no visibility or physicality.

The artist frequently employs critical humor. For example, for *Infiltración No 3: Estudio de Mercado* (Infiltration No. 3: Marketing Research), (Galería de Arte Nacional, 1988), D'Arago conducted a survey of the public's preferences regarding art. Expressed in percentages, those preferences (pertaining to size, color, subject matter, composition, or texture) became the basis of a performance installation, in which D'Arago created a painting based on detailed attention to the taste of those surveyed. Art thus reflects on art, language reflects on language, and theory reflects on demand, revealing the formation of habit in contemporary art. D'Arago reflects about the art market and how it imposes tastes, fixes codes, and intervenes in the very act of creativity. And he shows, with humor, that merchants are not the only ones working in the marketplace, but that many artists also end up producing works based on the preferences of someone else with money.

Juan Loyola

About the artist Juan Loyola (b. 1952), Pierre Restany wrote:

> I am aware of Juan Loyola's talent. I believe in his obstinacy and his faith in a fair cause. But he seems to be made of that emotionally hypersensitive skin that martyrs are made of. I admire him with great love and, quite honestly, I am afraid for him.[8]

Titles such as *Chatarra* (Junk Cars), *Yo Soy Venezuela* (I Am Venezuela), *Proyecto Bicentenario para un Libertador Que No Ha Podido Descansar en Paz* (Bicentennial Project for a Liberator Who Has Not Been Able to Rest in Peace), *Venezuela, Tú Me Dueles Demasiado* (Venezuela, I Hurt Too Much for You), *Venezuela, Entonces Yo Te Escucho* (Venezuela, I'm Listening to You), *Un Saludo de Amor de la Pequeña Venecia* (A Message of Love from Little Venice; a reference to Venezuela, a name whose original meaning is "Little Venice") (Venice Biennial, 1986), *Intervención y Diálogo con Paloma Tricolor* (Intervention and Dialogue with a Three-Colored Dove) (Venice Biennial, 1986), *Asalto a los Tribunales de Justicia* (Assault on the Courts of Justice) provide an idea of some of the themes in the work of Loyola, who made an impact in the Venezuelan art world of the 1980s because of his complex personality and his public confrontations.

Loyola mobilized the forces of order by means of transgressions, both informally and intentionally. His event titled *Chatarra, Intervención Urbana* (Junk Cars: An Urban Intervention) used humor and his knowledge of Venezuelan idiosyncrasy to mobilize the police in an unusual manner, making them take care of cases that should have been part of their daily tasks but would normally be ignored. Focusing on the numerous junk cars that were left abandoned, littering the streets, not removed by the authorities, Loyola made a series of performances in which he painted the damaged car bodies with the colors of the Venezuelan national flag (yellow, blue, and red). In so doing, he touched a patriotic nerve, and thus triggered police displeasure. Invariably, the authorities would remove such transgressions from the public way. By finally setting to the task of cleaning the streets, the police involuntarily *collaborated* with the artist, since they concluded the performance. Often, Loyola was required to appear at the police station.

Conclusion

Venezuelan cultural institutions gave support to the above-mentioned artists, but in general they did not initiate activities. The art world of that time was not like it is now, in which curators have a more creative participatory role and actually act as a catalyst. For that period, a person such as Marco Antonio Ettedgui, who died on stage in 1981, was key because he proposed many projects to institutions in which many different artists participated. These projects were then accepted and supported by key institutions – Fundarte: the National Gallery of Art, the Museum of Fine Arts, and the Ateneo of Caracas.

In many performances there was an implicit critique of the art market. It was evident, for example, in the work of Teowald D'Arago, Diego Barboza, and Rolando Peña. That critique was complemented by the critique that many artists made of political issues, above all over national politics, which was the focus of much of the work of Ettedgui, Zerpa, Peña, and Loyola. The critique of the oil industry as a national symbol aimed to show that the fact the country's entire economy was organized around one industry was in actuality evidence of a fundamental flaw. Another set of themes that were critiqued related to the myths of the fatherland and the hypocrisies of nationalist discourse.

Venezuelan performance artists have addressed issues from sexual violence to political violence; they have staged a birthday celebration for the artist doing a performance; and two artists conducted a real wedding ceremony. During the period in question (late 1970s to early 1980s), many performances focused on the poetic transformations of the body and of space, as explorations of the sublime by artists who had been influenced by dance, theater, Eastern disciplines, or psychology. Nature and ecology as a theme ranged from the transformation of a natural rose into a rose of culture and language, to the most direct interventions in specific Venezuelan natural sites, such as the salt pits known as Salinas de Araya or the sacred mountain in Gran Sabana.

In a more self-reflexive vein, other artists presented their performances based on figurative works of art by masters of Venezuelan painting throughout the centuries, incorporating new media and languages, to old themes and iconographies from the history of our visual arts.

Notes

1.   It should be noted that the 1970s witnessed the arrival of many international performance artists in Caracas who provided a great incentive. Charlotte Moorman (1975, Museo de Arte Contemporáneo de Caracas (MAAC)) presented works by Nam June Paik, Kosugi, Yoko Ono, Roberto Breer, and Joseph Beuys. In 1976, Antonio Muntadas presented his *Acción – situación Hoy* (Action – Situation Today) (MACC). Several Venezuelan artists participated at the 1980 Annual Avant-Garde Festival of New York: Carlos Zerpa, Rolando Peña, Diego Rísquez, and Rubén Núñez.

2.   Hernández, Carmen, "Chronology of Pedro Terán," in *Pedro Terán. Territorios de lo Ilusorio y lo Real. 1970–1995* (Caracas: Museo de Bellas Artes de Caracas, 1995).

3.   Flores, "Elsa, Introducción a la Obra de Carlos Zerpa," in the catalog *Cada Cual Con Su Santo Propio* (Sala Ocre, Caracas, 1981).

4.   Popper, Frank, *Art–Action and Participation* (New York: New York University Press, 1975), pp. 29–30.

5.   Stringer, John, *Contrastes* (Cali, Colombia, April 1984). Quoted in an article by Miguel González.

6.   *High Performance*, (volume 4, number 2, Los Angeles, summer 1981).

7.   Sosa, Antonieta, "Arte y Locura: Espacios de Creación," *Serie Editorial Reflexiones en el Museo*, Caracas: Museo de Bellas Artes, 1977) p. 136.

8.   Restany, Pierre, "El Arte de Juan Loyola," in the catalogue, *Exposición Torre ACO*, (Confinanzas, Caracas, April–May 1987).

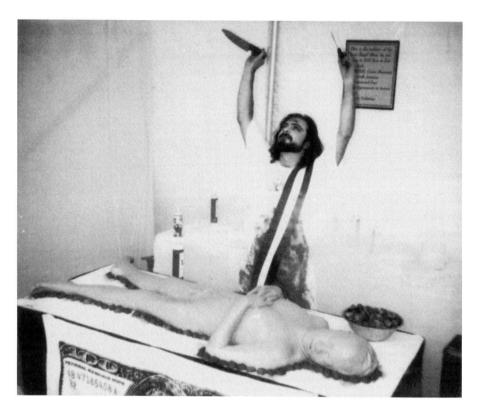

24. Cesar Martinez

PerforMANcena (Performance Meal), 1995–97

Photo courtesy of Cesar Martinez

After finishing his fine arts degree, Mexico City-based artist Cesar Martinez received training in the use of explosives to create sculptural and painterly "gestures" by activating gunpowder and dynamite. His performances and installations often reflect on the precariousness of the Mexican economy. PerforMANcena was first presented shortly after the institution of the North American Free Trade Agreement, the debilitating peso devaluation of 1994 in Mexico, and the introduction of Proposition 187 in California.

PerforMANcena (Performance-Meal)

Cesar Martinez

The Letter of Sagawa by the Japanese writer Juro Kara gave me the idea to create an edible sculpture. Kara was inspired by the letters that Issei Sagawa wrote to him from prison after killing – (for love) – a young Dutch artist and then devouring several parts of her body. This act of modern cannibalism occurred in Paris in 1981, and sparked an international scandal. Two years later the French judicial system declared him not responsible for his act.

I am also profoundly indebted to writers such as Apollinaire, the Marquis de Sade, and George Bataille, who wrote of the erotic savoriness of the human body.

I am drawing on popular cultural references as well: the symbolism of the unusual *panes de muerto* (bread of the dead), the macabre banquets, and the sugar skulls that are all part of the Day of the Dead in Mexico. Above all I was interested in the contemplation of horror that is so much a part of us as Mexicans, and that we inherited from both the indigenous peoples of Mexico and the Spaniards. During my adolescence, for example, I was fascinated by the macabre comics about Dr. Goyo Cardenas, a serial killer who would rape and dismember his victims, and then cook them and serve them as tamales in his restaurant. The sweetness of death, which is the taste of life, is the hunger of our living death.

The painting of the Italian artist Giuseppe Arciboldo (1530–93) was another important source of inspiration. Those magnificent portrait-plates made me think that at last I could consume a work with my eyes and palate. And so I began, in 1989, to create edible artworks; human heads made of transparent gelatin in a variety of tastes and colors, full of fruits and dramatically illuminated from below.

To digest a work, literally speaking, is to make it your own. You savor it as it circulates like a sweet inside of you. Then you can expel it by shitting, living with art up to that precise moment, and thus better comprehending the most routine task of your existence.

Of course, my sculptures were dietetic and were "sculpturally cooked" with electro-purified water, using the finest ingredients, chosen not only for their freshness but also for their shape, color, and taste (which were fundamental aspects of the artwork's conceptualization).

It was not until 1992, when I saw the illustrations by Theodor De Bry for *Americae Pars Tertia* by Johanes Staden von Humber (who recounts the tale of his capture by a cannibal tribe in Brazil), that I conceptualized my PerforMANcena.

The moment of political cynicism that we were living in my country, modernity's shameless historical amnesia, and the new Free Trade Agreement (play on words here between *comercio*/business and *comerse*/to eat) gave my piece a new context.

I took advantage of the rituals of Catholic Communion and those of Aztec sacrifice, and created a speech that was both political and religious, which I recited before a peach-flavored, flesh-colored corpse with a melon heart. The ranchero existentialism of certain Mexican corridos, and the amorous lyrics of the ballads of the 1950s, were blended together before the consumption of the cadaver of Ge-Latina America, in the era of the North American Cholesterol Free Trade Agreement, at the moment of this a-PRI-calypsis, at the end of the millennium:

> Everyone eat and drink from him
> for this body is the debt of blood
> the blood of the cadaver
> the one we see every day
> that everyday of all Mexicans
> The blood of our new and ethereal alliance
> that will be runneth over by the free economic transit
> and by all the governors
> for the forgiveness of sins.

25. Nao Bustamante
America the Beautiful, 1995
Mexico City
Photo: Monica Naranjo
Chicana artist Nao Bustamante first trained in postmodern dance before moving into the realm of performance in the mid-1980s. Well-known in San Francisco for the masterful comic improvisations that have made her the doyenne of the Bay Area's underground cultural scene, Bustamante's corporeal gestures form extended reflections on the social forces that confine and contain feminine creativity.

America the Beautiful (1996)

Nao Bustamante

America the Beautiful is a body-narrative that was developed over the period of a year as a structure of improvised moments within the skeleton of the tasks and tricks. I use the response of the audience to fuel my improvisation, providing the viewer with a grotesque and beautiful mirror in which to gaze.

    America the Beautiful begins with me, the performer, literally setting the stage. Through the rituals of feminine transformation, using clear packing tape and haphazard make-up, I create a distorted reality of beauty with all of its Eros and defeat. This tragic comedy takes the viewer on a bizarre circus-like adventure of ladder-climbing and breath-holding tension.

PART III

Stepping toward an oppositional public sphere

26. Marta Minujín
El Parthenón de Libros (The Parthenon of Books), 1983
Buenos Aires, Argentina
Argentine artist Marta Minujín studied in Paris in the 1960s and created her first
ephermeral works there before returning to Buenos Aires. In the late 1960s she participated in activities of Andy Warhol's Factory in New York, and eventually created a
performance in which she offered corn on the cob to Warhol as a way of paying off
Argentina's foreign debt. For her piece "The Parthenon of Books," she constructed a
replica of the Parthenon of books that had been banned by the military regime, and
invited people to dismantle the work.

Sunday, July 25, 1965

Marta Minujín

At nine in the morning, I read the dailies announcing my happening. In El Pais, it was stated that

> Today Sunday at 3pm, in the Cerro, an Art Event created by Marta Minujín will take place, in which spectators will be dragged out of their passive contemplative condition and coaxed, somewhat compulsively, into participation.
>
> The Event will not last more than twenty minutes, because the artist decided that due to the Event's intensity and element of surprise, it cannot be any longer. It is not about a spectacle because there is no established distance as in the theatre between the spectator and the actor. On the contrary the public itself is transformed into a protagonist.

The open buses were at the door of my hotel at nine on the dot, and I got onto the first one, giving the others directions to follow me. We headed south. It was a sunny Sunday in winter, and many people were out on the street. I was scanning left and right, looking for subjects for my next artwork. I looked for fat women, couples, beautiful women who dressed like chorus girls, adhesive cloth in large quantities, bags of flour, lettuce and live chickens. I had six marvelous hours to find them.

It was easy to find lovers walking arm in arm, or standing together in doorways. Stopping the buses, I would get out and invite them to participate, I told them to come to the stadium, that there was nothing to lose, that on the contrary they would part of a work of live art, that they would be creators, that they would live an adventure outside convention ... the only thing they had to do was to wrap each other in adhesive cloth, since it was a metaphysical game. It was a way of becoming part of a worldwide collage.

At first they looked at me somewhat doubtfully, but it soon seemed funny and new to get on the bus, take a ride somewhere to wrap themselves up, so few turned me down. That's how I got twenty couples.

At eleven in the morning the caravan proceeded. We went to the TV stations to look for extras, and we found people on line waiting to be chosen as members of TV audiences for Sunday morning shows: Now at this point I was looking

for fat women, and I found about nine or ten fat women on line at the two television stations. I contracted them, and I had to pay them from the budget that
the museum had given me.

The fat women had to roll around the floor in between people throughout
the entire event . . . Some of them didn't like this but since I was paying them they
accepted. It was twelve o'clock and I still needed more fat people and the chorus
girls. Then I went on to look for muscular types and motorcyclists, and to buy
chickens that had been ordered by phone, and the bags of lettuce and the talc.

Margins and Institutions: Performances of the Chilean *Avanzada*

Nelly Richard
Translated by Paul Foss and Juan Davila

The dimension of social exteriority in the production of art

The attempts to exceed the spatial limits of art, by moving away from the format of painting and the pictorial traditions toward the use of the landscape and the social body as a support for artistic creativity, represents one of the most dynamic transformations of Chilean art since the 1960s.

The gradual shift in creative thinking from traditional formats and supports to the use of the social landscape was anticipated by the work of Francisco Brugnoli, or that of his students at the University of Chile,[1] as well as in the work of the Brigadas Muralistas (Mural Artists Brigade). This organization, formed in the beginning as propaganda for Salvador Allende's 1958 and 1964 electoral campaigns, later on developed a popular form of graphics to illustrate the political program of the Unidad Popular, the most prominent examples of which were produced by the Communist Youth's Ramona Parra Brigade. Even though the Brigadas Muralistas were among the first in Chile to challenge individualistic and fetishized types of pictorial gesture, and despite the fact that they used the city, they remained within a tradition of realism by making the image subservient to an ideological message. They treated the painted wall as a monument portraying the saga of the popular movement, by means of precoded figures which *addressed the social imaginary through a program of political representation*. In other words, art continued to express a prefabricated reality by illustrating its discourse or by dressing up its stated aims. This mural art neither reformulated the urban experience by relocating the parameters for reading walls as a text of the city nor did it modify the casual perception that most citizens have of the those walls given their restricted trajectory through a grid of monuments and institutions.

Although they acknowledged the Ramona Parra Brigade as "their closest antecedent," the actual performances carried out by the group CADA (Colectivo de Actiones de Art – Art Actions Collective)[2] were different. The relationship between their art and its urban subject no longer took the form of a mural narrative of popular events. Rather, the group *redefined the conditions of their creative participation in the behavior and discourses of everyday life*. With CADA's "art actions,"

the Chilean on the street no longer saw the ornamented walls as a space for graffiti or political propaganda; he was no longer a passive spectator of images, but
actively involved in the creative process. By being urged to intervene in the entire
network of social conditioning that ensnared him, he became part of the living
material of the work through his own interaction with it.

It was from Wolf Vostell, whose works were exhibited in 1977 at the gallery
Epoca,[3] and his concept of "found lives" or the aesthetic reprocessing of the co-
ordinates of social existence, that the Chilean artists inherited their desire to
confront the dead time of the museum picture with the *living time of an art that
works with vital experiences.*

After the Exposicion de los Derechos Humanos (Exhibition of Human Rights)
at the Museum of St. Francis in 1978, the new work that evolved was based on a
different dynamic of space and time, leaving the artwork unfinished. All the works
of Lotty Rosenfeld, Juan Castillo, Parada, the Taller de Artes Visuales, Codocedo,
and Jaar have open structures; they use biography or community events as living
material so as to guarantee the *incompleteness* of the work and to solicit the viewer's
intervention to complement its meaning. The work that became the primary model
for the new Chilean art after 1979 was *Para No Morir De Hambre en el Arte* (Not to
Die for Hunger in Art). This work came from the group CADA, which was initially
composed of the artists Lotty Rosenfeld and Juan Castillo, the sociologist Fernando
Balcells, the poet Raul Zurita, and the novelist Diamela Eltit. The group's interdisciplinary composition to an extent explains its choice of approach.

Para No Morir was constructed from the actual social events. It diagnosed
the wants of the national body by using the symbol of milk to denounce poverty,
hunger, or other economic deprivations.

The overall panorama of malnutrition and lack of basic consumer or cultural
goods was presented by this work in the following manner:

- The CADA artists distributed powdered milk amongst families living in a
  shanty town on the edge of Santiago.
- A blank page of the magazine *Hoy* was made available as another support for
  the work: "Imagine that this page is completely blank/imagine that this blank
  page is the milk needed every day/imagine that the shortage of milk in Chile
  today resembles this blank page."
- A text recorded in five languages was read in front of the United Nations
  building in Santiago, thus portraying the international view of Chile as precarious and marginal.
- In the art gallery Centro Imagen there was placed an acrylic box containing
  some of the bags of powdered milk, a copy of the *Hoy* issue, and a tape of

the text read in front of the UN. The milk was left in the box until it decomposed. A statement on top of the box read: "To remain here until our people receive the proper amount of food. To remain here as a symbol in reverse of our deprived social body."

- Ten milk trucks paraded through Santiago from a milk factory to the Museum, thus highlighting for the passerby the general lack of milk.
- A white sheet was hung over the entrance to the Museum, both as a symbolic closing down of the establishment and a metaphorical denunciation of continuing hunger.

The interventions that were part of this work, and which were documented with photography and video, were attempts to modify the customary perceptions of the city. The unexpected sight of a parade of milk trucks and the altering the facade of the museum attracted attention to the social landscape, and to the way that it remained unnoticed. The groups sought to reveal the social norms that regulate the behavior of the citizens, by intervening in the field of social productivity – the milk industry, the networks controlling the distribution of magazines, and the institutional space of art discourse.

Another collective work performed by CADA in 1981 was *Ay, Sudamerica!* (O, South America!). Once again, they used the concept of interfering in the models of everyday life prescribed by society, but this time they engaged in "social sculpture"[4] to designate the degree to which their art practices could reconfigure interpersonal relations in the community in new aesthetic terms. For *Ay, Sudamerica!*, three airplanes dropped leaflets over poor sectors of Santiago. These leaflets included the following statement: ". . . the work of improving the accepted standard of living is the only valid art form/the only exhibition/the only worthwhile works of art. Everyone who works, even in the mind, to extend his or her living space is an artist."

The proposition contained in the leaflet was also stated in the magazine *Apsi*. It was an attempt to compel readers to unlearn the habits reinforced by the conventional press. Through this new poetics of word and image, the discourse of the imaginary collided with the discourse of political contingency.

Both *Para No Morir* and *Ay, Sudamerica!* were shaped by the multiple social dimensions of their artistic framework. The Chilean subject postulated by them is inserted in everyday community activities, while the works themselves incorporated this subject in their own procedures for socially and politically redefining the real.[5]

These two works from the group CADA significantly influenced the new work of artists such as Castillo, Donoso, Saavedra, and Parada, with their use of the city and its social landscape as a support for art. These artists operated in a space that provided an alternative to that of the art institution.[6] They produced a critique of museums and galleries, accusing them of endorsing, according to Fernando Balcells, "the bourgeois ideological space and the way that it separates art from reality" and "the elitism assigned to artworks by the authorities."

The official status of the museum and its discourse on art was thrown into question by the 1981 performance piece *Transito Suspendido* (No Through Traffic) by Carlos Altamirano. But CADA's metaphorical closing down of the sanctuary of art best epitomized the attempt to challenge such patrimony or preservation of the past from outside the museum through the interweaving of creative and social space-times. In the work of CADA, the city became its own museum, but only in the sense that its repressive structure was revealed by altering the landscape through art actions.

The institution of the Museum is based on material structures which ideologically condition the value of artworks, in particular those endorsing their ahistoricity. The illusion of eternity that is created places the artworks outside time by neutralizing all trace of the concrete historical circumstances under which they were produced. These were the sort of structures which CADA's "art actions" tried to dismantle, by reasserting the viewing subject's actual physical participation in the construction of the artwork; the actions refused to become trapped in the past under the extemporaneous gaze of the museum visitor. Thus, for these works, to question the Museum meant that they also had to question the rituals of perception consecrated by the ceremonial hanging of work, as well as the effect of confinement imposed on them by the institutional apparatus.

Both the Museum and the Gallery are inherently criticized by works displayed outside, and which contest "the private ownership of the salon work" or "the increasingly ritual nature" of its contemplation in those privileged areas[7] defined by CADA as a "concealed bomb": "the gallery is therefore absolutely analogous to that certain spatial notion we have of ourselves." It is not insignificant that one text from the group CADA condemning the *self-referentiality* of the gallery space, published on the occasion of an exhibition by Codocedo at the Galeria Sur in 1983, was called *Contingencia* (Contingency). The radical critique of the art concentrated in galleries happened to coincide with the celebration of ten years under military regime (September 1983). At this time, collective works emerged in which the artist "chose to address the walls of the city and voice their protest with the brief and simple cry, *No +*, which encouraged others to fill in the missing word: for instance, no more hunger, no more pain, no more death" (*Hoy*, September 1983). The walls, whose use was forbidden throughout the regime, were reconquered by the CADA artists as places for a popularly committed art.

This phase of production corresponding to the work of urban intervention came to an end because of the absence of new propositions and because, after 1982, many young artists returned to painting and to the gallery circuit. The retreat of art practice once more to the picture and to institutionalized spaces coincided with the failure of democracy, and destroyed any illusion of change. *The private*, or the subjective pictorial imaginary, replaced *the public* as the scene of art production. After all that effort to establish the outside as a place for art, the return to the picture protected the artist against their personal disillusionment with History. Thereafter, only a few works were concerned with the social space: for example, the 1983 *Paisaje* (Landscape) by Francisco Brugnoli and Virginia Errazuriz, or the 1984 *Que Hacer?* (What to Do?) by Gonzalo Diaz and Justo Mellado, tried to *invert* this space by theoretically relating the outside (the social) to the inside (the gallery, whose discourse of art about art is tautological). These works attempted to redefine metaphorically the conventions of the gallery, whether by parodying its architecture or by calling its visual topology a "landscape."

On the other hand, Lotty Rosenfeld has insistently remained outside the *protected* spaces of the institution, and continues to desecrate the cult of art as a market fetish by utilizing the streets. Since 1979, she has traced crosses on the road as a way of altering the codes of urban movement: in the desert of northern Chile, in front of the White House in Washington, on the border between Chile and Argentina, on the Pacific Coast, etc: "The dividing lines on the street are traversed by the white cloth to from a cross chain of crosses in order to transgress the road signs which regulate the traffic" (Balcells).

By rearranging the marks which regulate the social landscape, the work of Rosenfeld exposes the ideal expressed by a linear system of urban transportation. Her work not only symbolically alters this space by converting the minus sign into a plus sign, *thus contravening the one-way traffic of meaning*, but it also violates the grammar of order imposed by the inner network of social communication. She brings the road sign and its legibility into crisis by reconjugating the vertical and horizontal lines as a (feminine) act of dissidence.

The premise of Rosenfeld's crosses is that the road sign appears to be the most inoffensive of signs. She submits them to inversion. This not only makes the traveler alert to the possibility of violating the geography of transportation, but also has an even greater metaphorical impact in the Chilean context. Her gesture of *intersecting the code* is disobedient in that it provides a basis for rearticulation of meaning.

The rhetoric of the body

It is at the level of what we understand as everyday life, namely the intersubjective microcircuits existing within the couple or the family, work, domestic organization, urban movements, etc., that the division between *the public* (the sphere of social productivity) and *the private* (everything outside that sphere) can be traced. This division is necessarily strategic in countries like Chile: here authoritarianism penetrates the everyday (for example, through the familial myths surrounding the woman[8]) because it abolishes the distinction between the political and the apolitical, and disguises the fact that this distinction is itself inherently political.

The body is the stage on which this division primarily leaves it mark. It is the meeting place of *the individual* (or one's biography and unconscious) and *the collective* (or programming of the roles of identity according to the norms of social discipline). That is why its utilization as a support for art practice entails the dismantling of the ideological use of the body as a vehicle for images or representation of the rituals of day-to-day living, as a material bearer of the means of social reproduction and the models or sexual domination.

The body is the physical agent of the structures of everyday experience. It is the producer of dreams, the transmitter and receiver of cultural messages, a creature of habits, a desiring machine, a repository of memories, an actor in the theater of power, a tissue of affects and feelings. Because the body is at the boundary between biology and society, between drives and discourse, between the sexual and its categorization in terms of power, biography and history, it is the site *par excellence* for transgressing the constraints of meaning or what social discourse prescribes as normal.

There is no significant record of any use of the body in Chilean art prior to 1973. Then in 1975 two major works appeared, triggering the entired discussion of the body which took place after that time within the *avanzada* scene. One was Carlos Leppe's *Perchero* (Coat Hanger), performed at the Modulos y Formas gallery in 1975, which marked the first photographic treatment of the male nude disguised as a woman in Chilean art. The other was Raul Zurita's act of self-atonement in burning part of his face, thus initiating the form of poetry which he later on came to develop in his first book, *Purgatorio* (1979), which featured his mutilated face on the cover. These two events anticipated and encapsulated the double reference of the body that remained active during this period: the body as a place of sacrifice or painful acts (Zurita and Eltit), and the body as a place of mimesis or the use of simulacra (Leppe), one bordering on literature while the other on theatricality.

After his first live body performance, *Happening de las Gallinas* (Happening of the Chickens), in 1973 at the Carmen Waugh gallery, Carlos Leppe continues to stage photographic self-portraits. The pose in his 1975 *Retrato con Hilos* (Portrait with Strings Attached), which frustrates any indulgence in narcissism, shows his identity somewhat constrained in a social web of resignations and compromises, as a metaphor for the blackmailing of the self that is suffered by the Chilean subject. The same severe presentation occurred in his 1977 performance at Cromo, *Restitucion de Escena* (Scene of the Crime), in which the photographic document, again a self-portrait, was reflected in an entire arrangement of objects emphasizing the repressive social landscape of a body traversed by zones of incarceration (prisons or psychiatric hospitals) or by places of sexual exploitation (brothels).

Leppe followed this this first series of photographic references to the socially violated body with a long period of video performances. He used different techniques for disguising identity (the pose, make-up, theatrical costumes, and impersonations) as a response to the tyranny of social roles. This fantasy of *touching up one's image* defies that form of identity that remains identical to itself in the imitation of a model, which remains unique and definitive through unalterable marks of itself.[9]

Leppe's performances presented a parody of the self. This disguising of identity or role-changing was a strategy of appearances, of altering the substance of the body. The face was an expressive ruse of a merely rhetorical self, playfully falsifying that rogue's gallery or demand for an identity expressed by society in its photographic inventories. Leppe's "mountain of lies" was a response to the pressure to remain faithful to the roles that society deemed fixed or inexchangable.

From his first quotation of the male nude in *Perchero* to his use of feminine rhetoric or artifice of signs, Leppe postulated the body as a *tissue of quotations*, interweaving photographic, theatrical, and cosmetic references to different models of the body, and constructing identity in a game of otherness. His body quotations referred to a fragmented self that was never psychological or interiorized, but that defied all depth and challenged the essentialist notion of the self. His use of the body defined the subject as a combinatory of signs of collective identity within the discontinuous perimeter of the individual.

Whereas Leppe postulated the body as a game of appearances and reinvented its image by maneuvering its external signifiers, Zurita and Eltit promoted the body's "concrete substance of pain" in acts of resignation and self-denial. Their various mortifications of the body signaled a type of subjectivity modeled on *sacrifice* or martyrdom: Raul Zurita burned his face (1975) or attempted to blind himself (1980), Diamela Eltit cut and burned herself and then turned up at a brothel where she read part of her novel (1980). By inflicting these emblems of the wounded body upon themselves, Zurita and Eltit appealed to pain as a way of approaching that borderline between individual and collective experience:

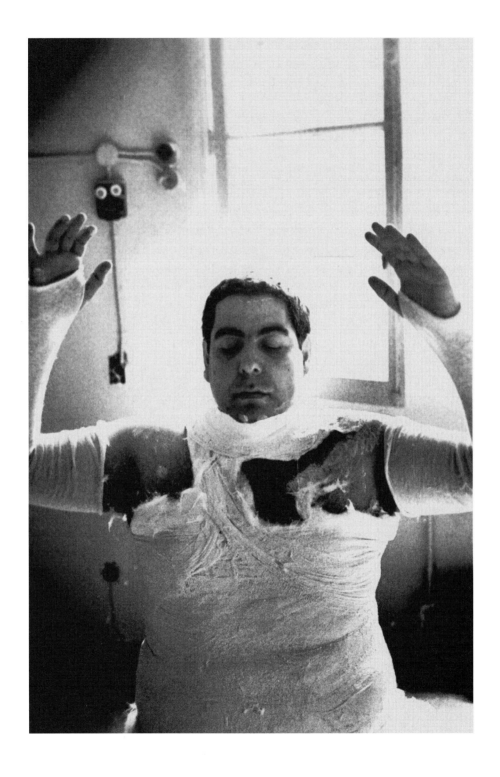

their self-punishment merges with an "us" that is both redeemer and redeemed. The threshold of pain enabled the mutilated subject to enter areas of collective identification, sharing in one's own flesh the same signs of social disadvantage as the other unfortunates. Voluntary pain simply legitimates one's incorporation into the community of those who have been harmed in some way[10] – as if the self-inflicted marks of chastisement in the artist's body and the marks of suffering in the national body, as if pain and its subject, could unite in the same scar.

The acts of mortification used by Zurita and Eltit belong to that primitive tradition of communal sacrifice, or the ritual exorcism of violence. Even though not every manifestation of marginality need pass through a process of self-torture, such acts do enable one to purge oneself through the mystical experience of going beyond the self. The register of the sacred in Zurita and Eltit, to which most of their rhetorical figures of the body refer, undoubtedly explain the fascination with their work in Chile. At a time when the real is forbidden, there is *demand for the symbolic*, a demand which their Christian message is able to satisfy.

There were two models of body art which influenced the Chilean art scene: the body of Leppe, who simulated the sexual categorization of identity in order to *denounce it or interchange its signs*, and the stigmatized body of Zurita and Eltit, who used pain in order to recapture the communal body of suffering. These bodies organized or even opposed two kinds of discourse regarding the ideological maneuvers that each favored or rejected: Leppe's materialistic body, or the theater in which the fiction of the body is dismantled, and the utopian body of Zurita and Eltit, whose sacrificial scars evoke the humanism (and not only Christian humanism) on which the metaphysics of identity depends. In spite of their many differences, the work of Leppe, Zurita, and Eltit all proposed the body as a vehicle for artistic language. This convergence can be explained in the following ways:

1   They all used *biography as a support for creativity*. Since 1980 and his installation "Sala de Espera" (Waiting Room), and without mentioning the earlier reference to castration in *Perchero*, Leppe has utilized his *mother*, who recites or sings in his videos. The maternal referent acts as a *vector of identity* to endorse his use of biography; it also acts as an intensive source of vocal activity.

27. Carlos Leppe
"Sala de Espera" (Waiting Room), video installation, 1980
Galeria Sur, Santiago, Chile
Photo courtesy of Nelly Richard
In "*Sala de Espera*" Leppe uses transvestism to address the fragmentation of identity.

The form of biography at work in Leppe and Zurita does not function as mere background to the psychology of the authors or their respective imaginaries. On the contrary, it is used to *objectify* the articulation of meaning in the subjective structures of artistic creation. Also, their work parodied the role of psychoanalytic interpretation in art, either by revealing the supposedly concealed figures of unconscious discourse (in Leppe, castration of the mother) or by utilizing clinical information concerning the artist's split personality or mental imbalance as a source of creativity (Zurita).

2   Both Leppe and Eltit have a dialectical relation to language and to the norms controlling all verbal communication by reassessing the perceptual parts of the body, like the skin or the voice, in order to make the verbal code heterogeneous. *They effect a dissolution of the word by replacing the sign's communicative function with non-linguistic textures.*

First, they used the gesture to deviate from a linear chain of information and establish a new semantic space. Second, the *voice* was made corporeal, either in the scream (Eltit) or the song (Leppe). Third, the *skin* becomes a surface of inscription (the wound in Eltit, cultural ideograms in Leppe).

Quotation provided Leppe with new modes of transcription: *cutaneous* in the case of his 1979 *Acción de la Estrella* (Star Performance), where Duchamp's star-shaped tonsure was duplicated on the artist's own head, or *vocal*, as in his 1981 *El Dia Que Me Quieraas* (The Day You'll Love Me), where Leppe imitates the singer Carlos Gardel by mouthing the words of his taped voice. This new mode of quotation through performance art reinscribes the cultural fragment in the living body as a web of *affects* and of enunciation.

3   In the work of Leppe, as in that of Zurita and Eltit, sexuality always has a symbolic function with regard to the reformulation of the categories of identity:

Leppe staged the Oedipal referent (castration, and the biographical overdetermination of the maternal role) and transvestism by playing with the formation of sexual roles.

Zurita postulated himself as a subject who challenges representation through the *sexual indifferentiation* of his categories of identity.[11]

Eltit made a dual criticism of the discourse which sexualizes the woman according to the dominant representations. First, the self-mortification of her

28. Diamela Eltit
Maipu, 1980
Santiago, Chile
Photo courtesy of Nelly Richard
Eltit washes pavement in front of a brothel.

body testifies to a refusal to accept the model of beauty which makes a fetish of the woman.[12] Second, because she gives a kiss in the street to an old tramp freely (which is depicted in her 1982 video performance *El Beso* (The Kiss)), she violates the law of amorous exchanges and disrupts the network of sexual transaction, including prostitution, where the woman is caused to offer herself for nothing.

In fact, in all of Eltit's work the woman is portrayed in situations that locate her on the edge of the social system, or on the verge of being excluded from its symbolic contract. These situations exacerbate her sense of alienation in a world ruled by masculine representations; borderline situations where she has to make the most of her relationship to language and its codes of representation and identity.

Zurita and Eltit both postulate the body as productive of signs, as something whose language wavers between that which is said or can be translated, and that which cannot be said or translated in the terms of existing thought. Marking the body, such as Zurita's gesture or scorching his cheek and then using it as a premise for writing his *Purgatorio*, is equivalent to bringing about an encounter between writing and what precedes it (that which cannot be put into words, or exceeds the system of symbolic structuring or *uncodified by any discourse.*)

Similarly, when Zurita responded to the provocation of Juan Davila's paintings by violently ejaculating in front of them as an art action, he was only emphasizing the power of the body to disrupt, sexualize, and bring into crisis the socio cultural norms of the dominant pictorial format.[13] The body was used to criticize the function of the imposed language and signification by disrupting the superior and ordered schemas of linguistic rationality. Zurita and Eltit staged the body as the indomitable Other – or inverse – of language. In their work, the body became the somatic and pulsional materiality which language represses, obliging the subject to renounce his unconscious and his flows of uncontainable energy. This manifestation of the forbidden or traumatic decimation of the body which overwhelms the codification of verbal behavior, resomatizes language and utters the body's marginality through rudimentary signification which order finds untranslatable or *in excess.*

For these Chilean artists, working with the body was perhaps the best way to expose the suppression of meaning or the positions of power in official discourse. Under circumstances where censorship is applied to vast areas of meaning in language, *any superfluous discourse or unspoken pressure which escapes or undermines the syntax of the permitted can only surface as bodily gestures.*

Since the body need not depend solely on the linguistic standards that code experience, it can offer a range of polyvalent expressions, of fragments of discourse and conceptual *residues*. Working with the body not only avoids the restrictive monopolies of language by releasing non-signifying particles or trans-semiotic flows, but it can also reintensify the censored areas of experience, areas which had virtually become impossible to express because of the broken link between the referent (reality) and its designatory model (language) in a society under-going a crisis of codes. The corporeal not only lies at the frontier of the sayable, it also becomes the domain of the unsayable.[14] Such body signals provide a carnal symptom of violence used by and against language. But they can also *recodify* that violence by translating the pre-symbolic or trans-symbolic potential of censored material into physical gestures.

This essay is excerpted from Nelly Richard's Margins and Institutions: Art in Chile Since 1973 *(Art & Text, 1986).*

Notes

1.   The mural work by college students was just as relevant . . . Some of Fernan Meza's students from the School of Architecture in Santiago, and those of Francisco Brugnoli from the School of Fine Arts, were the ones who went out into the city and intervened in its visual codes, along with their teachers and tutors.

Osvaldo Aguilo, *Plástica Neovanguardista: Antecedentes y Contexto*, Santiago, Ediciones Seneca, 1983.

2.   CADA editorial in *Ruptura* (August 1982).

3.   After years of being ignored internationally because of the ban by the Left on the Chilean military regime, and given that most of the cultural production going on inside Chile was suspected (both by the Left and by the Chilean exiles) of complicity with the administration, Vostell was perhaps the first avant-garde artist of any international standing to accept an invitation to visit Chile. Undoubtedly his favorable response to the invitation issued by Ronald Kay was due to this personal contact and to the fact that he was assured that he would not be involved in any official matters. Even so, one should stress the courage of his decision to bring to Chile works that ran the risk of being misinterpreted by the Left.

4.   We understand by social sculpture a work of art action that tries to organize, by means of intervention, the time and space in which we live, firstly to make it more visible, and then to make it more livable. The present work [*Para no morir de hambre en el arte*] is a sculpture since it organizes the material of art in terms of volume, and it is social to the extent that such material is our collective reality.

CADA, *La Bicicleta*, 5 (December 1979).

5. Their proposal is to rescue the latent creativity of the landscape and its social use, and to provide mechanisms for a possible reappraisal of it . . . thus creating an essential basis for experiencing what until now has escaped our attention.

> Fernando Balcells, "Acciones de Arte Hoy en Chile" (Art Actions in Chile Today), *La Bicicleta*, 8 (December 1980)

6. We are witnessing the construction of an 'art gallery' in the street, or inversely the destruction of that concept by the use of open and public spaces as markers or receivers of the artwork, whose ultimate aim is not personal profit but to remain in the eye and memory of the passerby who moves daily through the open landscape. The landscape is thus transformed into a creative space which forces the passerby to change his point of view, which obliges him by and large to question his surroundings and the conditions of his own becoming.

> Diamela Eltit, "Sobre las Acciones de Art: Un Nuevo Espacio Critico" (Concerning Art Action, A New Critical Space), *Umbral* (1980)

7. One thinks of the Gallery as a conventional place. Outside the Gallery . . . art generates history, that is, its most transgressive history, which it doesn't even have the words to express. This pre-history is the gesture, the physical and also emotional work from which the photo album or the gallery always profits. Every photo album is the non-savage part of the savage, its most innocent exhibition.

> CADA, "Una Bomba Cerrade" (A Concealed Bomb), catalog, Galeria Sur, 1983

8 The Chilean military regime extends its definition of 'being a woman' to the specific sense of 'being a patriot'. Thus any questioning of the patriarchal order is neutralized by the very discourse that treats politics as chaotic. The masculine is reinstated as an (apparently) apolitical sphere dominated by the figure of the Fatherland. Politics is conceived in similar hierarchical terms to those of the domestic sphere: the referent is no longer the Polis of Greek democracy, but the Paterfamilias of the Roman Empire . . . If the patriarchal order was previously based on the exclusion of woman from the political and public world, it now relies on the restriction of woman to the private or apolitical (familial-patriotic) sphere as the only legitimate one.

> Norbert Lechner and Susana Levy, *El Disciplinamineto de la Mujer* (The Disciplining of Woman), Santiago, Flasco, 1984

9. Carlo Leppe's *Sala de Espera* shows his body transformed through the medium of television and imprisoned in a plaster cast, with his face made up as the opera singer heard in the video. This particular kind of transvestism, already a transgressive act, presents an imaginary woman in a body which is also trapped in plaster. Thus it is not an act of exhibitionism or of personal liberation (which is proven by the plaster cast), but a statement on the fragmentation of identity. Its staging problematizes sexual identity in general, despite its performance by an individual. Its aim extends beyond the no less pertinent analogy between masculinity/ authority and femininity/affective . . . Perhaps we can add that a program of personal transformation is necessary to begin any attempt at social transformation.

The work of Leppe points to the establishment of a creative subject capable of recognizing in his own body the social conflicts which traverse him and which make him conform to 'society'.

Fernando Balcells, *Analisis* (December 1980)

10. Diamela Eltit herself works with what she calls "zones of pain," or marginal areas of social confinement: brothels, psychiatric hospitals, flop houses, jails, etc.:

My concern is to expose these places, to become one with them by my physical presence. My wish is not to morally change them, but only to show that they actually exist . . . It is a form of individual pain confronting the collective pain. Then you can grow and fuse with it.

CADA, "Como Matar el Arte y, de Paso, Cambiar el Mundo"
(How to Kill Art and, by the Way, Change the World),
La Tercera de la Hora (November 1982)

11. The subject . . . exists in such a precarious and fragmented situation that he doesn't even have access to his sexual definition. He occupies a space that cannot distinguish between masculine and feminine.

Raul Zurita, interview by Samuel Silva in *La Tercera de la Hora*
(November 1982)

12. I present my scars as a symptom of exclusion, as a ruptured model . . ., superimposing on my wounded body the signs favored by the system, like clothes, makeup, etc. These signs, by way of contrast, do not resolve but only make manifest the dichotomy that . . . exists between the maltreated body and its submission to the model of appearances.

Diamela Eltit, "Socavada de Sed" (Drained with Thirst),
Ruptura (1982)

13. It was work that seemed quite subversive to me, in the fullest sense of the word: not merely political, but breaking all the codes. And I thought that any verbal discourse about it would be a type of domestication, and that there were other ways to respond: action instead of words.

Raul Zurita, interview in *La Tercera de la Hora*
(November 1982)

14. I wished to distinguish between what cannot be written and what has already begun to be written, bewteen what can be talked about and what cannot be talked about. Faced with a personal experience that is extremely violent or painful, the wish to express it, even by going so far as to burn one's face, is already a sign.

Raul Zurita, "Una Aventura Poética Radical" (A Radical Poetic Venture),
El Mercurio (April 1983)

29. Lotty Rosenfeld
Operations (work in progress) Chile–England, 1996
The Bank of England, London
Photo: Douglas Cape

Operations (work in progress) Chile–England (1996)

Lotty Rosenfeld

"Operations" consists of art actions performed at locations of economic and social power: inside the Stock Exchange market of Santiago and outside Scotland Yard and the Bank of England.

Since 1979 I have been tracing crosses on streets as a way of altering the codes of urban circulation in Chile and abroad. My performances and video installation focus on exposing the operations of official power and the conflict zones in which bodies are submitted to margins and borders.

I have insisted on remaining outside the establishment's protected spaces, and have continuously desecrated the cult of art and its fetishization by the market by using the streets for my work.

For "Operations," I transformed a line painted on a street to direct the path of traffic into a plus sign. In this way I interrogated political and cultural signs. Powers circulate and collide vertiginously in this piece to talk about bodies of power and their confrontation with unprotected and subversive South American bodies.

In this work I connect the Stock Exchange, with its strident cries that celebrate the capturing of capital, with its police counterpart, Scotland Yard, the guardian of vigilance. With her Chilean corporeal craziness, Claudia appears as the body capable of organizing the most complex operations to endow herself with an identity by means of surgery that transforms her from a man to woman. In that way, the passionate hybridity of her body acts as a form of rebellion against the logic of official power.

"Operations" thus embraces fugitive identities together with the paroxysmal gestures of institutions that make surveillance and capital into the embodiments of their duties and powers. I present the conflict generated by "other" bodies; those that make a transgressive syntax out of amputation.

30. Las Yeguas del Apocalipsis (The Mares of the Apocalypse)
"Las Dos Fridas" (The Two Fridas), 1990
Santiago, Chile
Photo: Pedro Marinello
The Mares of the Apocalypse combine strident political critique of homophobia and misogyny in Chile with performance actions.

Las Yeguas del Apocalipsis (The Mares of the Apocalypse)

The equine lips of exile

Francisco Casas

Translated by Marcial Godoy-Anativia

We reinvented ourselves as a body, difference, morbidly sexed, and lumpen. We became a female animal, a mare, a warring machine from another time, beasts of burden; animals in disuse at the mercy of the spur.

Two plus two, four legs to turn back the homosexed centaur that neighed at the troop and sniffed the sadistic, syphilitic, and immune-deficient wound on the cadaver of the nation – that space where "the terrible mothers raised their heads" to denounce the raped and homicidal fatherland.

Territory is the body of the crime; the indigenous mares irrupt onto that cartography of orality, that unfettered lexicon that fills mouths, that vulgarity that reveals the established good and its trinket morality.

Las Yeguas map a utopian reconstruction of ethnicity, of our sexes, our social popular, our lets-do-it-all-over-again for the contruction of more just societies. We do this via urgent mobilizations in which we reimagine ourselves as warring machines on four legs.

In 1987, Las Yeguas marched to the School of Arts and Letters of the University of Chile. We rode on another mare, both nude, mare on top of mare, as Godivas, as Valkyries. But we did not march there to enter and remain inside, but rather to let the academy know that we are outside, that they have reinstituted the margin as aesthetic.

The museum was unable to peek underneath the fabric that cloaked the body of the crime. It closed its anemic doors to the old queens as they unveiled their shantytown chic at the ball of democracy.

In the midst of the listless spirit of the transition and before the eyes of the president-elect, the old burlesque beauties unfurled a banner that read "Homosexuals for Change" (1989).

In Patio 29 in the general cemetery, the clandestine unidentified graves were open for the horror of the encounter; a Guernican brushstroke kept the bodies anchored to the earth; embraced; fused into one body – that body of persistence that refuses to disappear from collective memory. The unidentified have an identity; they have sex, class; they have proof of their existence.

Las Yeguas reject the government's official decision not to name in order to disperse what's been lived.

In 1993, the School of Journalism of the University of Chile (located in a building which previously housed the headquarters of the regime's sadistic secret police) authorized us to open its cellars – those catacombs where the scream was buried; that torture center now decomposed and again decomposed into the academy; there, we made that past visible with multiple video screens facing each other that read "your pain disseminated." In the rooms downstairs, five hundred glasses of water, illuminated by flashlights whose dimming batteries slowly returned the (i.e., our) bodies to the darkness, as we read the names in the report of Chile's Truth and Reconciliation Commission out loud.

The unidentified, silenced, folded in the unfolding of torture; exorcism; memory ritual; narrative orality in the form of a politics of the margins against oblivion; our homosexual voices uttering a roll call in that underground class-room – one by one, thousands of names, dates – remaking sorrow; an identity hidden for twenty years by the impunity that veiled both the body and the crime.

The Street and its Conditions

Felipe Ehrenberg

31. Felipe Ehrenberg
The Street and Its Conditions, 1975
Photo: Felipe Ehrenberg

In the city of Xalapa, capital of the Mexican state of Veracruz, the state university (Universidad Veracruzana) maintained two show spaces for art, Gallery One and Gallery Two.

On the occasion of Felipe Ehrenberg's first major exhibit after returning from England, he temporarily converted these two galleries into what he called the "Museo Veracruzano de la Quincena" (Fortnight's Museum of Veracruz) and filled their spaces with both retinal and conceptual works of art.

The street area between the two galleries was also temporarily renamed "The Centro Regional de Ejercicios Culturale" (Regional Center for Cultural

Exercises). Whatever happened along the street space between the two galleries, and between very specific hours of the day, was identified by the artist as a performance piece: " . . . it could be a (faked?) car crash, or a (faked?) lovers quarrel, or . . ."

Non-objective arts in Mexico 1963–83

Maris Bustamante
Translated by Eduardo Aparicio

Performance art in Mexico must be understood in relation to the term "non-objectualism," or non-objective artmaking. The first person to use the term *"no-objetualismo"* (non-objective artforms) was theoretician Juan Acha. His texts, lectures, and courses contributed to our awareness of new artforms and their importance to us as Latin Americans. In order to explain and justify the birth, development, and wide acceptance of non-objective artforms in Mexico, as something other than a "conceptual contraband,"[1] it is necessary to explain their logic. They imply new forms of conceiving of and making art, which were as widely disseminated and forceful as their counterparts in Europe and the US. In Mexico, non-objectual artforms succeeded because they represented new ways of thinking.

Mexican non-objective aesthetics are essentially different from European ones, in spite of the fact that they appear to be direct heirs to the various types of conceptualism begotten by Futurism.[2]

The paradox, the contradiction, or the magic-uncanny sense that has come to characterize Mexican art gives it shape and qualities by which it can be identified, particularly from the outside. Seen from the point of view of a rationalist, European "order," or even from the US, the Mexican "order" often appears as a "disorder" or "non-order." It is precisely in this disorder or "non-order" that I believe lies the crux of the Mexican imaginary. I am noting here what I believe to be an original logic, revived in the artistic and aesthetic Mexican narratives of the twentieth century that had precedents going back to antiquity, which has made it possible, little by little, and through some intricate workings, for other ways of perceiving and imagining reality to come into being. This is evident in visual propositions provided by non-objective artforms since they "officially" appeared in Mexico.

This confrontation of orders corresponds to what some consider the encounter, for others the "mis-encounter," of two worlds, as the conquest, colonization, and neocolonization processes have come to be known, which processes have been extended over a period of five hundred years and about which so much has been said. It is a question of the conflict between two substantially different ways of thinking reality – the Meso-American way and the European way. The former one is associated with the concept of duality and the latter one with Western rationalism.[3] Both ways of thinking express bipolar values, but while European tradition argues in favor of an "eternal" struggle between opposites, out of which a single victor should emerge, the dualistic vision accepts opposites as part of harmonious whole.

From Surrealism to performance

Surrealism makes its appearance in European cultural scene in the year 1924, but became a presence in Mexico in the year 1940 with the International Exhibition of Surrealism at Galería de Arte Mexicano, organized by André Breton, Wolfgang Paalen, and the Peruvian poet César Moro, sixteen years after the publication of the *First Surrealist Manifesto*. A total of forty-nine Mexican and international artists exhibited as Surrealists. Among them were artists of Mexican origin or residing in Mexico: Manuel Alvarez Bravo, Alice Paalen, Wolfgang Paalen, Remedios Varo, Frida Kahlo, Diego Rivera, Agustín Lazo, Manuel Rodríguez Lozano, Carlos Mérida, Guillermo Meza, Moreno Villa, Roberto Montenegro, Antonio Ruiz, and Xavier Villaurrutia. Only Frida Kahlo, Diego Rivera, and Manuel Alvarez Bravo were presented in the international section.

The rest of the artists were exhibited as "Mexican painters," within an eclectic gathering of "primitive art forms."[4] Not all those who exhibited were Surrealists: among them were some artists who were affiliated with other schools of Mexican painting that had nothing to do with Surrealism. They never displayed interest in the materialization of the subconscious, nor were they concerned with innovative morphologies.[5] Instead, they were interested in conveying messages directly using straightforward realist content.

Quite possibly, the only ones who actually considered themselves Surrealist were Frida Kahlo, Alice Rahon,[6] and Remedios Varo. It is remarkable that all three are women. I venture to think that, in spite of being Surrealists, and even accepting themselves as such, the confessional aspect of their work,[7] in which the Surrealist proposal was made manifest, paved the way for a kind of feminism, or for a reclaiming of conscience from the position of the artist's own femininity. It is a fact that almost all women artists in Mexico have gone through this stage, as if it were a required rite of passage, in order to legitimize their sensibility as woman artists, and to affirm their knowledge and interpretation of the world in the midst of a patriarchal society.

I believe that in spite of the historical delay with which Surrealism was presented in Mexico, it was welcome here because it gave "permission" openly to value and give expression to narrative "a-logics" that were in the process of being conceptualized and concretized. They reflected the need for social change and, at the same time, we can now clearly see how they developed into actions that would later pave the way for the expression of non-objective artforms.

The appearance of the "Sphinx of the Night"[8] at the opening of the Surrealist exhibition in 1940, presented as a Surrealist action, could also be called a performance piece (however incipient or, even, of poor quality compared to the involutionary performance actions that were seen then and are seen now on the streets),[9] or as a proto-happening.[10] It had an impact on Mexican artistic production. This was perhaps the first artistic a-logic to be made known through the mass media, and it was in a sense authorized by Surrealists.

Ephemera: A step towards non-objective artforms

The so-called "Rupture" generation rose to prominence between 1952 and 1965. All the artists associated with this movement represented the internationalization of Mexican art. They were "lucky to be the ones to break away, both formally and ideologically, from the dogmatic and pro-establishment stance of what was known as the Mexican School."[11] They directly confronted the Mexican School's focus on recuperating and validating local and national culture, and those who are relevant in terms of the construction of non-objective art are Arnaldo Cohen, José Luis Cuevas, and Manuel Felguérez. Arnaldo Cohen is now a painter. Manuel Felguérez is a painter, a sculptor, and object maker. Both worked with Chilean artist Alejandro Jodorowsky in actions and happenings, making stage settings that today would be considered real environments between 1960 and 1963. They were also responsible for setting the proper surroundings for numerous daring actions and for living through the changes in attitudes related to the conceptualization and making of art.

An ephemeral work that made history occurred in 1963 at Deportivo Bahía (Bahía Sports Center), located on Ermita Zaragoza Street, considered today one of the most dangerous thoroughfares in the world because of the number of accidents and deaths that occur there. This is a heavily populated area that used to be reached by the Elba River and was known for its hot springs. Anyone could go for a swim at the 100-meter pool located in the sports center by simply paying an entry fee.

Manuel Felguérez finished a mural there, which was also 100 meters long, next to the pool. The mural, titled "Canto al Océano" (A Chant to the Ocean), comprised seashells, mother-of-pearl, and other sea materials. The unveiling took place with the support of the theater groups known as Teatro de Vanguardia (Avant-Garde Theater) and Teatro Pánico (Panic Theater), created by Alejandro

Jodorowsky, who at that time lived in Mexico. An ephemeral work was set to start when Jodorowsky, as main character, and dressed for the occasion, was to come down a rope from a helicopter over the center of the pool, while reading a poem by Lautréamont titled "Same." All other actions and improvisations were to take place simultaneously, among them those being presented in many dressing rooms alongside the pool. Each dressing room had a door. A large number of them would open and close, and by being lit differently they would reveal scenes of couples interacting, kissing, or making love. In the middle of the pool, a platform had been set as stage for several dancers. During general rehearsal the day prior to the event, the pilot of the helicopter came too close to the water while making his measurements. This caused a big explosion of the engine, violently thrusting the blades of the helicopter against the bleachers that had been set up for the audience in front of the dressing rooms. The helicopter was driven into the pool, fortunately without any personal injuries. And there it remained as part of an environment. The people who came to the opening, a total of about 1200, accepted this as a very daring idea for an environment.[12]

José Luis Cuevas presents an interesting case, since he is better known, both in Mexico and in the US as well as in Europe and throughout Latin America, for his art objects. His non-objective path, beginning with the period of the Rupture, is certainly one that had a big impact through the mass media. He is probably the only visual artist in Mexico who has been able to gain the kind of popularity usually reserved for movie actors, boxers, and what today are called "TV personalities." But what I would like to underscore about him is not his popularity in the media, but the means by which he constructed that popularity with actions, rude and polemical behavior, and articles. The structure of his work was taken from the happenings of the 1960s, which dealt openly with narrative a-logics in connection with Mexican culture and living conditions. I have actually been the one to rescue[13] the non-objective part of his trajectory for the historical record because I consider it to be one of the references without which these pre-non-objective structures would not have been known and accepted; they received a big impetus from him. At the time, many interpreted the actions by Cuevas as mere acts of exhibitionism, yet, thanks to his works, many people who generally have no ties to the world of culture accept as a given that visual artists would do what we do.

In 1967, the opening for "Mural Efímero" (Ephemeral Mural) by José Luis Cuevas turned into an open party for people or, rather, a kind of street fair. Misrachi gallery used every means to invite people to gather at the corner of Génova and Londres streets in Mexico City's Zona Rosa. The mural was made over a billboard and its purpose was to provide "a response to the stale muralism of the Mexican School." Fans, followers, curious people, ambulances, firefighters, and police officers, some surprised, some amused, witnessed this happening, which mobilized at the very least hundreds of people,[14] not to mention the wide coverage that this event generated, making it known to thousands of people.

Among the conceptual artists who had a great influence is also Matías Goeritz,[15] whose contribution was a catalyst for decisive changes ranging from the teaching of design and architecture to architectural proposals and urban sculpture projects. In 1955, Galería Proteo organized what was probably the "Primera Confrontación de Arte Experimental" (First Confrontation of Experimental Art).[16]

Grupo los Hartos (Group Fed Up), which also originated out of an initiative by Goeritz in 1961, presented an exhibition at Galería de Antonio Souza, which was titled in the catalog as "Confrontación Internacional de Hartistas Contemporáneos" (International Confrontation of Contemporary Fed-Up Artists). The catalog listed the names of the twelve participants, placing an "h" (from "*harto*" for "fed up") in front of their occupation. Thus Matías was the "hintellectual"; Pedro Friedeberg, the "harchitect"; Chelo Abascal de Lemionet, the "hhomemaker"; Agripina Maqueda, the "hteacher"; Benigno Alvarado, "the hlaborer"; Kati Horna, a well-known photographer, was the "hobjectivist"; Jesús Reyes Ferreira, the "paper hstainer"; Octavio Asta, the happrentice"; businessman Francisco Avalos, the "hindustrialist"; and José Luis Cuevas, the "hillustrator." Participant number twelve was Hinocencia (Hinnocent), a hen with her egg.

Alejandro Jodorowsky's vital presence and bold way of thinking about art have made a lasting impression on Mexican cultural milieu.[17] He was involved with painters, theater people, dancers, filmmakers, musicians, and writers throughout different stages in the history of Mexican art, and also produced within and among disciplines that at the time were quite rigidly defined and differentiated. Certainly, his ability to scandalize the most conservative sectors of the public, many artists, intellectuals, and cultural bureaucrats among them, helped push the frames of perception among viewers. I believe that he represents, without a doubt, the figure where we see the first manifestations of what today we call a multidisciplinary approach. His capacity to gain the attention of the media, secure sponsorships, and, above all, his power to summon, place them as the definitive figure in the period leading up to Mexican non-objectivism.

At the III Salón Independiente (Third Show of Independents) in 1970, installations, environments, and actions were clearly present. This third and last exhibition of independents was the result of the first one, held in 1969. It had been organized as a critical response to the so-called "Salón Solar", organized by Instituto de Bellas Artes (Institute of Fine Arts), as a cultural event running parallel to the Olympic Games being held in Mexico City that year. Several of the artists who called themselves the "Independientes" were founders of some of the groups in the 1960s.

Due to the lack of a budget for the third Salon, and in order neither to postpone or, cancel it, the proposed project was to work with paper and board. The sponsor was Cartonajes Estrella, S.A. For this event, a happening by Jodorowsky and Juan José Gurrola,[18] involved setting up a fashion show called "Moda Sí" (Fashion Yes), in 1970, where the word "sí" referred to both an affirmation, but is also the acronym for Salón Independiente. Cuevas participated with an installation piece, "El Dibujo Más Largo del Mundo: 307 Metros" (The World's Longest Drawing: 307 meters).

By 1971, Dirección de Acción Cultural y Social del Departamento del Distrito Federal (Cultural and Social Action Office, Government of the Federal District) organized Tribuna de Pintores (Painters' Tribune), on the esplanade at Bosque de Chapultepec, where the Rufino Tamayo Museum is located today. There was already talk of "el arte en la calle (street art), Op Art, el arte efímero (ephemeral art), arte público (public art), el trabajo en equipo (team work), el taller activo (active studio), and actions against visual and environmental contamination."[19] The year of 1968 had left its imprint.

The formation of groups in Mexico

A publication in 1963 had a preface written by Alejandro Jodorowsky titled "Hacia el Efímero Panico O ¡Sacar al Teatro del Teatro" (Towards an Ephemeral Panic Or, Let's Take Theater out of the Theater!)[20] I consider this to be the first theoretical text that gives a foundation to the aesthetics of performance art in Mexico. This writing by Jodorowsky proposes to take painting out of painting, the theater out of the theater, to mix them, then see what happens. He called the result a "concrete manifestation." According to Jodorowsky, this new attitude in artistic practice would eliminate friction and everything that would happen would be real. He was surely the first artist in Mexico to write in defense of new attitudes and their narratives. At the same time, he related them to the concept of ephemera, making it intersect with the notion of party and the "party spectacle." To establish a relationship in Mexico between non-objective artforms, ephemera, and partying is to point out the indisputable dichotomy in order to understand the creation of new narratives.[21] In some of his statements about new art, I can detect his reference to a duality:

- The panic-man "is" not, but "is being."
- Intelligence-panic is capable of affirming two contradictory ideas at the same time.

- Panic-man has no "style" because he encompasses them all.
- The man-panic is pro-constructive and pro-destructive at the same time.
- Panic sees time not as an ordered succession, but as a whole where things and events, past and present, are part of a euphoric mixture.

Following these statements and the actions that had been done and those about to be presented, the development and gradual unstoppable ascent of non-objective artforms would continue to this day. And a direct consequence of this, was the *grupos* movement.

Due to the fact that we still do not have a written, "officially" accepted history regarding the development of these a-logics, we can affirm that to this date they were lived experiences, lodged in memory and, particularly, in the archives of some of the main players, in addition to speculations, opinions, dates, and data on invitations and catalogs. This is why I would like to refer to an interesting account of the events, the one which is found in the catalog for the exhibit *De los Grupos, los Individuos* (From Groups, Individuals).[22]

In this first text written about the group movement, the date given for the start of the movement was 1976, the year when four of the groups were invited to the *X Bienal de Jóvenes* (X Young Artists Biennial) in Paris. These four groups were: Proceso Pentágono (Pentagon Trial), comprising Víctor Muñoz, Carlos Finck, José Antonio Hernández, and Felipe Ehrenberg; TAI (Taller de Arte e Ideología) (Art and Ideology Atelier), headed by critic Alberto Híjar; Suma (Sum), with Ricardo Rocha; and Tetraedro (Sebastián).[23] Naturally, the participation of these groups in the Paris show was a major event. However, even more important was what was happening in Mexico, since members of all groups saw the possibility of legitimization and encouragement, their diversity notwithstanding, which, rather than differentiating them would enrich them. This kind of participation and reinforcement of collectives was not only the result of the activity of their members, but was also due, it should be noted, to Helen Escobedo,[24] herself an installation artist. At the time, she was the director of the Museum of Arts and Sciences at UNAM (Universidad Nacional Autónoma de México). In addition, she was appointed curator of the Mexican representation at the *X Young Artists Biennial*. Later, while Helen was director of the Museum of Modern Art, she organized the first exhibition of the groups so that they would be part of her permanent collection.

The essay for "De los Grupos, Los Individuos," written by Dominique Liquois does not mention the group Polvo de Gallina Negra or other smaller groups. There were also groups outside Mexico City, in such areas as Mérida, Yucatán, which have always characterized themselves by their intellectuals and cutting-edge artists. And, certainly, there were also some ephemeral and very small groups, as well as individuals, who worked alone but with a collaborative attitude. Some of them were literally "a flower for a day;"[25] others were shaped by the feverish activity of those times. At any rate, they all participated in a decisive way, or in ways that deserve at least to be mentioned.

These participants included: Zalathiel Vargas, who designed several comic strips or "panic fables" for Jodorowsky, and who created installations and interdisciplinary actions with dancers and cutting-edge rock music. Someone who must also be mentioned is the undeniable figure of Marcos Kurtycz who always preferred to work alone, but whose critical contributions and impacting actions are remembered for contributing to enrich the ground from which these groups emerged.

The chronology made by Liquois recognizes only twelve groups, which (according to his chronological ordering) are: Tepito Arte-Acá (1973), Peyote y la Compañía (Peyote and Company) (1973–75), TAI: Taller de Arte e Ideología (Art and Ideology Workshop) (1974), TIP de Morelia: Taller de Investigación Plástica (Art Research Workshop) (1974–76), Proceso Pentágono (Pentagon Process) (1976), Suma (Addition) (1976), El Colectivo (The Collective) (1976), Grupo de Fotógrafos Independientes (Group of Independent Photographers) (1976), Mira (Look) (1977), Germinal (Germinal) (1977), No-Grupo (Non-Group) (1977–83) and Março (1978).

Mira, which is listed above as originating in 1977, in fact started in 1965. It was then known as Group 65 and played a very active role in the events of 1968[26] – a decisive year.

Proceso Pentágono, which adopted that name in 1976, still maintains the majority of its members – Víctor Muñoz, Carlos Finck, and José Antonio Hernández – from the days when they were at La Esmeralda Art Academy,[27] this being the reason why they maintain that they originated in 1968. The name "Pentágono" (Pentagon) was taken up when Felipe Ehrenberg joined them.

Although it is arguable whether or not this explosion of groups can be dated to 1976, it is even more difficult to establish an end date, since some groups have remained active to this day. Personally, I believe that the end of the group movement came when we exhibited at Museo de Arte Moderno (MAM) in 1983. That is simply because, even though we were presenting actions at museums and official cultural spaces from the beginning, we were never sparing in our subversive attitude, present in all as a common denominator (in spite of the differences in our works). I believe that when we became part of the "permanent" collection at MAM that marked the end, whether by means of accepted censorship or self-censorship. After all, the desire to be, or to be recognized, took hold. It was all over as far as groups were concerned.

No-Grupo (Non-Group)

The No-Grupo was active from 1977 to 1983 and included Maris Bustamante, Melquiades Herrera, Alfredo Núñez, and Rubén Valencia. I came from La Esmeralda and the others came out of San Carlos. The four of us were members of the same generation. We had been trained in the visual arts. Remarkably, we were all first-born. We presented eleven pieces between 1979 and 1983. At each event, we made texts that we distributed to the audience with small props in order for the public to contribute from where they were and to make it something ludicrous and even fun. We always anticipated about three hundred people in the audience, and thus made that number of text and prop sets.

Humor, sometimes black, or at least iconoclastic, was always part of our events. Beginning in 1979, we started calling them "Montaje de Momentos Plásticos" (Staged Artistic Moments), a suggestion I made and which was accepted by the rest of the group. We always self-financed our work and we met at least once a week. Unlike other groups, we never accepted a leader or a chief among us. We were interested in giving the right to credit the author of the piece, but we would always have to agree as to what each one would be presenting. We fought often, but never at our meetings did strong polemics or direct criticism deter us from the creation of our work as our most important objective. We started off by critiquing ourselves, then the political and cultural institutions, and then our colleagues, whether they were friends or not.

We did not even take art critics into consideration. This was clearly reflected in our events, where, on several occasions, we had very strong exchanges, both during and after the presentation, and this in front of the audience. We always looked for a way to find sponsors for our work, but we never let lack of funds stop us. In addition to the texts, we usually produced our own posters and releases. We formed something like a small aggressive gang, sometimes even being rude, when we went to exhibitions. We made jokes and we openly poked fun at work that we considered "contaminating" or plain stupid. Our laughs could often be heard even before entering the sacred precincts of art. For that reason, many feared our visits. We spent a lot of time with each other, and it could even be said that we trusted each other completely and became friends.

In 1979, we were invited to the First Salon of Experimentation, organized by the Fine Arts Department of the National Institute of the Fine Arts. The No-Grupo decided not to take part as a group. Nonetheless, we were invited to create an event to take place outside the Salon, and we accepted. It took place on March 4, 1979 and began at 2pm. Since the piece was scheduled to take place at the time when Mexicans have their most substantial meal of the day, we decided that eating was

32. Maris Bustamante
"Caliente-Caliente" (Hot-Hot)
Mexico City, 1981
The No-Grupo collaborated with Venezuelan artist Carlos Zerpa on this event at Mexico City's Museum of Modern Art. Bustamante created her masks in response to Sigmund Freud's theory that a woman who wanted to engage in professional endeavors suffered from penis envy. Bustamante replaced the nose on each face mask with a penis that had a sign on it that said "work instrument." She placed a mask on each spectator's seat and asked them to wear them while she read a translation of a song by Nina Hagen about how it was better to be a boy because girls didn't have as much fun as they did.

more important than art. We placed a white lunch box on each seat designated for an audience member. Inside each box was the following "artistic food."

- A Coca-Cola bottle with a tag on it stating that Andy Warhol had taken this well-known beverage out of mass circulation and turned it into art. If the person wanted to maintain the status of the bottle as art, he or she was not to drink it; but those who wanted to return the beverage to mass circulation were to drink it (Melquiades Herrera).

- A print with a image of Marcel Duchamp with a hole in his mouth. On the back was a little bag with tiny sweets. If the person decided to eat the sweets, he or she was to do so through the mouth of the Dadaist. That way they would be "vitamins" that would help them to understand conceptual art (Rubén Valencia).
- A small print by Alfredo Núñez made from a reduced photograph of a cow with powdered milk.
- A little cake, in the center of which was a tiny little plastic bag, which would be discovered upon eating it, designed to make you speak in another way. Together with the little cakes were prints of many mouths with a text that said, "Art is because you said so" (Maris Bustamante).

Each lunch box was accompanied by our written critique of the fact that the minimal sponsorship of new artistic projects by cultural institutions had created a milieu in which all the artists were fighting with each other for very little.

We worked at Museo de Arte Moderno in Mexico City and in several other well-known cultural centers. We were guests at Museo de Arte Moderno in Medellin, Colombia, during the Primer Coloquio de Arte No Objetual (First Colloquium on Non-Objective Art), chaired by Juan Acha. After participating in the exhibition that we titled *La Muerte del Performance* (The Death of Performance) at Museo de Arte Moderno in 1983, and after having worked together for six years, we decided to break up in December. Alfredo Núñez went to live in Los Angeles, California, and the rest of us remained in Mexico City. In a very personal way, we continued to work with the legacy of the group, unlike individuals from other groups who changed their work substantially after breaking up.

Polvo de Gallina Negra

The group Polvo de Gallina Negra (Black Hen Powder) worked consistently from 1983 through 1991. Mónica Mayer had completed an off-site MFA program through Goddard College that enabled her to study at the Woman's Building in Los Angeles. She had a family history of women struggling for women's rights, among them her paternal grandmother and her own mother, whom she used to accompany at marches and stand-ins. I had only struggled for my own rights within my own family, which was pretty conservative. We were familiar with each other's work and, in the midst of the group movement, it was very easy for us to become very good friends. When we decided to do something for women in Mexico, we organized a meeting with about eighty women artists who were friends and all specialized in different fields. We presented our ideas for a feminist art group.

When we realized that none of those present at the meeting was interested in the project, we learned that there were only two possibilities: to forget the entire idea or for the two of us to continue by ourselves. In 1983, we went from "the exogamous to the endogamous group" permanently and took part in several demonstrations. The first one, against rape, was on October 7 of that year. At that demonstration, having our name and logo, we did our first political-artistic action at Hemiciclo a Juárez, in Mexico City, in front of an audience numbering a thousand people. The name "Polvo de Gallina Negra," was proposed by me, based on the powders that are sold in small bags at traditional herb markets. They purport to offer a perfect protection against "evil eye." Seeing a connection between "evil eye" and our professional role as visual artists in a male-dominated medium, we found the name sufficiently humorous and made it public.

One of the objectives our project was to modify the image of women in mass media through performances on radio, television, and the printed media. Another was to assert the condition of women and our claims in a patriarchal society in general, and within our male-dominated medium in particular, by means of non-objective art pieces, using themes such as domestic work, motherhood, the age of 15, etc. At that time such themes were scorned with contempt as "a woman thing." We organized several projects based on these thematic pretexts. We also offered lectures and did mail and fax projects to about three hundred individuals on a routine basis, addressing not only intellectuals and artists, but also media personalities. We attended television and radio shows and published articles in feminist magazines, such as *FEM*, and others. We gave numerous lectures, including a series of thirty-six lectures sponsored by Dirección General de Promoción Cultural de la Secretaría de Educación Pública (Office for Cultural Promotion, Department of Public Education). We titled the series "Las Mujeres Artistas Mexicanas o se Solicita Esposa" (Mexican Women Artists, or Wife Wanted).

I believe the event-action-performance that really identified the group and its work, and which caused much surprise – both in Mexico when it took place as well as when the video has been shown in other countries – was the one which was part of the project *¡Madres!* (Mothers!),[28] and which also materialized in several smaller projects. One of them, "Madre por un Día" (Mother for a Day), was a televised performance. In addition, since both Mónica and myself were really pregnant, we had toyed with the idea that the methods used by the group were really scientific. In order to address the issue of motherhood, we needed to be really pregnant, something we were able to accomplish within a period of four months in 1987, "with the support and solidarity" of our husbands. We decided to choose a very high-profile media personality, so we approached Guillermo Ochoa, a journalist who is very well known for his news broadcasts on Televisa. I knew him from my 1979 presentation "Patente del Taco" (Patent for a Taco).

We did him the "great honor" of going with the whole group, all two of us, to talk with him about the project and turn him into a "Mother for a Day." He agreed to be part of the action and to put on an apron with a fake pregnancy tummy underneath for about twenty minutes, not only for national broadcast, but international as well (about 200 million viewers). Ochoa became the first Mexican man ever to become pregnant by the only Mexican feminist art group. The phone lines were jammed with calls, many of them against the event, which they considered to be disrespectful of motherhood. Since then, Mónica and I have shared the feeling that we were able to take a stab at one of the strongest archetypes in our culture. At the very least, we were able to leave a scratch.

Conclusions

Non-objective artforms, before they became known as such in the 1970s, have numerous antecedents, which can be traced back at least to the beginning of the century. They correspond to psychological, cultural, and political structures that we could call non-objective manifestations. This allows us to venture the thought that we did not require external influences for their development in Mexico. The social and political upheaval of 1968 was decisive in giving impetus to a-logical artistic narratives that have imposed themselves in radical ways.

This notwithstanding, there is evidence of a tendency for them to be mediated through subsidies from official sources due to their subversive character. This is why we are noticing a tendency among young artists to "copy" what comes from outside, rather than focus on and develop from traits that are particular to our geographical location. Nonetheless, we hope that these narratives will continue to help bring about the hoped-for change in our national culture.

Notes

1. Term coined by artist Ruben Valencia, member of No-Grupo.

2. Even today, the attempt to find and justify a cultural origin and development different from the European one is considered sacrilege.

3. It was not gratuitous for Mexican university researcher Pablo Moctezuma (UAM-Azcapotzalco) to propose that we do away with the habit of using the term "pre-Hispanic period" in favor of the notion of "pre-Cuauhtémoc period."

4.   Raquel Tibol in *Frida Kahlo: Una Vida Abierta*, Editorial Oasis: Mexico, 1990, p. 72. Originally published in 1983.

5.   I believe that they were more innovative in developing new techniques than in altering or transforming existing "visual grammars." On the other hand, Estridentistas (Stridentists) were indeed interested in modifying narrative structures; in their case, literary narrative structures.

6.   In the exhibit, it appears as Alice Paalen.

7.   Interesting research topic on women artists in Mexico: Why do most women artists work on confessional topics? That research, though intended, was left undone by the group Polvo de Gallina Negra (Black Hen Powder).

8.   Represented by Isabel Marín "dressed in a large white tunic, her head covered with an enormous butterfly," in *El Surrealismo y el Arte Fantástico de México*, (Surrealism and Art in Mexico) by Ida Rodríguez Prampolini, Instituto de Investigaciones Estéticas de la UNAM: Mexico, 1969, chapter 5, p. 53.

9.   I have used the term "involuntary non-objective actions" for a variety of actions, performances, and installations that are seen on the streets, in the buses, the subway, and traditional Mexican markets.

10.   The acceptance and use of terms such as "performance" and "happening" speak also of submission and acceptance of foreign values as the only valid ones. Certainly, we cannot reject everything, since that would leave us without a language, given that language and speech, though imposed from the outside, are modified and transformed by means of adaptations that provide them with values and concepts they did not have before, such as in the case of puns.

11.   Manuel Felguérez in the chapter titled "La Ruptura 1935–1955" page 93, catalogue for the exhibit *La Ruptura 1952–1965* (Rupture 1952-1965), held at Museo de Arte Alvar y Carmen T. de Carrillo Gil y Museo Biblioteca Pape, Mexico 1988.

12.   From a personal interview with Professor Felguérez.

13.   José Luis invited me to participate at a round table, as part of the tribute paid to him at Centro Cultural San Angel in Coyoacán on September 3, 1990. I explained to him that I would participate in order to rescue his trajectory as a non-objective artist, something that had not been done before

14.   Article titled "El Mural Efímero, Treinta Años Después" (The Ephemeral Mural: Thirty Years Later) by Maris Bustamante, *Viceversa* , issue 48, May 1997, p. 12.

15.   Matías Goeritz was born Danzig (then Germany, now Poland) in 1915 and died in 1990. He arrived in Mexico in 1949. In 1961 he developed and organized the exhibit of works by Los Hartos, cited in *Una Década de Crítica de Arte* (A Decade of Art Criticism) by Ida Rodríguez Prampolini, Edición Sepsetentas No. 145, Secretaría de Educación Pública, 1974, p. 126.

16.   Raquel Tibol: *Confrontaciones*, Ediciones Sámara, 1992, chapter titled "Confrontación 66" (Confrontation 66), p. 85.

17.   Alejandro Jodorowsky, born Iquique, Chile in 1929. Writer and filmmaker. Directed the films *El Topo*, *La Montaña Sagrada* and *Santa Sangre*. Author of the novel titled *El Oro de Siete Leguas*. Creator of comics known as "Fábulas Pánicas" (Panic Fables). He currently lives in Paris, where he lectures, reads the tarot, and is a guru for politicians and fans.

18.   Juan José Gurrola, who considers himself an architect, has been part of actions that are now legendary. A theater person, drawing artist, painter, and writer, he has remained a "professional provocateur," without whose presence it would not be possible to understand the current state of the arts.

19.   Raquel Tibol in *Confrontaciones*, Ediciones Sámara 1992, chapter titled "Inconformidad Generalizada" (Generalized Inconformity), p. 183. My emphasis.

20.   Ephemeral Pánico (Panic) or Fábulas Pánicas (Panic Fables), referring almost certainly to the god Pan, the Greek god of shepherds.

21.   This celebration exists in all cultures, but it seems that in Mexico it is part of an ancestral tradition that opposes itself to European rationalism and which we see reflected in the contemplation that Octavio Paz discusses in his book, *The Labrynth of Solitude* (New York: Grove Press, 1961). Here I speak of a particular sense of humor, black humor, the sexual pun (*albur*), and a sense of time that is evoked by a refusal of punctuality, etc.

22.   Exhibit at Museo Carrillo Gil from June through August 1985, Mexico City. Work shown by artists still active. First chronology of the group movement. Catalog, Edición INBA-SEP 1985.

23.   Enrique Carbajal has been called Sebastián since his days at the San Carlos school. He was part of Escultórico space. Currently, he is Mexico's best-known sculptor. In Mexico City alone he has more than 150 urban sculptures. He was a student of Goeritz and later became his assistant in his architecture courses. Since 1968, he has been a promoter and organizer of exhibits inviting young artists to show their work.

24.   Escobedo is a pioneer in installation art in Mexico, where she presented the first installation piece in spring 1969.

25.   The literal meaning of "ephemeral."

26.   In fact, as part of their activism in this political movement, they prepared a publication to rescue the graphics of 1968 entitled *The Graphics of 1968* (Mexico City: Edición Escuela Nacional de Artes Plásticas de la UNAM, 1982). It contains all the graphics that circulated during this period of protest. Research was carried out by el Grupo Mira: Arnulfo Aquino, Rebeca Hidalgo, Jorge Pérez, Melecio Galván, Eduardo Garduño, Silvia Paz Paredes, Salvador Paleo, and Saul Martínez.

27.   Escuela Nacional de Pintura y Escultura (National School of Painting and Sculpture), known as "La Esmeralda," part of Instituto Nacional de Bellas Artes (National Institute on Fine Arts) and Secretaría de Educación Pública (Department of Public Education).

28.   ¡Madres!, May 10, 1987.

Orphans of Modernism:
The Performance Art of Asco

C. Ondine Chavoya

Formed in the early 1970s by four Chicano artists from east Los Angeles, the Asco collective set out to test the limits of art – its production, distribution, reception, and exhibition. Its founding members,[1] Harry Gamboa, Jr., Gronk, Willie Herrón, and Patssi Valdez, engaged in public, performance, and conceptual art in a direct response to the social and political turbulence in Los Angeles in the late 1960s and early 1970s.[2]

The contributions of Asco have remained largely unrecognized or underestimated in accounts of American art from the 1970s. A decade ago in the MIT exhibition *LA: Hot and Cool*, Asco was identified as a pioneer of contemporary conceptual work; the curatorial essay outlined how in 1987 (the year Asco broke up) their contributions were only beginning to be acknowledged.[3] However, in more recently published histories on performance, conceptual, and public art Asco is suspiciously written out altogether.[4] In response to the acknowledged need for new narratives and genealogies of the avant-garde that complicate its past and support its future (Foster 1996: 5), I will discuss the intersections of performance, interventionist public art, and intermedia technologies in the work of Asco. While insisting upon the value of the avant-garde as a model, I suggest that the palpable absence of Asco from the historical record reveals a pattern of exclusionism in the construction of the Euro-American avant-garde.

To understand the dynamic interaction in Asco's work between critique and seduction, play and provocation, and activism and abstraction, one needs to contextualize their tactics. Between 1968 and 1973, Chicanos in Southern California protested about the disproportionate number of Chicano casualties in the Vietnam War and the relationship between this statistic and inequities of education and other opportunities for Chicano youth.[5] As Mexican Americans became more active in organizing and voicing their social demands, law enforcement became increasingly suppressive. Historians argue that during this era of increasing "police–barrio confrontation," the colonial status of Chicanos had rarely appeared so palpable. In effect, Chicano civil rights actions and protests were regarded and dealt with as insurrection.[6]

Gamboa, Gronk, Herrón, and Valdez all attended Garfield High School in East LA, a locus of political organization and violence, and were part of a Chicano youth movement that "rebelled against social victimization by adopting 'an extreme and flamboyant use of language and fashion'" (Dubin 1986: 2). Known as Jetters, this group was noted for their wild dress, tricky talk, and sardonic attitudes, and their "extravagance of dress and manner served as a placard for social impotence" (Gamboa 1985).[7] In a city where only one-fourth of all Mexican Americans graduated from high school, Garfield High "boasted the highest dropout rate in the nation, with 59 percent of students failing to complete the curriculum" (Gamboa 1987: 13).

On March 5, 1968, more than 1000 students walked out of five high schools in protest of the substandard educational system in the nation's largest barrio – East LA.[8] Outside the schools, signs were raised that read "Education not Eradication," "Ya Basta Con Reagan," "Viva La Raza!" and "Education not Concentration Camps." By the end of the week, sixteen high schools were involved, and over 10,000 students were on strike during the fifteen-day period.[9] This student boycott for educational reform, known as the Chicano Blowouts, was the first urban mass protest against racism undertaken by Mexican Americans in the history of the United States. This organized non-violent student strike "brought the largest school system in the nation to a standstill and made news across the country; a *Los Angeles Times* reporter interpreted the strike as 'The Birth of Brown Power'" (Muñoz 1989: 64).

Gronk, the first member of Asco to engage in performance art, contributed to the political newspaper *Grassroots Forum* and college Chicano activist publications.[10] Harry Gamboa, Jr. served as the vice-president of the Garfield High School Blowout Committee and contributed to the activist-news periodicals *Chicano Student News* and *La Raza*. Gamboa's role in organizing the Blowouts made him the target of surveillance for "New Left" internal subversives and unAmerican activities. In testimony before a US Senate subcommittee in 1970, Gamboa was named one of the hundred most dangerous and violent subversives in the USA, along with black activists Angela Davis and Eldrige Cleaver, and Chicano activist Reies Lopez Tijerina; Gamboa's part in organizing the Blowouts was deemed "antiestablishment, antiwhite, and militant" propaganda (Committee on the Judiciary US Senate 1970: 12).

The military resonances of the term "avant-garde" are doubly relevant when discussing Asco. At a time when Chicanos accounted for less than 1 percent of the University of California's total student population, as a group they suffered the highest death rate of all US military personnel (Guzman 1969). Asco's avantgarde strategies were "urban survival techniques" (Gamboa in Brookman and

Brookman 1983: 6) that emerged from the organized protest movement against
the use of Chicanos, and other people of color, as the literal avant-garde in the
war in Vietnam.

In 1971, Gamboa was appointed an editor of *Regeneración*, a Chicano political
and literary magazine first published by Mexican anarchist Ricardo Flores Magon
in the early 1900s. He enlisted Patssi Valdez, Willie Herrón, and Gronk to work
on the publication. This was the first time the four artists came together to
collaborate on a single project.[11] With no formal training, few available models,
and even fewer venues for exhibition, *Regeneración* was Asco's educational collaborative training ground.

As Gronk often muses, "We went into the garage, but instead of coming
out rock stars, we became artists" (Gronk 1993). Between coffee, make-up tips,
and fashion crises, the artists formed what Gamboa has retrospectively described
as a surrogate family. As Patssi Valdez remembers,

> We were all having dialogues about the different things that bothered us.
> The school we went to was horrible; the teachers didn't teach. You'd look
> at television and you didn't see yourself there, and if you did you were a
> cholo or a chola. And, . . . [I was] like where am I in this picture? I don't
> exist anywhere.
>
> (Garza 1994)

Out of these dialogues came Super-8 films, photography, and performance. United
by their shared sense of displacement, they formed an art collective and merged
activism with cultural production. The artists recognized the power of public
representation and documentation and became expert at overcoming their exclusion from mainstream institutions by using alternative methods of access and
distribution. Their multimedia works were inspired by their own urban experiences and intended to galvanize a response from the community (Gamboa n.d.:
2). It was in these works that the geographic and social space of Los Angeles
became the focus of Asco's conceptual art.

Performances

On Christmas Eve 1971, Gamboa, Gronk, and Herrón performed their first walking mural, *Stations of the Cross*, and iconoclastically transformed the Mexican
Catholic tradition of the Posada into a ritual of remembrance and resistance against
the deaths in Vietnam.[12] The trio arrived at the corner of Eastern Avenue and
Whittier Boulevard in outlandish make-up and costume. Carrying a brightly
colored cardboard cross, Herrón led the procession as a stylized skull-faced Christ

wearing a long flowing white robe with an emblazoned Sacred Heart.[13] Following him were Gamboa, as a zombie-like altar boy wearing an "animal skull headpiece to ward off unsolicited communion," (Gamboa 1991: 124) and Gronk as Pontius Pilate in clown-like make-up, a burgundy velvet gown, and his signature accessories: a green bowler hat and an oversized fake-fur, beige purse.

Performing *Stations of the Cross* along a one-mile stretch of Whittier Boulevard, the procession's final rite was held before the US Marines' Recruiting Center at the Goodrich Boulevard intersection. Gronk blessed the site with Kress dime-store popcorn, the trio observed a ceremonial five minutes of silence, and then placed the fifteen-foot cross at the door of the recruitment center before they fled the scene. *Stations of the Cross* was an urban disturbance designed symbolically to block Chicanos from enlisting at the center on that day.

Patssi Valdez joined Gamboa, Gronk, and Herrón for their encore Christmas Eve Whittier Boulevard performance in 1972, titled *Walking Mural*. As a result of the National Chicano Moratorium Against the Vietnam War (1970),[14] a peaceful demonstration that turned into a police riot and several subsequent retaliations,[15] the Annual East Los Angeles Christmas parade had been canceled.[16] Assuming the traditional course of the countermanded parade, the artists staged a public spectacle in which they were both the participants and floats. In the process, they advanced the convention of street murals from a static media to a moving, performance medium.

Stations of the Cross and *Walking Mural* are more than reminiscent of social protests: both performances subverted authority in order to (temporarily) reclaim social space. Whittier Boulevard is East LA's central commercial thoroughfare and, because it had been a central site of riots, the Los Angeles Police were particularly repressive in that area. During this time of paramilitary police occupation, any group or gathering of Chicano youth was considered suspect and potentially subversive; as a result groups were routinely stopped and interrogated by police and, to prevent "cruising" on the boulevard, passage to cars on weekend nights was blocked. Asco chose to perform on Whittier Boulevard repeatedly because they would be assured a public there, because of the role the site played in the riots, and in response to the rapacious prohibitions on public behavior and assembly exercised in order to protect public space from ongoing contestations. Improvising absurd imagery and environmental interventions was Asco's tactic to disrupt the quotidian perceptual responses of their spontaneously generated audiences. As Herrón states, "We wouldn't plan it so people could actually come and see it, we would just drop in on everything in its normal pattern" (Brown and Crist 1985). Even if startled spectators and unknowing participants could not precisely decipher their allusive critique, the artists hoped that the very occurrence of these bizarre activities in public thoroughfares would raise questions in the minds of their viewers.[17]

Momentarily retaking control of the landscape, the artists enacted an alternative interpretative practice from the position of those subordinated by urban spatial politics.[18] Moreover, "they were situating their critique in a space that Chicanos did not have access to – public space" (Noriega, in Chavoya 1996). Asco's engagement of the city and their performative contestations in (and over) public space are a part of what anthropologist James Holston has called the "spaces of insurgent citizenship."[19]

Underpinning the dominant social geography of Los Angeles is a disciplinary structure maintained by various policing activities and organizations (Davis 1990). These enforced practices of exclusion are racialized and made manifest via a spatial formation that segregates and contains the Mexican and Chicano population. The spatial cultural hegemony of Los Angeles has historically labored to implement and reproduce the systematic containment of the Chicano population through "consciously constructed economic and racial barriers" (Rios-Bustamante and Castillo 1986: 125).

The urban history of Los Angeles is ripe with examples of its exclusionary spatial formation, both physical and symbolic. As early as the 1850s, shortly after the Mexican–American War, "Mexican residents were literally and figuratively forced out of what was fast becoming an industrial boom town" (Rios-Bustamante and Castillo 1986: 104). By the 1880s, LA was a two-tiered city of mutually exclusive cultural entities, with the Mexican population concentrated in specific areas and relegated to a second-class status. A Mexican removal project, allegedly "to rid the city of slums," in practice between 1906 and 1913, demolished the historic central plaza barrio (Rios-Bustamante and Castillo 1986: 113); segregation was additionally fortified with the institution of racially restricted real-estate covenants.

More than one million Mexicans and Mexican Americans were deported in 1954. According to the attorney general, this massive deportation program, known as Operation Wetback, was initiated by the federal government primarily to rid the country of political subversives. These practices and the ideologies that supported them gave credence to the popular expression used by Mexican Americans to describe their status: "Strangers in one's land." As historian John Chávez outlines, "regardless of their place of birth or citizenship, Mexicans were intimidated, separated from families, and deported as if they were enemy aliens in the Southwest" (J. Chávez 1984: 125). In this same era, urban development and renewal consistently displaced or intruded upon Mexican and other minority residential areas at the same time as cultural institutions were continuously established apart from the very same neighborhoods. The development of the freeway system, an icon of Los Angeles mobility and modernity, destroyed count-less Mexican neighborhoods along its path between 1953 and 1957; the construction of Dodger Stadium prompted the eviction of several thousand Mexicans from Chavez Ravine in 1957.[20]

Such efforts at social-spatial control attempt to relegate Chicanos "to a sphere outside the public, to bar admittance to the discursive construction of the public, and in this way, prohibit participation in the space of public communi-cation" (Deutsche 1996: 38). The experience of this disciplinary exclusion was poignantly conveyed in testimony presented to a US Commission on Civil Rights investigating continued allegations of police brutality and violations of federal law by law enforcement agencies during the East LA riots of 1970. As one commu-nity representative proclaimed, "Whether the law knows it or not . . . . we're the public, even if we are brown" (Commission 1970: 13).

Asco addressed the issues of "minority" public representation and access with the 1972 performance "Project Pie in De/Face" or "Spraypaint LACMA." At a meeting Gamboa requested with a curator at the Los Angeles County Museum of Art, the artist was told that the museum did not collect or exhibit Chicano art because Chicanos didn't make "fine art"; they only make "folk art," or were in gangs. In reply, Gamboa, Gronk, and Herrón signed their names to all the LACMA entrances in gang-style fashion, thereby claiming the institution and all its contents as the artists' own conceptual art piece.

First Supper (After a Major Riot) was performed on December 24, 1974, during rush hour on a traffic island at Arizona Street and Whittier Boulevard in East Los Angeles. In this performance, Asco deployed the act of occupation in lieu of their previously mobile tactics. The traffic island the artists occupied had been built over a particularly bloody site of the East LA riots as a part of an urban "redevelopment" project in 1973. Following the riots, the surrounding buildings, sidewalks, and streets were leveled and rebuilt to prevent further public demonstrations. Transforming the traffic island into a stage for a macabre re-enactment of the Last Supper, including elements from Days of the Dead celebrations, the artists memorialized the death and destruction that occurred at the scene years earlier.[21] Identifying the site as a spatial symbol of subordination, *First Supper* is a symbolic attempt to thwart the onset of historical amnesia.

Immediately following the occupation of the traffic island, Asco initiated another performance involving forced immobility and bound constraints. Gronk invented the "Instant Mural," when he fastened Humberto Sandoval and Patssi Valdez to the exterior wall of a liquor store with masking tape. The performance renders ideographic the "relations of power and discipline inscribed in the apparently innocent spatiality of social life" (Soja 1989: 6). Asco's *Instant Mural* can be seen as making us, in the words of Edward Soja, "insistently aware of how space can be made to hide consequences from us . . . how human geographies become filled with politics and ideology" (Soja 1989: 6). In this way, *Instant Mural* (symbolically) challenged the fragility of social controls while "actualizing the adhesive relations between society and space, history and geography" (Soja 1989: 223), with specific attention to the locations and functions of cultural identity and gender within this paradigm.

The "symbolized space of place" constitutes the very material for Asco's performances. Given their spatial and historical contexts, *Walking Mural*, *First Supper*, and *Instant Mural* are tactical forms of symbolic resistance and spatial interventions. These spatial-conceptual actions map out the hegemonically enforced yet tacit limits and exclusions of urban space and official culture in Los Angeles.

No-Movies: the art of false documents

Asco sensed that the presence of violence in their environment was profoundly problematic, but the methods they chose to engender awareness of it were purposefully disruptive. Herrón remembers, "We wanted to reach inside and pull people's guts out" (Benavidez 1981). As Kosiba-Vargas suggests, "Asco rendered new interpretations of the Chicano urban experience which emphasized the irrationality of an environment shaped by violence, racial oppression, and exploitation" (Kosiba-Vargas and Zaneta 1988: 4). For the artists such work was a means to combat the power of the stereotype as a system of subjection and its role in the promotion of violence.

Decoy Gang War Victim (1974) was both a performance and media intervention "designed to provoke the viewer to commit acts of perceptual sabotage" (Gamboa 1994: 7) and then to question "objective" sources of information and meaning. After closing off a residential city block with flares in the Li'l Valley area of East LA, Gronk sprawled across the asphalt posing as the "victim" of a gang retribution killing with ketchup all over him. As Gamboa explains, "We would go around and whenever we heard of where there might be potential violence, we would set up these decoys so they would think someone had already been killed" (Brookman and Brookman 1983: 7–8).

The performance's status as media hoax and counter-spectacle depended upon the way that the documentation was put to use. Asco distributed a photograph of the performance to various publications and television stations, which was accepted by the local media as a real scenario of violence. The image was broadcast on KHJ-TV LA Channel 9 as an "authentic" East LA Chicano gang murder and condemned as a prime example of rampant gang violence in the City of Angels.

The artists were all but too familiar with the power of photographic documents "to structure belief and recruit consent; the power of conviction and the power to convict" (Tagg 1994: 146). Not only did the mass media represent crime and violence as East Los Angeles' specialty, but Gamboa was the target of "internal subversives'" surveillance sponsored by the FBI's COINTELPRO agency. This was possible, Gamboa argues, because "they had pictures and I didn't have pictures to prove my point" (Noriega 1996: 214).

Thus, by inverting the documentary sign function of the photograph, the aesthetics of the image were mediated by an ethics of the image (as stereotype) intent on reversing the terms of everyday media manipulation. "So much death had been occurring and does occur in East L.A. without any meaning attached to it," Gamboa said in an interview, "we wanted to give people a certain kind of almost gastro-intestinal response" (Sandoval 1978). That the decoy restored peace to the barrio or effectively revealed the media's biases to all is unlikely; however, the artists became aware of the possible uses of mainstream media to communicate their messages. The group did not seek to create spectacles for spectacle's sake but to bring attention to the spectacular condition of everyday life in the barrio and, through counter-spectacles, to destabilize the power of the media to represent it as such.

The "No-Movie" was Asco's signature invented medium – conceptual performances that invoked cinematic codes but were created for a still camera. The "No-Movies" were staged events in which performance artists played the parts of film stars in photographs that were distributed as film stills from "authentic" Chicano motion pictures. "No-Movies" alluded to two models of presentation: the Latin American *fotonovela* and the Hollywood film still. Bearing the signature red stamp "Asco/Chicano Cinema," No-Movies were distributed to local and national press and media, and to film distributors, and reached an international audience through mail-art circuits. Chon Noriega has succinctly described the No-Movie format as an "intermedia synesthesia" that uses one affordable medium (the still 35mm camera) as another more expensive medium (a 16mm or 35mm motion picture camera) (Noriega 1991: 192). The "No-Movies" circulated as examples of "authentic" Chicano-produced motion pictures, creating the specious illusion of an active body of Chicano cinema being produced from the periphery of Hollywood.

The "No-Movie" operated as an ideological "rebuff to celluloidic capitalism of contemporary cinema" (Gamboa and Gronk 1976: 31). "No-Movies" were

33. ASCO (Gronk, Patssi Valdez and Harry Gamboa Jr.)
No-Movie announcement poster (1977), featuring "A La Mode" (1975)
Photo courtesy of Harry Gamboa Jr.

both a critical assault and evasion of the Hollywood studio system, foregrounding the absence of Chicano access to and participation in mass media. The "No-Movies" were not only critically satirizing Hollywood cinema but also parodied the utopian nationalism of the Chicano Art Movement.[22] In a mock interview that Gronk and Gamboa wrote for the magazine *Chismearte*, they sarcastically critiqued nationalist Chicano filmmakers.

> *Chismearte*:   At what point did you reject the celluloid format of cinema?
> *Gronk*:   When I realized Chicano filmmakers were making the same movie over and over again.
> *Gamboa*:   When I discovered for myself that a multimillion dollar project could be accomplished for less than 10 dollars and have more than 300 copies in circulation around the world
> (Gamboa and Gronk 1976: 32)

The "No-Movie" that most clearly addresses this issue is appropriately titled "Chicano Cinema" (1976). The image of a gunshot victim fallen to the floor resembles those from the sensationalist Mexican true crime magazine ¡Alarma!. His white tank-top T-shirt is saturated with blood, but he remains propped up in the corner of the room. Fiercely yet blankly staring ahead, his eyes confront the viewer. The cinematic *mise-en-scène* suggests a cheap motel room. The words "Chicano Cinema" have been painted on brown butcher paper above the fallen casualty. However, the final letter of the title drips off the paper on to the floor, indicating that perhaps the bullet penetrated the author while in process. Cryptically scrawled out on the wall below is a signature – "Gamboa," and opposite him a pile of bank notes is aflame. One hand is placed inside his unbuttoned trousers, the other holding a gun pointed at the viewer; it is unclear whether this figure is a rebel with a cause or a victim of his own art and ideology. Regardless, "Chicano Cinema" has become his final rite and epitaph.

Gamboa notes that Asco's theories of performance crystallized with the "No-Movies." The "No-Movie" format facilitated the circulation of their performances by taking "the barrio out of the barrio" (Goldman 1980). Gronk has described the "No-Movie" concept as follows: "We were using Hollywood by mimicking it – we became its characters," as well as its technical staff, producers, directors; "LA, the city, became our canvas and we became the pigment" (Gronk 1993).

Asco's spatially politicized aesthetics embodied resistant meanings in order to mobilize resistant readings. The frequent object of their critical investigations was the normative landscape and official culture of Los Angeles. In one series of performances, Asco appointed themselves municipal officials to East LA, a predominantly Mexican-American populated unincorporated county territory. (To this day, East LA remains unincorporated and, thus, does not have a City Hall.) Asco toured their municipality on random site-visits, designating various spaces and objects to be civic landmarks, monuments, and preservation zones. In one such "No-Movie" performance, a storm drain was anointed the illustrious title "Asshole Mural" (1975). Traditionally monuments mark, embody, and make visible power relations. Steve Pile describes this process as making space incontestable "both by closing off alternative readings and by drawing people into the presumption that the values they represent are shared" (Pile 1996: 213). Asco's spatial aesthetic is an example of an enacted heterotopia that embodies and actualizes alternative readings.[23] Their ephemeral performance challenges the sanctioned durable autonomy of monuments as grids of social meaning and state power and intervenes in the control and manipulation of space (both real and metaphorical) exerted in the production of monuments.

"Asshole Mural" is a performative subversion of the historical process that has produced Chicanas/os as the categorical blind spot – the "disposable phantom culture" (Gamboa 1981: 15) – of dominant media as well as political and cultural institutions. The tactic utilized is to usurp the authority and power invested in the civic heritage industry as spectacle. Jonathan Crary has described similar strategies employed by the Surrealists and other Euro-American avant-garde artists as "turning the spectacle of the city inside out through counter-memory and counter-itineraries," arguing that this strategy incarnates "a refusal of the imposed present" (Crary 1989: 107). But whereas such Euro-American avant-garde artists may have attempted to refuse an imposed present by reclaiming fragments of a demolished past in order to implicitly figure an alternative future, Asco's performance is clearly not one of cultural reclaiming; instead it marks an absence.[24] Asco's aesthetic strategies and interventionist tactics emanate from neither the fragment nor the ruin, but from the absence.

As non-celluloid dramas, "No-Movies" produce the affect of cinematic reality. As barrio-star vehicles, "No-Movies" explored and exploited the power of the image. "Vogue" (1978), featuring Billy Estrada and Patssi Valdez (looking remarkably like Sophia Loren), appropriates the aura of stardom by referencing the photographic conventions of fashion advertising. Occasionally "No-Movies" were far more explicit in their cinematic references, such as "Fountain of Aloof" (1978), the Patssi Valdez and Billy Estrada remake of the Anita Ekberg and Marcello Mastroianni fountain scene in *La Dolce Vita* (1960). Concepts for still other "No-Movies" included: "Asco Goes to the Universe" (1975); "The Gore Family" (1975), a cannibalistic sci-fi thriller, in which descendants of Lesley Gore are mugged while attempting to pawn a camera, and transformed into city terrorists from City Terrace; the "Hollywood Slasher Victim" interview and press conference (1978); and "Stranglers in the Night" (1978), a domestic mass-murder plot that unfolds in a showerstall.

Gronk often invokes the celebrated postmodern photographer Cindy Sherman in discussion of the "No-Movies." In his influential essay "The Photographic Activity of Postmodernism," Douglas Crimp surveys the history of technological challenges to aura, and identifies the work of a group of young (at the time of the essay) artists that reflexively contest the auratic fetishization of the original. These artists, of which Sherman is a stellar example, demonstrate how the photographic medium is primarily and always "a representation, always-already-seen" (Crimp 1993: 118), and do so by turning the medium's axiomatic claim to originality against itself. The aura is thus only an aspect of the copy.

Although there is a formal and conceptual convergence in Asco's "No-Movies" and Sherman's "Film Stills" through their "rhetoric of the pose,"[25] there is a crucial distinction to be made. For Sherman the rhetoric of the pose is utilized to effect a sense of cinematic unreality. Working within an established, if entrenched, series of signifiers and overdetermined narratives, the effect of cine-matic unreality is a strategy to destabilize or denaturalize normative gender codes. As Crimp describes, Sherman's "Film Stills" function to expose an unwanted dimension of fiction. Created in the images of "already known feminine stereo-types," Sherman's photographs "show that the supposed autonomous and unitary self out of which other 'directors' would create their fictions is itself nothing other than a discontinuous series of representations, copies, fakes" (Crimp 1993: 122).

"No-Movies," in contrast, were "designed to create an impression of factu-ality" (Gamboa in Norte 1983: 12), to produce the affect of cinematic reality. In their impersonating an institution they wish to see themselves in, the strategy employed is to construct a series of signifiers and narratives. While Sherman's "Film Stills" constitute a simulation of overdetermined signifiers, the "No-Movie" is simulacrum for which there is no original.[26] As Gronk coyly proclaims, "It is projecting the real by rejecting the reel" (Gamboa and Gronk 1976: 31).

Asco's production of barrio stars – "survivors on the periphery" (Gamboa in Rupp c. 1985) and "the elite of the obscure" (Gamboa in Sandoval 1980) – mimics the glamor and explicit sexuality of Hollywood in a manner similar to Andy Warhol's production of Factory Superstars. "No-Movies," like Warhol's early films, take as their main points of reference the notion of stardom and the discourse of fashion and advertisement. Though rejected by New American Cinema, the star system was reformulated and reborn in its "most pristine state" in Warhol's films (Barrios: 1968: 31).

The superstar was often the only recognizable figurative element in Warhol's early film work, and he is credited with the contribution of the "Superstar" to the iconography of the underground art film.[27] Soon after, the superstar as device was expanded into structuring idea and content (Battock 1968: 25). The Warhol film factory has been described as a flip Hollywood[28]: "Hollywood's nemesis, its Wonderland looking glass" (Berlin and Bruce 1986: 54). In this manner, Tally Brown described the Factory as:

> creating a Hollywood outside Hollywood, where you don't have to bother with learning to act, making the rounds, going to agents, getting your 8 x 10 glossy, doing small parts being an extra, and gradually working up to becoming a star. You just got on camera and were a Superstar.
> (Suárez 1996: 229)

The creation of a Factory Superstar hinged upon "the awareness that rather than transmitting a pre-existing 'substance' – artistry, beauty, acting skill – the media created stars as an effect, a supplement, of recording apparati and of media circu-lation" (Suárez 1996: 229–30). In many respects, this concept complements, rather than complicates, Warhol's fascination with the simulacral surface and insistence that the surface was the only source of meaning.[29]

Hollywood cinema is often accused of furnishing the appearance of art with none of its intellectual demands. "No-Movies" achieve the appearance of Hollywood cinema through the guise of art demanding intellectual and cultural response.[30] While Warhol's strategy may have been not to direct his films, Gamboa's was not to make movies; while Warhol may have attempted to create a Hollywood outside Hollywood, Asco created the affect of Hollywood from the periphery of Hollywood.

The social body and the dematerialized object of art

Asco's performance and multimedia production were social commentaries in non-traditional form. Their bodies provided the most immediate form, and the social space of Los Angeles provided the most effective forum for the materialization of their concepts. As a whole, Asco's work can best be characterized and understood as social, spatial, and aesthetic infractions of place (place here as a regulative and hierarchical location that is both social and spatial).

For Asco it was imperative to shatter "people's preconceptions of what Chicano artists should do" (Gamboa in Benavidez and Vozoff 1984: 51). Asco did not adhere to the prescribed agenda for Chicano artists within the Movement to unite and educate "the family of *La Raza* towards liberation with one heart and mind" (First Chicano National Conference 1969: 3). Instead, Asco cannibalized the mediums of film and muralism to stage movement and possibility in exchange for static, iconic, and mythical representations. Neither obviously didactic nor consumable, their work was seen by many of their peers as an unproductive expenditure that did not fulfill the tenets of nationalism within the Chicano Movement and potentially obfuscated a nationalist ideology:[31] "[Despite such dismissal] Asco's work was a dynamic fusion of avant-garde theory and social practice, and demonstrates how politically engaged art need not be rigid and conformist" (Ybarra-Frausto c. 1983: 13).

How, then, do we account for the exclusion of Asco from the histories of the US American avant-garde? Coco Fusco alerts us to the narrative devices through which the genealogies of the avant-garde, particularly in performance, preserve an exclusionary discourse:

> It is generally understood that performance as a term was introduced in the early 1970s to describe art that was ephemeral, time-based and process oriented, that incorporated the body as an object and as a subject of inquiry,

and explored extreme forms of behavior, cultural taboos, and social issues. It is also used retroactively to refer to the experiments of the 1960s, the Black Mountain College group of the 1950s, Dadaist and Surrealist events of the 1920s and 1930s, and so on. This genealogy is flagrantly Eurocentric, and lends credence to the assumption that American artists of colour started doing performance thanks to multicultural policies of the 1980s.

(Fusco 1995: 160)

How do we work within, and yet against, such genealogies? We must begin by acknowledging that there are other sources and trajectories for "avant-garde" practices and that these histories have been ignored and/or subjugated.

While some Euro-American conceptual artists were questioning or rejecting the art object, others investigated the apparatuses that produced and controlled them. The efforts undertaken by Euro-American artists and collectives to subvert the museum–market war machine, was, "of course, to make art which was object-less, art which was conceived as uncollectable and unbuyable because intangible" (Sayre 1989: 14). This intentional self-absenting from commodification, Henry Sayre argues, "became a useful instrument of change." Sayre is speaking directly to and exclusively about the physical aspects of the medium, when he describes the strategies utilized "to defeat or at least mitigate, the exploitation of their material manifestation" (Sayre 1989: 12–13), and not material means of production – that is, its economic features or requisites.

Sayre's argument marks the limits of what can be considered productive for either aesthetic or political agendas. These same limits have denied Asco entry into the accepted canon of the Euro-American avant-garde. Asco's strategies differ from those of the Euro-American avant-garde because Asco's work addressed the experience of absence and exclusion and because their means and methods of production were directly related to this.

The conviction that the dematerialized object could necessarily effect a de-reification of the art establishment solely by undermining its economic and aesthetic norms is a cornerstone of vanguardist accounts. Lucy Lippard has recently characterized such "particularly tangled account[s]" of the past as escape attempts:

Communication (but not community) and distribution (but not accessibility) were inherent in Conceptual art. Although the forms pointed toward democratic outreach, the content did not. However rebellious the escape attempts, most of the works remained art-referential, and neither economic nor esthetic ties to the art world were fully severed.

(Lippard 1997: xvi)

Asco's performative assault and rejection provides a counterexample to the Euro-American avant-garde history of self-absenting. Given their social situation of exclusion, the dematerialized object or action was not a strategic decision, but Asco's only alternative. Recent definitions of the dematerialized object would have us believe that it was a process of reduction so that "[b]oth the materials of the art and its subject are ephemeral and insubstantial" (Prinz 1991: 52–53). The idea may have been placed over the object in Asco's work, and their materials were certainly disposable and ephemeral, but the founding fables that art was a relative value, a language game, or function of frame and context (Suárez 1996: 216), do not account for the ways in which Asco actualized or extrapolated these concepts in order to make social statements. As Gronk relates, "the true avant-garde works within the community to change a real situation, not a manufactured one" (Benavidez 1982: 30).

Notes

1.   Humberto Sandoval has also been considered one of the original members of Asco, as he was involved in Asco performances as early as 1973. However, unlike the other core members, he is not, nor never has considered himself, a visual artist.

2.   Asco's work should also be understood in relation to the larger international context of alternative youth cultures and radical politics of the period.

3.   See Dana Friis-Hansen's (1987) essay "L.A. Hot and Cool: Traditions and Tempera-ments." The exhibition was organized by the MIT List Visual Arts Center in 1987 and divided into two parts: "Pioneers," which included Asco, Michael Asher, John Baldessari, Chris Burden, Edward Kienholz, Bruce Nauman, Edward Ruscha, and Betyre Saar, among others; and "The 80s," which included two members of Asco in the 1980s, Barbara Carrasco and Daniel J. Martinez. Two years earlier, on the occasion of the inclusion of Asco artists in *Summer 1985*, an exhibition at the Museum of Contemporary Art, Los Angeles, the largest Spanish-language newspaper in the USA proclaimed, "Sufficient praise has been set forth by both critics and specialists so that they may be considered a fundamental part of the most important artistic movement presently existing in the US" ("Calendario Cultural," La Comunidad section, *La Opinion*, July 14, 1985; author's translation).

4.   See, for example: Loeffler and Tong (1989); Sayre (1989); Raven (1993); Goldstein (1995); Felshin (1995); Ferguson (1998); Lacy (1995); Nittve and Helle (1997); Foster (1996). One exception to this structural omission is the exhibition catalogue *Outside the Frame: Performance and the Object: A Survey History of Performance Art in the USA since 1950* (1994), edited by Gary Sangster, where Asco is listed in the chronology but not included in the exhibition.

5.   In Vietnam between 1961 and 1969, 20 percent of US American casualties were Chicanos and other Latinos, who at the time accounted for only 10 to 12 percent of the

population of the southwestern states and a much smaller percentage of the country as a whole. California was the home to the greatest number of all US casualties regardless of ethnicity in the Vietnam War (Guzman 1969).

6.   See Chávez (1984: 147). Several antiwar protests orchestrated by the National Chicano Moratorium Committee (founded by the Brown Berets) were held in East LA at this time: the first on December 20, 1969, with 2000 people in attendance; the second on February 28, 1970, with 6000 protesters; and another on July 3, 1970. A demonstration to protest the deaths of six Mexican-American inmates at the East Los Angeles Sheriff's substation broke out in violence on July 4, 1970. Historian Rudolfo Acuña has described this period of the early 1970s activism and community-police relations as "Chicanos Under Siege" (Acuña 1988: 345–50). See also, Gutiérrez (1986) and the following government reports, Commission on Civil Rights California Advisory Committee (1970), and the Commission's earlier report on *Mexican Americans and the Administration of Justice in the Southwest* (March 1970).

7.   As Gamboa recounts,

> With over three thousand predominantly Chicano students faced with unequal opportunities at home and probable overrepresentation in the fields of death in Vietnam, . . . [Garfield High School] gained notoriety as the trendsetter of Chicano fashion, etiquette, violence, and slang . . . The mutual awareness of the musicians and artists in the midst of social and political change allowed them to convey their shared experience through personal and group expressions of music or art.
>
> (Gamboa 1991: 127)

8.   On March 4, 1968, the day before the first planned Blowout, FBI Director J. Edgar Hoover issued a memo to local law enforcement officials across the country urging them to place top priority on political intelligence work to prevent the development of nationalist movements in minority communities. At a national level, this was specifically directed against the Black Power movement; in California the political units of the Los Angeles City Police and County Sheriff's Office were additionally ordered to investigate the "Brown Power" strike (Muñoz 1989: 67–68). See also "Taking Back the Schools," part three of the video documentary series *Chicano!: A History of the Mexican-American Civil Rights Movement*, which includes interviews with Patssi Valdez and Harry Gamboa, Jr.

9.   The largest of all the walkouts occurred at Garfield High with 2700 students (72 percent of total student population) participating (Commission 1970: 11).

10.   Gronk's early art actions were designed to take art "out of the galleries and into the alleys" such as: the "Skid Row Manicurist" and the "Boo Report," chronicles of life in downtown LA sneaking up behind people and saying, "Boo!" Working with two other East LA artists, Mesa and Cyclona, Gronk engaged in public art actions that dealt with gender diffusion. Patssi Valdez met Gronk through his directorial debut, *Cockroaches have no Friends*. Perhaps his most important performance was his draft-dodging performance in US Military Service. After being inducted into the army, he managed to be discharged as undesirable after six weeks of service (Gamboa in Kosiba-Vargas and Zaneta 1988: 25).

11.   A 1974/75 issue of *Regeneración* (vol. 2, issue 1) is the first to identify Patssi Valdez, Willie Herrón, Harry Gamboa, Jr., and Popcorn (one of Gronk's pseudonyms) as members

of Asco. In the archives of Shifra M. Goldman, it is indicated that between 1972 and 1974 they worked as Midnight Art Productions, taking on the name "Asco" in 1974.

12.   The Latin American festival of Las Posadas dramatizes Mary and Joseph's search for lodging on each of the nine evenings before Christmas.

13.   The *calavera*, or animated skeleton, a traditional Mexican death motif often associated with Days of the Dead, was popularized by José Guadalupe Posada, the celebrated caricaturist and printmaker. The Days of the Dead, or Dias de los Muertos, observed on November 1 and 2, are dedicated to the preparation for and celebration of the return of the dead. Dias de los Muertos observances and practices are the syncretic product of the encounters between pre-conquest indigenous cults of the dead and the Spanish Catholic rituals of All Souls' and All Saints' Days.

14.   Over 20,000 people participated in the largest Chicano Moratorium Against the Vietnam War on August 29, 1970. Organized by former UCLA student body president, Rosalio Muñoz, the demonstration was meant to "to expose the fact that second to Vietnamese, the heaviest burdens of the war have fallen on the Chicano community." Eighty percent of the protesters were under 25 years old, the group to which Muñoz wanted to stress that "the front line for Chicano youth is not in Vietnam but is the struggle for social justice here in the United States" (E. Chávez 1994: 108).
   Once the march on Whittier Boulevard was complete, participants gathered in Laguna Park for a rally and scheduled entertainment. Police determined that the number of people in Laguna Park, which reached an estimated 30,000, was critical and ordered that the demonstrators disperse and vacate the park. Tear gas and violence were utilized to achieve this end. Thousands of previously non-violent protesters sought retaliation against the assaulting police officers. By evening 158 buildings were damaged, 4 destroyed, 400 people arrested and 3 dead, and an unestimated number of civilian and police cars were charred (E. Chávez 1994: 116). One of the casualties included Ruben Salazar, a reporter for the *LA Times* and news director of KMEX (LA's Spanish-language television station), who was killed by a tear-gas projectile fired by a sheriff's deputy that tore through his head while he was seeking shelter inside the Silver Dollar Cafe on Whittier Boulevard.

15.   Although the Moratorium Committee had kept the police fully informed of its program and provided monitors to accompany marchers and maintain order (Commission 1970: 14), Gamboa describes it as a "target of a well-orchestrated plan for disruption by the Los Angeles Police Department, the Los Angeles County Sheriff's Department, and other police agencies" (Gamboa 1991: 122). Indeed, what began as a peaceful demonstration turned into police riot, which in turn provoked the first violent Chicano retaliation in a major US city. With each subsequent parade (September 16, 1970, Mexican Independence Day), protest against police brutality (January 9, 1971, Hollenbeck police station), and demonstration (January 31, 1971, Belvedere Park, East LA), disturbances arose and participants were attacked by the police, which only increased existing tensions between police and community.
   A sense of the general public attitude toward the Chicano protests, urban disturbances, and police riots that were centralized in, but not limited to, East LA during this period can be surmised in the following statements. An editorial in the *Los Angeles Herald Examiner*

argued, "The attacks against people and property were planned by anarchists who have no respect for the country and the American system of righting grievances and obtaining justice" ("Riot Aftermath," *Los Angeles Herald Examiner* September 2, 1970, p. 12.). Contrary to such popular and vehement statements, an advisory committee to the US Commission on Civil Rights, assigned to study police–community relations in East LA, concluded that "Whenever police were present, disturbances erupted; when the police stayed away, the demonstrations were orderly and calm." Their findings that "peace is kept best in East L.A. when the police aren't around" (Commission 1970: 11), sharply contrasted Los Angeles County Sheriff Peter Pitchess's contention that Chicanos "can not control their own people" ("Violence Breaks Out after Chicano Rally in East LA" *LA Times*, February 1, 1971 part 1: 1,3).

16.   The canceling of the parade and other restrictions on public space are examples of what José Angel Gutiérrez has described as the official legal and extralegal repression of the Chicano community, particularly when public opinions and actions are enacted in protest of injustice (Gutiérrez 1986: 28, 30).

17.   Two accounts regarding the reception of *Walking Mural* significantly, and interestingly, contrast one another. While one member remembers that "Several individuals converted in passing, joined their silent walk through the crowds," essentially producing "art converts" (Gamboa 1991: 125), Herrón remembers, "They ripped my cape . . . They tore my tail off as they screamed 'putos' [faggots]" (Gamboa 1976: 30).

18.   As Rosalyn Deutsche reminds us, "the unity of public space depends on repressing – on establishing – as external to 'the public' – the differences and conflicts as well as outright injustices of urban life, public space becomes an appropriated territory subject to, rather than representing the limit of, regulatory power" (Deutsche 1996: 38–39).

19.   See James Holston, "Spaces of Insurgent Citizens," *Planning Theory* 13 (1995): 35–51.

20.   Rios-Bustamante and Castillo (1986).

21.   In addition, Asco conceptually allied their resistance with the literal occupation of islands as an act of anti-colonial protest, such as the Native American occupation of Alcatraz Island and the Chicano occupation of Catalina Island. Gronk's diptych painting "Terror in Chile," attached to the street sign, generates yet another political alliance with the victims of the Pinochet regime.

22.   "No-Movies" appropriated the spectacle of Hollywood even as they critiqued the absence of Chicano access and participation in the mass media; moreover, albeit somewhat ironically, "No-Movies" fulfilled the goals of the nationalist Chicano cinema movement to gain control of the means of production by inverting its methods. See: Cine-Aztlan "Ya Basta con Yankee Imperialist Documentaries" (1974) and Francisco X. Camplis "Towards the Development of a Raza Cinema" (1975), both reprinted in *Chicanos and Film: Representation and Resistance*, Chon Noriega, ed., Minneapolis: University of Minnesota Press, 1992.

23.   On the heterotopia, please see Michel Foucault, "Of Other Spaces," trans. Jay Miskowiec, *Diacritics* (Spring 1986): 22–27; Edward W. Soja (1996) "Heterotopologies:

Foucault and the Geohistory of Otherness," *Thirdspace: Journeys to Los Angeles and Other real-and-imagined Places,* Oxford: Blackwell, 145–63; Jennifer A. González and Michelle Habell-Pallan, "Heterotopias and Shared Methods of Resistance: Navigating Social Spaces and Spaces of Identity," *Inscriptions* 7 (1994): 80–104.

24.   For recent art historical accounts on flânerie to dérive in such Euro-American movements as Dada, Surrealism, Situationist International, and their contemporary influences, see: Mirella Bandini (1996), "Surrealist References in the Notions of Dérive and Psychogeography of the Situationist Urban Environment, in *Situationsists: Art, Politics, Urbanism,* eds. Libero Andreotti and Xavier Costa, Barcelona: ACTAR/Museu d'Art Contemporani de Barcelona 40–51; A. Bonnett (1992), "Art, Ideology, and Everyday Space: Subversive Tendencies from Dada to Postmodernism," *Environment and Planning D: Society and Space* 10: 69–86; Christel Hollevoet (1992), "Wandering in the City: Flanerie to Dérive and After: The Cognitive Mapping of Urban Space," *The Power of the City/The City of Power,* eds. Christel Hollevoet, Karen Jones, and Timothy Nye, Whitney Independent Study Program Papers no. 1, New York: Whitney Museum of American Art, 25–57.

25.   On the "rhetoric of the pose," see Craig Owens (1992) "The Medusa Effect, or, The Specular Ruse," and "Posing," 191–217; Henny Sayre (1989: "The Rhetoric of the Pose: Photography and the Portrait as Performance," 35–65).

26.   For a different interpretation of the simulacral structure in Sherman's "Film Stills," see Rosalind Krauss' (1993) essay in *Cindy Sherman 1975–1993,* NY: Rizzoli. Perhaps another way to approach this debate would be through Barthes's discussion of the "third" or "obtuse" meaning – the signifier without a signified – and the specifically filmic existing not in the moving image but in the still; see "Third Meaning: Research Notes on Some Eisentein Film Stills," in his (1977) *Image-Music-Text,* trans. Stephen Heath, NY: Hill and Wang, 152–68.

27.   The underground's first and leading Superstar was Mario Montez (a.k.a. Dolores Flores), the "man-queen-star" (Tavel 1966: 44) of films by both Jack Smith and Andy Warhol. Ronald Tavel recounts how the unparalleled rise to stardom in underground movies of this "square, strong shoulder[ed] . . . lithely dark Puerto Rican" (Tavel 1966: 41) "was so traditionally Hollywood as to again defy belief" (Travel 1996: 57). This is the subject of my current research, for it affirms not only a history of Latino participation in the US American avant-garde, but exemplifies how this history is far more "American" than is represented by its annalists.

28.   Critics such as Dwight MacDonald, however, argued that Warhol's films were just as self-defeating as the Hollywood product (Barrios 1968: 32), while it was more generally asserted that Warhol's put-on was mistaken for content and his indifference for will (Gavronsky 1967: 48–9).

29.   Above all, Warhol represented himself as a "pure artist" (Berg 1967: 39), a definition premised on the negation of social content and critique.

30.   As Gamboa explains, "The conceptual works were designed to provoke the viewer to commit acts of perceptual sabotage" (Gamboa 1994: 7). The "No-Movies" manipulated

content and context in order to "oppose reality" with only "a camera, film, and a concept" (Gamboa 1994: 2–3). Gamboa explains that the performances were designed for

> actual documentation, analysis and explanation to the audience, to show them how things are done ... We ... manipulate images, texts, nuances, and turn them back on the people – with a different message. We trick people visually and verbally, then stop the joke in midstream and explain to them how it was done.
>
> (Geyer 1981: 18)

31.   El Plan Espiritual de Aztlán declared that "Cultural Values of our people strengthen our identity and the moral backbone of the movement ... We must insure that our writers, poets, musicians, and artists produce literature and art that is appealing to our people and relates to our revolutionary culture" (First Chicano National Conference 1969: 3). A substantive distinction between Asco and other Chicano artists and collectives of the time relates specifically to their location within identity politics and divergent investments in reclaiming cultural traditions and effaced histories. In this respect, Gronk contrasts Asco's work with identity-based and/or community oriented work: "A lot of Latino artists went back in history for imagery because they needed an identity, a starting place ... We didn't want to go back, we wanted to stay in the present and find our imagery as urban artists and produce a body of work out of our sense of displacement" (Durland and Burnham, 1986: 57).

References

Acuña, Rodolfo (1988) *Occupied America: A History of Chicanos*, 3rd Edition, New York: Harper and Row.

Barrios, Greg (1968) "Andy Warhol's Hedy – Hollywood's Goetterdaemmeruner," *Film Culture* 45: 27–32.

Battock, Gregory (1968) "Superstar-Superset," *Film Culture* 45: 23–26.

Benavidez, Max (1981) "Interview with Willie Herrón," radio broadcast, KPFK-FM Los Angeles, June 8. Audiocassette, Gamboa Collection, Stanford University Libraries Special Collections.

—— (1982) "The World According to Gronk," *LA Weekly* August: 13–19: 30.

Benavidez, Max and Vozoff, Kate (1984) "The Wall: Image and Boundary, Chicano Art in the 1970s," in Leonard Folgarait (ed.) *Mexican Art of the 1970s: Images of Displacement, Monographs on Latin American and Iberian Studies*, Nashville, TN: Vanderbilt University.

Berg, Gretchen (1967) "Nothing to Lose: Interview with Andy Warhol," *Cahiers du Cinema in English* 10: 38–43.

Berlin, Gloria and Bruce, Bryan (1986) "The Superstar Story," *CineAction!* December: 52–63.

Brookman, Philip and Brookman, Amy (1983) "Interview with Asco," *CALIFAS: Chicano Art and Culture in California, Transcripts*, Book 3, Collección Tlogque Nahuaque, University of California at Santa Barbara Davidson Library.

Brown, Julia and Crist, Jacqueline (1985) "Interview with Willie Herrón," *Summer 1985*, Los Angeles: Museum of Contemporary Art, unpaginated.

Chávez, Ernesto (1994) Creating Aztlán: The Chicano Movement in Los Angeles, 1966–1978, Ph.D. Dissertation, Department of History, UCLA.

Chávez, John R. (1984) *The Lost Land: The Chicano Image of the Southwest*, Albuquerque: University of New Mexico Press.

Chavoya, C. Ondine (1996) Unedited interview transcript, published as "Images of Advocacy: An Interview with Chon Noriega," *Afterimage* 21.10: 5–9.

Commission on Civil Rights California Advisory Committee (March 1970) *Mexican Americans and the Administration of Justice in the Southwest*, Los Angeles: The Committee.

—— (October 1970) *Police–Community Relations in East Los Angeles: A Report of the California State Advisory Committee to the U.S. Commission of Civil Rights*, Los Angeles: The Committee.

Committee on the Judiciary United States Senate (1970) *Extent of Subversion in the "New Left"; Testimony of Robert J. Thoms [and others], Hearings before the Subcommittee to Investigate the Administration of the Internal Security Act and Other Internal Security Laws*, Part I, Ninety-first Congress (second session), Washington, D.C.: US Government Printing Office.

Crary, Jonathan (1989) "Spectacle, Attention, Counter-Memory," 50 (October): 97–106.

Crimp, Douglas (1993) [1980] "The Photographic Activity of Postmodernism," in Crimp, *On the Museum's Ruins*, Cambridge, MA: MIT Press, pp. 108–24.

Davis, Mike (1990) *City of Quartz: Excavating the Future in Los Angeles*, London: Verso.

Deutsche, Rosalyn (1996) *Evictions: Art and Spatial Politics*, Cambridge, MA: MIT Press.

Dubin, Zan (1986) "Artist Won't be Confined to Gallery," *Los Angeles Times* June 6: Part VI.

Durland, Steven and Burnham, Linda (1986) "Gronk" interview, *High Performance* 35: 57.

Felshin, Nina (ed.) (1995) *But is it Art? The Spirit of Art and Activism*, Seattle: Bay Press.

Ferguson, Russel (ed.) (1998) *Out of Actions: Between Performance and the Object 1949–1970*, organized by Paul Schimmel, New York: Thames & Hudson/Museum of Contemporary Art, Los Angeles.

First Chicano National Conference (1969) "El Plan Espirtual de Aztlán," in Rudolfo A. Anaya and Francisco Lomelí (eds) *Aztlán: Essays on the Chicano Homeland*, Albuquerque, NM: Academia/El Norte Publications, 1989, pp. 1–5.

Foster, Hall (1996) *The Return of the Real: The Avant-Garde at the End of the Century*, Cambridge, MA: MIT.

Friis-Hansen, Dana (1987) "L.A. Hot and Cool: Traditions and Temperaments," in *L.A. Hot and Cool*, Cambridge, MA: MIT List Visual Arts Center, pp. 6–13.

Fusco, Coco (1995) "Performance and the Power of the Popular," in Catherine Ugwu (ed.) *Let's Get it On: The Politics of Black Performance*, London: ICA, pp. 158–75.

Gamboa, Harry, Jr. (n.d.) "Chicano Art of Los Angeles: Serpents, Shadows, and Stars," Manuscript, Gamboa Collection, Stanford University Libraries Special Collections.

—— (1976) "Gronk and Herrón: Muralists," *Neworld* 2.3: 28–30.

—— (1981) "No Phantoms," *High Performance* 14 (4.2): 15.

—— (1985) *Jetter's Jinx Playbill*, Los Angeles: Los Angeles Theatre Center.

—— (1987) "Reflections on One School in East LA," *LA Weekly*, February 6–12.

—— (1991) "In the City of Angels, Chameleons, and Phantoms: Asco, a Case Study of Chicano Art in Urban Tones (or Asco was a Four-Member Word)," in R. Griswold del Castillo, T. McKenna, and Y. Yarbro-Bejarano (eds) *Chicano Art: Resistance and Affirmation*, Los Angeles: Wight Art Gallery, UCLA, pp. 121–30.

—— (1994) "Light at the End of Tunnel Vision," paper presented at Armand Hammer Museum, Los Angeles, April 26. Gamboa Collection, Stanford University Libraries Department of Special Collections.

Gamboa, Harry, Jr. and Gronk (1976) "Interview: Gronk and Gamboa," *Chismearte* 1.1: 30–33.

Garza, Juan (1994) *ASCO: Is Spanish for Nausea. Heritage: Latino Arts Independent Documentary Series*, K-RLN, San Antonio, Texas: Corporation for Public Broadcasting.

Gavronsky, Serge (1967) "Warhol's Underground," *Cahiers du Cinema in English* 10: 46–49.

Geyer, Anne (1981) "Artists' Exhibits are Street Performances," *The News (Mexico City)* September 11: 18.

Goldman, Shifra M. (1980) Transcript of interview with Harry Gamboa, Willie Herrón, and Gronk, January 16, Collection of Shifra M. Goldman, used with permission.

Goldstein, Ann (ed.) (1995) *Reconsidering the Art Object: 1965–1975*, Los Angeles: Museum of Contemporary Art.

Gronk (1993) "Artist's Talk," Cornell University, October 28, audiocassette, collection of author.

Gutiérrez, José Angel (1986) "Chicanos and Mexicans Under Surveillance: 1940 to 1980," *Renato Rosaldo Lecture Series* 2: 28–58.

Guzman, Ralph (1969) "Mexican American Casualties in Vietnam," [US] *Congressional Record*, 91 Congress, 1 Session, October 8.

Kosiba-Vargas, S. Zaneta (1988) "Harry Gamboa and ASCO: The Emergence and Development of a Chicano Art Group, 1971–1987," Ph.D. dissertation, Department of American Culture, University of Michigan.

Lacy, Suzanne (ed.) (1995) *Mapping the Terrain: New Genre Public Art*, Seattle: Bay Press.

Lippard, Lucy (1997) [1995] "Escape Attempts," in Lucy Lippard (ed.) *Six Years: The Dematerialization of the Art Object from 1965 to 1972* (1973), Berkeley: University of California Press, pp. vii–xxii.

Loeffler, Carl E. and Tony, Darlene (eds) (1989) *Performance Anthology: Sourcebook of Californian Performance Art*, San Francisco: Contemporary Art Press.

Muñoz, Carlos, Jr. (1989) *Youth, Identity, Power: The Chicano Movement*, London: Verso.

Nittve, Lars and Crenzien, Helle (eds) (1997) *Sushine and Noir: Art in L.A. 1960–1997*, Humblebaek: Denmark.

Noriega, Chon A. (1991) "Road to Aztlán: Chicanos and Narrative Cinema," Ph.D. dissertation, Department of Modern Thought and Literature, Stanford University.

Noriega, Chon A. (1996) "Talking Heads, Body Politic: The Plural Self of Chicano Experimental Video," in Michael Renov and Erika Suderburg (eds) *Resolutions: Contemporary Video Practices*, Minneapolis: University of Minnesota Press, pp. 207–28.

Norte, Marisela (1983) "Harry Gamboa, Jr.: No Movie Maker," *Revista Literaria de El Tecolote* (San Francisco) 4.2 (July): 3, 12.

Owens, Craig (1992) "The Medusa Effect, or, the Specular Ruse," in Scott Bryson, Barbara Kruger, Lynn Tillman, and Jane Weinstock (eds) *Beyond Recognition: Representation, Power, Culture*, Berkeley: University of California Press.

Pile, Steve (1996) *The Body and the City*, London: Routledge.

Prinz, Jessica (1991) *Art Discourse/Discourse in Art*, New Brunswick, NJ: Rutgers University Press.

Raven, Arlene (ed.) (1993) *Art in the Public Interest*, New York: Da Capo Press.

Rios-Bustamante, Antonio and Castillo, Pedro (1986) *An Illustrated History of Mexican Los Angeles, 1781–1985*, Chicano Studies Research Center Publications, UCLA Monograph 12, Los Angeles: Chicano Studies Research Center.

Rupp, Beverly Jones (c. 1985) *Harry Gamboa: Conceptual Artist*, Television Broadcast, Falcon Cable Company, Los Angeles, Videorecording, Gamboa Collection, Stanford University Libraries Special Collections.

Sandoval, Alicia (1978) *Let's Rap with Alicia Sandoval*, television broadcast interview with Harry Gamboa, KTLA Channel 5, Los Angeles, April, Audiorecording, Gamboa Collection, Stanford University Libraries Special Collections.

—— (1980) *Let's Rap with Alicia Sandoval*, television broadcast interview with Harry Gamboa, KTLA Channel 5, Los Angeles, Videorecording, Gamboa Collection, Stanford University Libraries Special Collections.

Sayre, Henry M. (1989) *The Object of Performance: The American Avant-Garde Since 1970*, Chicago: University of Chicago Press.

Soja, Edward W. (1989) *Postmodern Geographies: The Reassertion of Space in Critical Social Theory*, London and New York: Verso.

Suárez, Juan A. (1996) *Bike Boys, Drag Queens, and Superstars: Avant-Garde, Mass Culture, and Gay Identities in the 1960s Underground Cinema*, Bloomington and Indianapolis: Indiana University Press.

Tagg, John (1994) "The Discontinuous City: Picturing and the Discursive Filed," in Norman Bryson, Michael Ann Holly, and Keith Moxey (eds) *Visual Culture: Images and Interpretations*, Hanover: University Press of New England, pp. 83–103.

Tavel, Ronald (1966) "The Banana Diary (The Story of Andy Warhol's 'Harlot')," *Film Culture* 40: 43–66.

Ybarra-Frausto, Tomás (c. 1983) *CALIFAS: Socio-Aesthetic Chronology of Chicano Art*, in [Tomás Ybarra-Frausto (ed.) *CALIFAS: Seminar Essays*] s.i.: s.n., National Museum of American Art Library, Smithsonian Institution, Washington, D.C.

The End of the Line, 1986

The Border Art Workshop (BAW)/El Taller de Arte Fronterizo (TAF)

San Diego/Tijuana
Photo courtesy of BAW/TAF
Founded in 1985 in San Diego by Isaac Artenstein, Sara Jo Berman, Jude Eberhard, Guillermo Gómez-Peña, and Michael Schnorr, BAW/TAF began with a series of site-specific performances at the US–Mexico border that addressed human rights violations in the region, the conditions of undocumented workers, and cultural hybridity in the border zone. Though the Chicano arts movement of the 1970s had already revindi-cated the poetics of Spanglish, introduced the notion of border culture, and had also made landmark visual arts and theatrical representations of Mexican laborers in the Southwest, BAW/TAF's emergence coincided with the intensified industrialization of the border that generated unprecedented population growth in the area and concomi-tant media attention, and with the new centrality of multiculturalism to American art debates. Stylistically, BAW/TAF performances, early exhibits, and multiples resembled the work of Mexico City conceptualist *grupos* and the LA-based collective Asco. In their 1986 performance "The End of the Line," BAW/TAF placed a table directly on the US–Mexico border. Members, which now also included David Avalos, James Luna, and Victor Ochoa, sat on both sides and proceeded to exchange goods and gestures illegally across the divide.

Performance in Cuba in the 1980s: A Personal Testimony

Leandro Soto
Translated by Coco Fusco

I offer this text as a reflection on the performances that I did in Cuba. I would like to distinguish between culture and politics here, and separate what I consider to be artistic creation from ideology. It is clear to me that Marxism as a totalizing vision of the world and of culture is obsolete. Having been educated according to this philosophical tendency "by official decree," I now see Marxism as one of the many European discourses that has been used to colonize the rest of the world. Despite this, what is specifically Cuban has survived. In the final analysis, is it not a way of looking at things, a way of feeling and a particular way of organizing the world that makes us Cuban? Those who think that Cubanness disappears when one leaves Cuba are mistaken – the best of Cuban culture has always been produced in exile. Cuban culture defines itself by absence, by lack, by nostalgia. Even the author José Lézama Lima invented the term "internal exile" to define how one does not physically leave the country but instead makes creation the route of an adventure away from home.

Performances in Cuba began to crystallize in 1976, when a group of my peers and I were in our last year of study at the National School of Art in the Cubanacán section of Havana. A cultural bureaucrat decided to impose one of the many absurd elements of the antiquated educational system of the Soviets on us: we were forced to paint a model who would maintain the same boring positions for hours, days, even months. Until then, we had enjoyed a curriculum based on the most contemporary aspects of art from Cuba, Spain, and Paris, and had studied all the avant-garde movements of the twentieth century.

We seniors reacted against this new limitation by making "actions," which took place during the intervals when the model would rest. These actions lasted no more than ten or fifteen minutes, but they were planned with great anticipation. We gave them titles, and shaped them conceptually, so that they would be seen as artworks in and of themselves. Humor was never absent, nor was a sense of playfulness, but on a deeper level these were acts of protest against the absurdity of limiting spontaneity. We wanted a space for surprise, and we wanted to experiment with non-verbal languages, since the use of words was very risky. These events generated a sense of interactivity among all twenty-five of us in the class.

Of course, we were not innocent; from the beginning of the 1970s we could read in all the art-school libraries and throughout the country books such as *New York: Scene of a New Art*. The National Library had the latest issues of *Art in America*, *Art News* and European art magazines. We were also affected by the influence that Dadaism has had in the twentieth century, the films we saw at the Cinemathèque, and the intellectual and artistic climate in Cuba, which had always been intense.

After my graduation from the National School of Art, I was sent to work in Cienfuegos, my home town. At that particular moment, there was not much going on there artistically. Cienfuegos is like a phoenix – every once in a while it has artistic movements that are very strong, and then for long stretches it lays dormant. Nonetheless it was possible to see original works from other countries in private collections. Several international artists had exhibited there since the mid-nineteenth century, and there were vanguard artistic groups with independent art magazines, and other publications. In 1957, there was a group exhibition at the art gallery, in which those who participated were, according to the catalogue, Robert Altmann, Wifredo Lam, Joan Miro, Yves Tanguy, W. S. Hayler, Harry Elstrom, Salvador Dali, and Paul Klee.

In addition, many artists and intellectuals who achieved international fame were born or had lived there. I remember perfectly that when I was 9 years old I went to visit the studio of artists like the sculptor Mateo Torriente who had lived in Paris and had original works by Wifredo Lam, Paul Klee, Jean Dubuffet, Robert Altmann, and Yves Tanguy hanging in his studio; the studio of Leopoldo Suarez; and the house of Samuel Feijoo, with his original works by Jean Dubuffet and other Primitivist painters. The works of the Cienfuegan sculptor Guayacon were practically installations. There were the decorations made for the annual Carnaval – a project in which all the Cienfuegan artists strove to be considered the most original. Young artists such as Pedro Damian, Aldo Menendez, and Andres Ugalde met regularly. All of this created an atmosphere that was perfect for the creation of unusual things.

All these artists worked in the Decoration Workshop of Cienfuegos, which was directed by my father, Vitorino Soto, and which I visited regularly as a child. To bid farewell to 1966 and bring in 1967, they decorated a Cabaret in a Surrealist style, which created quite a sensation at the time for its unexpected extravagance.

During the years between 1977 and 1980, while I was still in Cienfuegos, I dedicated myself to two artistic explorations. One was focused on visual art issues – I looked for objects and materials in my environment that were waste products but that I could use as art. The other investigation was anthropological and conceptual – it involved investigating the traces of the cultures in

Cienfuegos so that I could see what corresponded to me from that inheritance. Since its foundation, the city was inhabited by descendants of indigenous Cubans, Africans from different parts of Africa, Spaniards, French, Chinese, and Arabs. These investigations converged in the "plastic actions" that I would undertake either alone or with a small group of friends. The pleasure of feeling that my two investigative tendencies coincided on a common point made me develop several performances of this kind.

Plastic actions

Performances, or what I call "plastic actions," started "officially" in Cuba with *Volumen Uno*. That was the first time a Cuban gallery exhibited a testimony of the making of a visual event. This testimony consisted of photographs and of the objects that had been used to create the event itself.[1] This created a particular aesthetic that suggested pages in a grand photo album that had been extended across the walls. They were accompanied by graphics on the floor and the objects that had been used. In this way, we explained our aesthetic principles, and we even invited the public to engage with these elements.

The works that were presented had been made in Cienfuegos, between 1979 and 1980, at the time I lived and worked there. "Ancestors," "Mutable on Avenue Zero," and "Man and the Slings" were the three works that I showed there and which I had made in my own neighborhood, Punto Gorda. I was helped by curious visitors who knew me as an artist since I had exhibited in the Cienfuegos art gallery since 1975, and my solo shows were infamous social and cultural events in my home town long before *Volumen Uno*.

It is difficult to explain to people who have not lived in Cuba how important all the artistic manifestations are for Cuban people, as well as how relevant the collaborative element is for everyone. It is worth noting that the Cuban Carnaval, as the Cuban painter Rene Portocarrero once told me when he was being interviewed about the novelty of plastic actions, "is a great collective plastic action." When I first heard it, the comment seemed retrograde; today, twenty years later and 1500 miles away, as I now write from Buffalo New York, I find it very apt.

The three works that I exhibited in *Volumen Uno* were closely related to my life in the city of Cienfuegos, the sea, and the anthropological and cultural investigations that in those times I was drawn to and that even today are present in my work. "Ancestors" consisted of offering guitars made of cardboard to an urban ceiba tree (all the ceibas are sacred, no matter where they are). I had decorated the insides of the guitars based on the notion of sacramental drums.

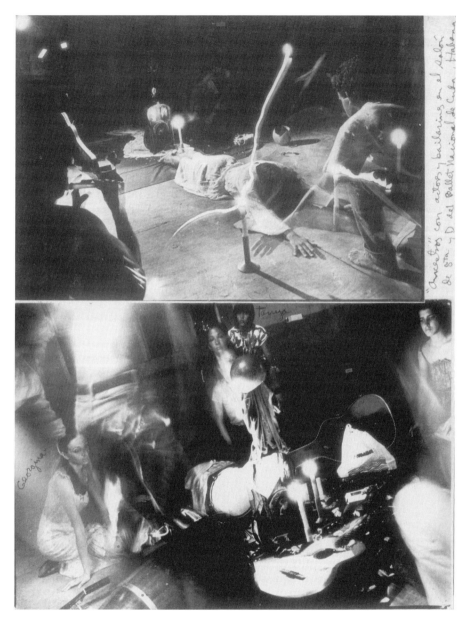

35. Leandro Soto
"Ancestros" (Ancestors), 1979
Cienfuegos, Cuba
Photo courtesy of Leandro Soto

To have a "toque de santo" (a drumming session in offering to the gods), the drums must attract the Orishas, the gods of the Afro-Cuban pantheon. For this they prepared a ritual in which certain secret elements are introduced that only the initiated know. Inspired by the concept I prepared the guitars, and presented them to the ceibas so that they would become "charged." In this piece the concept was to integrate the three basic cultures of Cuba: the indigenous one, symbolized by the sacred tree the ceiba; the Spanish or European one, represented by the guitars; and the African one, which was conveyed by the concept itself.

It was black people in Cuba who integrated these elements into a single entity. Blacks renamed everything. They renamed the ceiba *Iroko*, referring to the sacred tree where the ancestors from Africa lived. What we now understand as conceptualism in terms of artistic expression was brought to Cuba by blacks. Only through the naming of an object can it be related to a god. The Orishas are made manifest in the placement of an object, in its ordering, in the arrangement of one object in relation to another.

"Ancestors" stirred great interest among artists from different areas – the composer Leo Brower, the director Flora Lawten, the theater director Roberto Blanco, the choreographer Humberto Gonzalez, and the poet Eliseo Diego, among others. It also drew a strong reaction from the official more conservative communist sectors that saw the piece as a dangerous attack on Marxism-Leninism: "a step backward," a return to recreating the past that had been transcended by the Revolution. Marxism was accepted as the official religion in Cuba; it had inherited the paraphernalia of Catholicism and also its intransigience.

"Mutable on Avenue Zero"

This plastic action was realized on the smallest avenue of the city. I had been noticing for a while how some beer cans, once empty, would appear on the street flattened by traffic. The idea of something that was mass-produced in series becoming unique thanks to an "accident" seemed to be to a perfect metaphor for social life in Cuba, in which we were all supposed to be the same. The people who stood out the most in that cultural milieu were generally the ones who had had "accidents"; those who were "burned" by the political system; those who were "thrown away"; those had been been "ironed out" – in general those who had strayed from the official Marxist line.

I wanted to call attention to those cans – that garbage that had individuality, character, and beauty – as a metaphor for what was happening to people. I used the lines on the pavement of the street as mathematical points of reference. I arranged the cans in such a way that no one could pass through without stopping to look and think "What the hell is going on around here?" Throughout the period in which this action took place, the cars that passed would veer to avoid running over the cans that I had placed in order; the very same ones that usually went unnoticed. Every once in a while I would change the ordering of the "chatas," a popular term for the crushed cans, but I always followed the same concept. I did this for several days and the children in the neighborhood followed suit. The critic and curator Tony Morales, who now lives in exile in Toronto, was one of those kids.

"Man and the Slings"

To be born and live by the sea is a vital experience that many Cubans have from childhood onward. Those who have had this experience know that whatever object you give to the sea will be returned, transformed into something marvelous and unusual. During this period I dedicated myself to picking up the pieces of rope that the boats would discard after long periods of use. The changes in color, in malleability, and texture of those fragments caught my attention when I would go swimming in the afternoon by the sea. The basic idea of this piece consisted of creating an artistic composition on a white sail, one that the sailors used for propelling their boats by the wind. During the brief fifteen minutes that it takes for the sun to set in the tropics, I would arrange the ropes in different configurations, some spontaneous and others premeditated. The alternating of control and spontaneity at the hour of dusk recalled the work of the fisherman as they returned to shore after the day at sea. The afternoon of my action, there was a breeze that interfered with my work. The neighbors gathered around the area. At that time I already knew I was the son of Yemaya, the goddess of the sea in the Yoruba pantheon, and that I was also a Pisces.

Something about the environment that sparked this work

That these actions constituted significant social events was perfectly understandable within the context of artmaking in Cuba in the 1980s. This openness to renovation had existed in the country since the times of the vanguard art movements of the 1920s. The idea that all of Cuban culture began with the 1959 Revolution was an historical falsity created by the current government as part of a policy of erasing the past. In the interior of the country the official policy was to remove from all the textbooks any mention of Cuban culture before 1959. All the particularities of the different Cuban towns were melted into one insipid homogeneous mass. One lived in the "New World" without a relationship to the past. We were the "new men" that Che spoke of, although we did not know exactly what our novelty consisted of. We were supposed to avoid all knowledge of, and contact with, the country's bourgeois past and its pre-revolutionary culture, which was also bourgeois.

If the artists of my generation had problems with identity, they were provoked by that loss of historical continuity. The history of the international communist movement substituted our local history, our particularity. Local discourses did not matter, and personal and familial history were not seen as valid.

After the exhibition *Fresh Paint*[2] in Cienfuegos and the success of *Volumen Uno* in Havana, I experienced many difficulties with cultural bureaucrats in Cienfuegos who sought to curtail artistic experimentation. I had no choice but to go to Havana to live. Many of my "plastic actions" were seen as politically suspect because they attracted youth and "were not very clear ideologically." In Havana my main source of income and of social exchange came from doing stage work as an independent set designer. Without knowing it, I was the first freelance artist of the revolutionary period. The theatre scene at that time in Cuba enjoyed a bit more formal liberty. It had been practically destroyed prior to this by political " cleansing." There was less ideological control over the process, if not the product, than there was over writers and visual artists. It was in this open environment in which I developed experimental exercises and applied them as training for actors, that "plastic actions" acquired many followers.

I was invited by several theater groups around the country to execute "plastic actions" as a mode of training in creativity for the actors. That which first had taken place behind closed doors started gaining ground in galleries and museums, thanks once again to the impact of *Volumen Uno* and the exhibitions that followed, and to my generation's need for an opening that would allow them to make themselves present in history. The "plastic actions" in Cuba became so attractive that there came a point when there could not be an opening of a show without them. Many other artists from earlier generations joined the movement, as was the case of Manuel Mendive. There was never a written or published definition of what a "plastic action" was, and in some cases the term was applied to events that were not at all creative. But a space for experimentation under that name was established so that each could use it in a different way.

The fundamental characteristics of what was done under the rubric of this term were: the use of non-artistic contexts as artistic spaces; the use of waste and other materials that were found by chance; the actualization of the event without any previous rehearsal; the interest in documenting the process and event; the management of communicative elements that were decodifiable by the spectators; a veiled intent to contest a totalitarian regime or the open attempt to broaden the concept of art and its themes (in certain cases later on, these plastic actions sparked politically motivated arrests); and an explicit sense of humor. The canonization of these "plastic actions" occurred at the International Conference of Young Creators organized by the Ministry of Culture and the Casa de las Americas in Havana in 1983, to which I was invited to present a retrospective of my work and where I was surprised to receive a standing ovation at the end of my presentation. The fact that this occurred within the context of an international event gave me a certain liberty that was very important for the image that Cuba projected of itself abroad.

"Plastic actions" began to be called performances after a while. We started using the English word "performance" because of visits to Cuba by critics, academics, and artists from the US such as Coco Fusco, Ana Mendieta,[3] Carl Andre, Luis Camnitzer, and other artists who were drawn to Cuba by the arts renaissance that began with *Volumen Uno*.

I was the first person to use the term "plastic action," which was my translation of the French term "action plastique." I am convinced that the success that this term has had in Cuba has very much to do with the Cuban predilection for social events. I have seen performances in many countries and in many different cultural milieus, and I have never seen a public that reacts as viscerally to artistic propositions as a Cuban audience does. We are oriented culturally toward direct communication, toward the tactile, toward the exchange of emotions. We want things to happen, we want our conversations to be remembered, we want to be present in people's minds.

Sometimes we playfully say that a friend "became an Orisha," which means that s/he demanded attention, or wants to be present and attended to in a special manner. We Cubans tend to change ourselves easily into Orishas. The artists of the 1980s managed to draw attention to the visual arts from practically all the social sectors through a series of rapid and comunicative events. We managed to change the course of art history in Cuba in spite of limited materials and access to information, and political constraints and totalitarian control. As cultural beings, Cubans are interdisciplinary and multicultural by nature. The small size of the island combined with the diversity of its cultural components makes for a very particular cultural reality. The best way of explaining it is to say that the country is like a pressure cooker and the culture is an *ajiaco* [a traditional stew made of many vegetables and meats].

In my opinion traces of this spirit of renovation from the 1980s remain alive today, but there are blind spots. Many young artists who work within the medium today do not have any idea of who their antecedents were, since the documentation of those events was not extensive, due to limited materials. Also, performance is not taught in art schools, although I remember directing the theses of students from the Higher Art Institute who chose to work with this medium. The limited resources and the massive emigration of artists from the 1980s has ruptured historical continuity.

Notes

1.   The photographers who documented these actions in Cienfuegos were Alexis Maya and Francisco Ruiz, both from the city and specialists in sports photography.

2.   *Fresh Paint* took place in December 1979. It was the first group show that the artists of *Volumen Uno* organized and it was presented in Cienfuegos with support from the city's cultural bureau. At that time the art gallery didn't have a curator and so I volunteered for the job. I coordinated various exhibitions, including this one, which created a huge scandal because I asked a rock group called Liga Social (Social Bond) to play at the opening to attract young people to the show. The music filled San Fernando Street and the young people danced in the gallery and outside. The local police intervened because of the ruckus and the next day rumors spread that we had all gotten naked in an act of rebellion. Once more the popular imagination exaggerated things – someone had taken their jacket off because of the heat of the lights and the crowd.

3.   Ana Mendieta joined the *Volumen Uno* group on many trips and activities. We were her hosts in Cuba. One of our most memorable encounters was a week on a boat from Varadero to Caibarien. I was in one boat with Ana Mendieta, Gustavo Perez-Monzón, Juan Francisco Elso, María Elena Diartes, and José Bedia. In the other boat were Flavio Garciandia, Carmen Bedia, Rogelio Lopez Marín (Gory), Lucia Ballester, and José Manuel Fors. Many arrangements were made to accommodate Ana, who complained about everyone. In the end she decided to travel with the first group. Our artistic investigations coincided with hers on many points. Ana was interested in Afro-Cuban traditions and the traces of indigenous culture. At that time I was the only one of us working on Afro-Cuban issues and popular culture. Together with Gustavo Perez-Monzón, Ana extracted Aboriginal artifacts from Guanabo Beach and Gustavo took her to Jaruco, where she made three works inside the caves. This happened on a trip she made with Carl Andre, who was invited with her to Cuba.

Art Attack: The Work of ARTECALLE

Aldo Damian Menendez

Translated by Coco Fusco

As I reflect on the Cuban art boom of the 1980s from 90 miles away in search of the original causes that led to its explosive period in the late 1980s, I determine once again that to understand it I must look at it sociologically rather than aesthetically. All artistic movements relate to the times in which they are born, but in this case the sociopolitical circumstances were so extraordinary that they shook up the course of everyday life in a small country.

The 1980s was the decade when the first generation to be born and raised within the Revolution reached their twenties. They were living out one of the few utopian projects of the twentieth century. It was an imperfect utopia, but it did generate some fantastic experiences, such as the avant-garde movement of the 1980s, which has left an indelible mark on Cuban art.

While the rest of the world was talking about the death of art, and many vanguard movements were held back by a return to painting and to other conventional forms dominating an increasingly frivolous and implacable art market, in Havana hundreds of young people took on the most daring means that modern art had at its disposal and transformed them into weapons to intervene in the process of Cuban history. Some were artists, many were students; others were just sympathizers who got involved as active spectators.

Perestroika, the beginning of the fall of the socialist bloc in Europe, signs of the decadence in Cuban political discourse, the growing influence of capitalist tourism, the worsening economic crisis, the mixing of social sectors that the equality enforced by the Revolution engendered, religious syncretism, the language and methodology of Marxism-Leninism, the women's movement, sexual freedom, the open wounds of the wars in Angola and Ethiopia, etc. – all of these were factors that transformed the streets of the capital into a incandescent scenario where anything could happen and anyone could be a protagonist.

Cuban people, and especially youth, felt the need to express themselves, to vent their worries and doubts, to criticize, to make their opinions known, to establish a dialogue with power and assume an active role in the development of the country. But this communication was cut off; all that existed was a boring monologue that came from the top. All dictatorships fear their intellectuals, and

Cuba's ferociously controlled its musicians, journalists, philosophers, dramatists, and all those who in one way or another used the spoken or written word as an instrument of expression. In the mid-1980s, the visual arts, on the other hand, had a bit more freedom. The official censors in Havana, with their bizarre ideas of art, saw visual artists as extravagant but inoffensive, incapable of going beyond the ambiguity of form and color. They did not know that the visual arts incorporated text, sound, video, action, collective work, interaction with the public, popular discourses, as well as philosophical and scientific analyses of reality. In sum, they did not know about conceptual and ephemeral art. If we combine this ignorance with all the sociopolitical factors that I have already mentioned, we can understand why in the second half of the 1980s there was a microworld of freedom and modernity in the art schools, the principal places where this phenomenon gestated.

The explosion of performances started in 1986 with the appearance of two groups – PURE (puree) and ARTECALLE (street art), – and lasted until 1989, when the grand exodus of artists to other parts of the world began. The moment of splendor of these groups was 1987 and 1988. It took the Cuban government two years to dismantle this phenomenon which, like a child, had slipped between its legs. During this period, several different groups emerged, such as Art-De, Provisional, Pilon Projet, BTVT, and the duo Rene and Ponjuan. Debates and group shows took place in galleries, museums, universities and all kinds of cultural centers, and in private homes, parks, and streets. We were not focused on personal benefit or transcendence, but rather on fraternal collaboration based on common goals. Not a week passed without something taking place, and sometimes as many as two or three events took place in one night. Artists met almost every day, since there was a strong sense of the historic role that we were playing, and the leaders of the movement wanted to achieve certain goals by setting out collective strategies to meet them before we were neutralized. We were working against the clock, and immediacy and the ephemeral were the only means of achieving transcendence.

None of this would have been possible if it had not been for the popular support we received from the outset. Nothing was easier for the experienced and efficient Cuban censors than to repress a bunch of crazy youths, but the massive popular participation in our events created international repercussions that made the work of the censors quite difficult. Here we must ask: Why did the Cuban people support modes of expression that were strange and incomprehensible? Very simply because the same worries and needs that motivated us were shared by them, and because these angry and rebellious methods established an alternative mode of public communication that compensated for the lack of liberty in the mass media. Our works expressed popular sentiments, and the public ratified this by their approving presence.

I remember that, in 1987, a group of neighbors in the Vibora neighborhood of Havana contacted ARTECALLE to ask us to make a street mural. These were people who had little familiarity with contemporary art, but on the day we arrived who had our cans of paint we discovered that not only was the entire neighborhood waiting for us, but that they had set up a sound system with microphones and speakers so that we could all talk. To top it off, some of the neighbors worked at the local fire department. They had brought over one of the fire trucks to stage a simulated evacuation to make the entire event more colorful. We went with the idea of making a simple mural and ended up with the surprise of being involved in a colossal happening, which we would never be able to recreate. Those insignificant streets were teeming with people for hours, people who came from all over the city and who began to paint murals with us, to paint the sidewalks and the fronts of houses; people who danced in the streets with music that we played on the sound system, and who participated passionately in debates around the microphones, while the firefighters scaled the walls to take local residents out of their homes through their windows, and drew across the sky with streams of water from their hoses.

People had a need to express themselves and we were the Robin Hoods who transgressed the censors for and with them. When we would paint a text on a city wall at night, the next day a rumor would spread like wildfire, and when it got back to us the single phrase that we had actually written would have grown to an entire paragraph, embellished by the rebellious popular imagination. When, for example, we made the mural that said "Art is just a few steps from the cementery" in front of the Colon Cemetery in Havana, the rumor that spread was that a group of youngsters had painted a poster on a tomb in the graveyard that said "Freedom has been buried by the Revolution." Or, when we abbreviated our group name in signing a mural as "AC," people would interpret it as "Abajo Castro" (Down with Castro). Our works functioned as collective texts with multiple meanings, and in our inscriptions people saw reflected their own obsession with the suffocating reality in which they lived.

It was this experience of working directly with people on the streets of Havana that gave us the keys to developing a language and method that we would continue in our subsequent work. Other artists' groups that were part of this movement, such as the Pilon Project group, had similar experiences – they would go to small towns in the interior of the country to live and make work with the inhabitants. There was also Art-De, who would mount shows in the parks in Havana that resembled popular fairs. There were the street performances of the

Provisional group that were put on by rockers and break dancers and other marginal tribes of the city.

The language of the ephemeral was preferred by all of us. It was the only way to get around the censors, since the actions were short and often took place without prior notice. Even when certain events were publicized, the censors would not know what was going to happen until the last minute. These performances had another advantage – while the art object, because of its durability, had a more universal and atemporal character, ephemeral art allowed us to deal with more local and topical themes, without having to undergo the bureaucratic processes needed to put on a conventional art show. In Havana there were incredible things happening every day, and this vertiginous rhythm could only be articulated via a medium that was rapid, simple, and effective.

The members of ARTECALLE (Ofill Hecheverria, Ariel Serrano, Pedro Vizcaino, Ernesto Leal, Erick Gomez and Aldito Menendez) were adolescents between 15 and 18 years old. ARTECALLE was born in the living room of my house in central Havana, when the original group members, all in our last year of junior high school art training, collectively decided to create street performances together. We conceived of our work as clandestine, seeing ourselves as art terrorists. We always signed our work "ARTECALLE" so that our real names would never be shown. This was also our way to avoid egotism and individualism, which we considered fatal to artistic labor. We kept our projects secret, and took advantage of any kind of event in the city to make surprise interventions, in the way that one might prepare an assassination. We would study the site, the context, the kind of public, and the risk and implications of what might happen, and on that basis we would plan our strike as a way of manipulating or altering reality violently to give it another meaning.

A classical example of this was the performance "We Don't Want to Intoxicate Ourselves," which we did at the Cuban Artists and Writers' Union in 1987 in order to foment debate on the concept of art that was being utilized there. That night, we barged in on an event witnessed by artists, critics, journalists, and students, dressed in white robes that said "ARTECALLE experiment: we don't want to intoxicate ourselves." Our faces were covered with gas masks and we carried placards (as if we were engaging in a mini-protest) that had texts that parodied revolutionary slogans and popular sayings like: "Art of Death, We will Win"; "Let it be known, critics of art, that we are not afraid of you"; "In closed carriages no flies can enter"; "Revolution and Culture" etc.

This way of using performance as a strategy of direct action and to make fun of censorship continued even after the termination of the ARTECALLE collective. On my own, I created two performances that demonstrate this clearly; "*Reviva la Revolu*" and "The Indian."

36. ARTECALLE
"We Don't Want to Intoxicate Ourselves," 1987
Havana, Cuba
Photo courtesy of Aldo Menendez

"*Reviva la Revolu*" was an installation that I made in 1988 at the College of Philology at the University of Havana. The installation consisted of a painting that was 1.80 meters by 2 meters high, placed on the floor against the wall. In front of the painting, on the floor, there was a receptacle, and by its side a piece of paper on which was written, "As you can see this work is almost blank. I could only start it due to a lack of materials. Please help me." The first time I showed it was in a show called *This is not only what you see*. I was sure that it would be censored, so I covered the canvas with newspaper to make the organizers think that the work was supposed to look that way and would let me show it as such. When the piece was mounted, and the audience filled the room, I executed a quick performance in which I tore away the newspaper and unmasked the real work, which read, "*Reviva la Revolu*," a phrase that literally means "revive the mess/confusion," but plays on the political slogan "Viva la Revolución" or (Long Live the Revolution). I later presented this piece in the group show *Smooth and Fresh* at the National Museum of Fine Arts, where the staff stole the piece and never returned it.

That same year at the National Museum of Fine Arts, I undertook the performance "The Indian," during a conference Robert Rauschenberg was giving about his tour of Havana. For this piece I did not publicize anything beforehand. On the contrary, I took advantage of the massive public attendance and entered the museum as just another observer. However, I was dressed as an indian, with a loincloth, feathers, bow, and arrow. With my piece I was trying to establish a symbolic presence, since my behavior was the same as any other person there. The anachronistic character of my dress and its implications in this context parodically revealed that the encounter between the public and the visitor was an obvious act of cultural colonization.

Too many performances and events took place during that period to recall them all in this brief testimony. I would like, however, to end by mentioning a group performance that to me represents the final moment of the Cuban art boom of the 1980s. I am referring to "The Baseball Game." It took place in 1989, at the Marcelo Salado Sports Center in Havana. Around that time the movement had been infiltrated by informers for State Security. Certain important members began to separate themselves from the group, and those who remained were repressed and threatened. Censorship had been reorganized, and now it was so difficult to organize an art show that more than sixty artists and cultural figures (including Gerardo Mosquera) decided to engage in an ephemeral artwork together as one last act of rebellion. Several signs were printed, which were distributed around the city. On them appeared a list of all the participants and the date and address of the sports center, under the slogan "Cuban art has decided to dedicate itself to sports." The censors could not reproach us though we knew that they were furious at our sarcasm. That afternoon, the much-awaited baseball game took place without any incidents. I suppose that any observer who did not know what was going on would have surely found it peculiar that there were hundreds and hundreds of people in the bleachers watching the most clumsy baseball players imaginable.

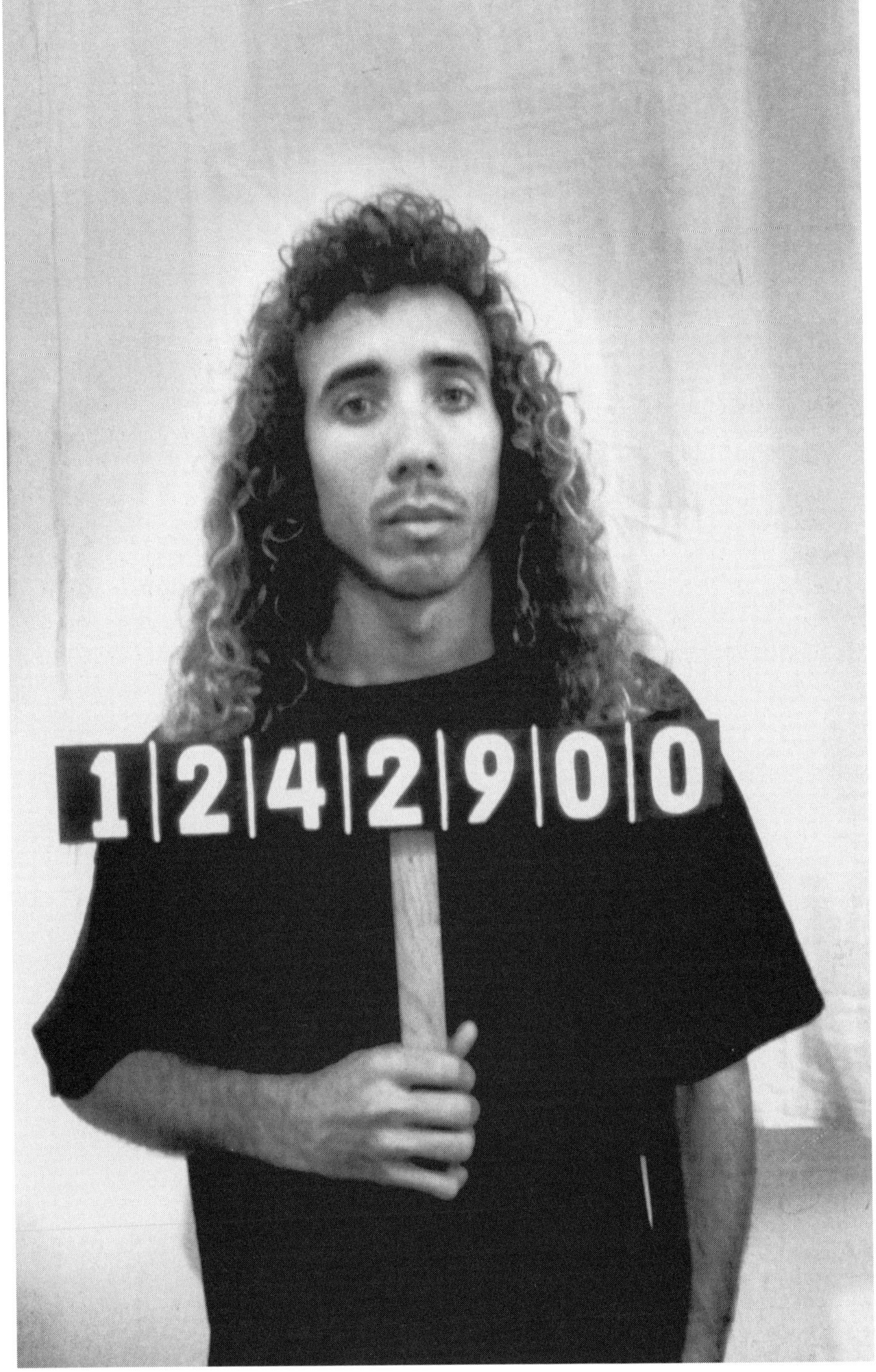
1242900

"1242900 (Parte I)", 1996

Angel Delgado

Espacio Aglutinador, Havana, Cuba
Photo courtesy of Sandra Ceballos
In 1990, young Cuban artist Angel Delgado decided to make a performative statement at an opening at the Center for Development of the Visual Arts in Havana – he defecated in public on top of a copy of *Granma*, the Cuban Communist Party's daily newspaper, literally acting out a vulgar Cuban expression "Me cago en eso" (I shit on this), which means that one doesn't give a damn. This provocative act could be interpreted as a comment of the excessive rigidity of Cuban cultural institutions at the time, on the state of Cuban art, or on the contents of the newspaper. For having deposited his scatological sculpture in the gallery, Delgado was charged with public scandal and imprisoned for six months. His excrement was left in the gallery until the day after his arrest so it could serve as proof of the "crime." In 1996, Angel Delgado exhibited the artefacts from his prison experience at El Espacio Aglutinador in Havana, a gallery located in the home of artists Sandra Ceballos and Ezequiel Suarez.

Electronic Disturbance Theater

Ricardo Dominguez

Disturbance networks

> We are all the network, all of us who speak and listen
> | The Zapatistas

The Electronic Disturbance Theater (EDT) was created by myself, Carmin Karasic, Brett Stalbaum, and Stefan Wray in April 1998. EDT recircuits agit-prop actions to mobilize micronetworks to act in solidarity with the Zapatistas in Chiapas by staging virtual sit-ins online. This networked performance is structured as narrative, the temporal frame of which is bound by the length of the struggle and its needs. The staging of the action is html and a javascript-based tool called FloodNet, which reloads a URL several times a minute, and which slows the site down if a critical mass join the sit-in. The masses, the media, and site on which the virtual sit-in will take place – which 90 percent of the time is the Mexican president's Website – are hailed via e-mail postings on multiple listservs.

Since its inception, EDT has staged nine "acts." Each act takes place from 10am to 12pm, and from 4pm to 6pm (Mexico City time) on a designated day. Our actions have marked such historic dates as the anniversary of Emiliano Zapata's death, Mother's Day, the fourth anniversary of the Second Declaration of the Lacando Jungle, the third anniversary of the Aguas Blancas Massacre, the tenth anniversary of the biggest election fraud in recent Mexican history, Mexican Independence Day, the thirtieth Anniversary of the Tlatelolco Massacre, 506 years of colonization, the fifteenth-year anniversary of the birth of the EZLN, the first anniversary of the Acteal Massacre in Chiapas, and the fifth anniversary of the Zapatista Revolution. We also organized an action as civil disobedience against the infamous School of the Americas military training site.

This reconfiguration of street theater facilitates direct access between macronetworks and non-digital networks. The Electronic Disturbance Theater has also been able to reroute the conduits of information in the media to focus on issue of Chiapas, Mexico. The strategy has been to push the mythology of CyberZapatistas to a new level of activity in order to counter the rise of the

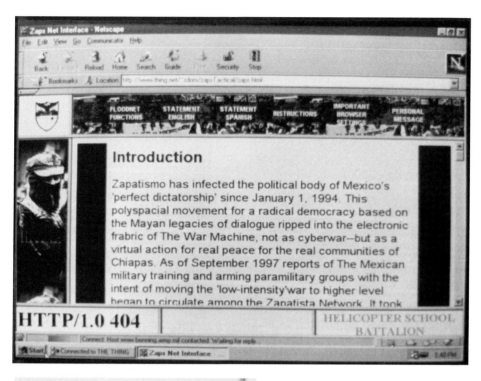

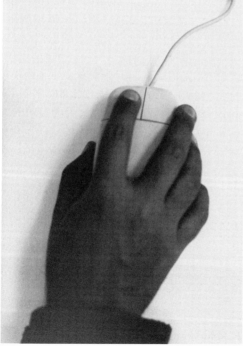

38 and 39   Electronic Disturbance Theater
FloodNet Performance Action, 1998
Electronic Disturbance Theater's virtual sit-ins involve jamming the Mexican government's Website with EDT's specially designed URLs that explain the history and motives of the Zapatista Liberation Movement.

Mexican Goverment's "low intensity warfare" after the Acteal Massacre at the end of 1997. These internet actions have caused not only the Mexican government to respond, both online and offline, but the US Department of Defense on one occasion counterattacked EDT by using browser-based code. The digital highway has become the site for a new mode of non-violent actions for human rights.

The Electronic Disturbance Theater has also become the staging area for the heated debate about electronic civil disobedience and hacktivism. Many on the Left and the Right speak of these virtual sit-ins as digitally incorrect actions that block bandwidth. These networks believe that clogging communication pipelines is not only immoral, but an act of cyberterrorism. Politically concerned network actors must only put up signs of protest and never walk out into the middle of the highway. Individuals and groups who lack the exact knowledge to hack into a system should just be good netcitizens and simply click.

The digital agitprop actions of the Electronic Disturbance Theater call for research and development of html democracies and the right to block data for human rights. These networked performances have also opened access and communication between three important micronetworks: net.art, net.activism, and net.hackers. What mutation will arise from this swarm is impossible to foresee.

Index